The Time Trip

Novels by Rob Swigart

Little America
A. K. A./ A Cosmic Fable
The Time Trip

ROB SWIGART

The Time Trip

Houghton Mifflin Company Boston
1979

A portion of this book has appeared in *Penthouse*.

Copyright © 1979 by Rob Swigart

Library of Congress Cataloging in Publication Data

Swigart, Rob.
  The time trip.
  I. Title.
PZ4.S9763Ti [PS3569.W52]   813'.5'4   78-31271
ISBN 0-395-27756-6   ISBN 0-395-27757-4 pbk.
Printed in the United States of America

S 10 9 8 7 6 5 4 3 2 1

This book is for friends:

Lyn Ballard
Buff Bradley
Jack Erwin
Bob Hass
Frances Mayes
Peter Steinhart
Jane Swigart

A special thanks to John Daniel, who wrote the words and music for *A Copper Rooster Crows in Sunnyvale*, © 1971 John Daniel, all rights reserved. He sold Mel Mellows the song for $1.

And to my father,
who will recognize his share.

BIBLIOGRAPHICAL
NOTE

Some readers may want to pursue the story of Gilgamesh a bit further. There are two translations of the epic of interest: first, the complete prose version by N. K. Sandars; second, a verse narrative by Herbert Mason that concentrates on the themes of death and grieving. Both are beautiful stories in their own ways and can easily complement each other.

The books of Samuel Noah Kramer mentioned in the text are extremely valuable and interesting, particularly *The Sumerians*.

The idea that ancient people heard actual voices comes from a wonderful book by Julian Jaynes, *The Origin of Consciousness in the Breakdown of the Bicameral Mind*. He is, of course, not responsible for the way I have used this idea.

And finally, the *Tao of Physics* by Fritjof Capra was an invaluable source of information and excitement about the relationship between physics and Eastern philosophy; he is not responsible for the spurious high-energy physics theories Josh MacIntosh has developed.

The signs are clear: The Age of Brass is coming to an end. It is the beginning of the Age of Irony.

— *Avery K. Augenblaue*

PRELIMINARY REPORT

Buddha said, "Don't bother me. I'm busy."

He was seated in full lotus and his left foot had fallen asleep.

Buddha, this Buddha, was known to the scientists of earth as LMC X-1, a 4200-year-old supernova remnant in the Large Magellanic Cloud, roughly twenty parsecs away; it put out approximately 3×10^{52} ergs of energy and was a powerful X-ray source. He was, at the moment, concentrating on his left foot, the tingling sensation.

"Damn," he muttered. "My foot's died again."

He gulped a high-energy mu meson bar and blinked; suns flared and died in the blink. Life structures formed on three planets, amino acids, proteins.

"Things are happening on earth," the voice repeated.

"Things are always happening on earth," Buddha said, yawning. "That place is a nuisance. Besides, my left foot died. Now I'll have to re-form it."

"It's connected, you know," said the voice.

"Of course it's connected," Buddha grumbled. "Everything's connected. I've always said that, so it must be true. See the Avatamsaka Sutra. The universe is a network of pearls, each pearl has all the others reflected in it, and so on and so on, et cetera. Now don't bother me. My foot died."

"Please," said the voice. "They've discovered computers."

"Oh, Christ!" Buddha said.

"Right," said the voice. "And your left foot is death. Wake it up. It's connected."

PART I

Today

Cuneiform lesson:

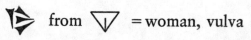 from ▽ = woman, vulva

1

Shortly after she died, Penny Gamesh checked into a Holiday Inn. The marquee under the green sign that ordinarily welcomed bowlers now welcomed PENNY G., SUICIDE OF THE YEAR.

"Does that mean me?" Penny wondered, struggling with her soft-sided beige suitcase with the belt strap and zippers. The pressure-sensitive front doors sighed open at her approach. "Cripes," she said, looking up at the familiar green and yellow entry. "They have one of these goddam places everywhere!"

The desk clerk had a baby face and wore a broad-striped purple and lime polyester shirt, casually open at the throat. Its long pointed collar arrowed toward his armpits. "Welcome, Ms. Gamesh," he said in a peculiar computerized rasp through an electronic device he put to his throat.

"Cripes," Penny repeated, to the clerk this time. "Do they have one of these things everywhere?"

An eyebrow lifted on the pink-scrubbed face. "Things?" the gadget rasped. "Things?"

"You know. Holiday Inns. I guess I expected something a little different."

"Gnkaaah. And what did you expect?"

"Oh, I don't know." Penny, always a bit exasperated, let out a small puff of breath. "Floating around, maybe. Smoky lights. Choiring angels with harps or red guys with pointed tails tossing people around like a salad. Or nothing at all, more likely. I certainly didn't expect a Holiday Inn."

"Allow me to take your bag. I'll show you to your

room." The tulip-shaped device at the man's throat warbled unpleasantly, and Penny noticed that his lips were not synchronized with the words coming out.

"What *is* that thing?" she asked, and the clerk had to put down her suitcase to grope again for the gadget, swinging from a plastic lanyard around his neck.

"Translation," he said. "This is an international Holiday Inn."

"Oh, thank God. I thought you had some kind of disgusting *cancer* or something. Barney was always playing around with crap like that, machines that talked and all. I hope that bastard's suffering now." She curled her lip.

Room 101 was a pleasant green and yellow single with a queen-sized bed, a dresser, a color television and a table with two chairs beside the window. Penny looked out the window.

Fields as far as her eye could see. Fields the color of fresh-sliced pickle, pale, sickly, pale green pickled fields, fields faintly phosphorescent and utterly repulsive.

"Oh, dear," she said softly and turned back to the baby-faced clerk. "Where am I, anyhow?"

"Are you?" the mushroom-colored tulip rasped. "This is the Holiday Inn Deathwest. Like Iowa."

"Like Iowa? But there isn't even a *town* out there. Just those hideous green fields. I hope I'm not to stay here forever." A slight lift at the end, half question, half hope.

"Oh, no-o-o," the clerk quavered with a pleasant smile. "No indeed. Just until things get straightened out. The dining room opens at six. You should meet some of the other guests then."

"Guests," Penny humphed to the closed door when the clerk had left. "I just hope that bastard Barney is suffering now. God almighty, those fields look like pickles!"

Barney was so devastated by his wife's nasty finish that he went out and bought $4000 worth of videotape equipment and passed the next 473 hours in front of his television set. His machines would record what was on every channel all the time, whether he was watching or not, so he had an endless supply of cassettes to watch when there was nothing on but test patterns or *Sermonette* or *Captain Kangaroo*. Barney drew the line at *Captain Kangaroo*. But he faithfully recorded and watched *Love of Life* and *Hollywood Squares* and *The Young and the Restless* and *The Doctors* and *Guiding Light* and *Another World* and *One Life to Live* and *Edge of Night* and reruns of *I Love Lucy* and *Merv Griffin* and *Gomer Pyle USMC* and *General Hospital* and *The Price Is Right* and *Marcus Welby M.D.* He watched *Dialing for Dollars* and *The New Mickey Mouse Club* and *Mike Douglas*. He watched re-reruns of *My Three Sons*. He watched *Mighty Mouse* and *Bugs Bunny* and *Porky and Friends* and *Cross-Wits* and *The Match Game* and all the news twice a day.

So it could not have been said that Barney was too miserable. He sat in his tastefully furnished model living room in his $232,000 Sunnyvale model home with wall-to-wall shag carpeting and exposed-beam ceiling and watched *The Brady Bunch* one night, holding in his hand a bottle of Kirin beer, and had an idea.

Sunnyvale is in the Santa Clara Valley, called by many of the residents Silicon Gulch, so Barney was embedded in a matrix of some 247,352 engineers of various types who worked for corporations with names like Syntex and Interface and Movonics and Eidetic Designs and Polymorphic Peripherals and Heuristics Inc. and Xybek and Rigel Four and Microtronics and Ibex and Isis Inc. and Icom and Imsai and Q and Intergalactic Orgone Computers and Augenblaue AeroSpace.

Barney wasn't suffering, exactly, but he was pissed. Off. At Penny. A sullen rage smoldered damply in his rastered brain; gray horizontal lines from screen to eye flickered with that rage. Penny had put her dainty head into the $575

microwave oven and set the timer for seven minutes and os-
cillated herself right out of Barney's life and universe, and
Barney decided in that moment of sudden illumination (rage
flickering up, a brief flare of light), as *The Brady Bunch*
faded rapidly into an advertisement for a new artificial beef
made from petroleum that "tasted just like the real thing,"
that he would get his wife Penny back. From wherever she
was.

"Somebody'd make a fortune if they could make petroleum out of cows," Barney muttered, thinking, I guess I
want her back.

So for the first time in 473 hours Barney turned off the
television set, shut down the automatic timer that was responsible for recording *The Brady Bunch*'s competition on
four rival channels, finished his Kirin beer, and threw the
empty bottle onto the heap of empties beside the real wood-
burning fireplace. He went into his all-electric kitchen,
averting his eyes from the gaping hole in the birch cabinetry
where the microwave oven had nestled. He opened his
Whirlpool electric refrigerator-freezer and pulled out a frozen Châteaubriand dinner for two. He slid the aluminum
tray into the electric oven, set the touch-activated temperature control to 375 degrees F and the touch-activated timer
to twenty-five minutes. The oven hummed into life, and
under the wrinkled aluminum the juices began to thaw and
bubble.

Barney stared through the dark glass door and thought
about the nature of microwaves. About frequencies and du-
rations and indeterminacy. He thought about antimatter
electrons, called positrons, which could be said to be traveling backward in time. There might be a way to get Penny
back.

Barney ate his Châteaubriand without tasting it. He
chewed and swallowed tirelessly, as automatic as his oven
or his magic garage door picker-upper or his Tappan trash
compacter or the mindless timers that in wetter years when

water was available turned the lawn sprinklers on and off.

When he finished, he tossed the crumpled aluminum Châteaubriand container onto the heap beside the fireplace, which was itself already filled with frozen food cartons, milk containers, cigarette boxes (Barney had barely noticed when he ran out of cigarettes during *Hollywood Squares* and had painlessly stopped smoking), beer cans and engineering magazines. Then he sat down in front of his seventeenth-century escritoire (not a nail in it) and lifted the front lid.

Upper right, the blue and red front panel of his ETC 1000, white buttons. The little red light burned steadily: power on. Upper left, floppy disk storage, and directly in front of him his Omron terminal. Below and to the left, on a sliding tray, his Diablo hard-copy printer. Below and to the right, his vocoder, modem and cassette recorders and disk file storage. He flipped on the rocker switch of the terminal and heard the fan start up. Slowly the cursor started winking on the screen, brighter and brighter, and Barney hit the carriage return.

"What do you want?" the screen asked him.

"I . . ." Barney typed, and 473 consecutive hours of television caught up with him, his hollow-hooded eyes sank into his skull, lids drooping over their reddened dimness, and his face crashed down onto the keyboard, setting off a stray program that generated endless random numbers that soon filled the screen and scrolled upward off the top, above his unwashed, dirt-caked hair, the cursor flying frantically across the screen, number after number, line after line of numbers between 0 and 10,000. On into the night while Barney slept and a thin thread of crimson blood uncoiled from his bloody nose and pooled in the shallow pad of the CHARACTER DELETE key of his terminal. The bloody thread dried and solidified and turned to rust, so when Barney stirred once in the middle of the dark morning, it broke with a slight tug on the end of his nose.

When he finally awoke his computer had generated on the

CRT screen 86,640,000 random numbers. He had slept for ten hours, and his nose ached like the very devil.

The devil didn't really exist, of course. As such. But the hostess in the dining room of the Holiday Inn Deathwest came as close as Penny ever cared to meet.

She muttered to herself, "She looks like the woman at the Department of Motor Vehicles."

"I used to *be* the woman at the Department of Motor Vehicles." The woman displayed preternaturally keen hearing. Her voice was salt corroding the underside of a 1968 Chevrolet three-quarter-ton pickup. "You sit at Table Three. With Mr. Despot."

"Mr. Despot?"

"Table Three." A long yellow finger pointed the way. Penny's eyes traveled from the face, a face that had never been young, a face that looked as if powerful midgets were pulling hard on the loose skin at the back of her head, an all-bone-and-parchment face, down across the sharpened shoulders that looked as if they could be used to slice cheese, along the arm wreathed with knotted blue veins and sharply etched long muscles (her hostess gown had short sleeves) to that rock-steady yellow finger pointing straight at Table Three. There was no small talk in that finger, no pleasant chitchat. Penny went meekly to dine with Mr. Despot.

"Hiya, hiya, Haig Despot here, Haig's my name and stereo's my game, also CB radios and television sets, don't take no wooden nickels, don't take no bets, what's yer handle?"

Haig stood there with his hand outstretched, a little fellow with an electric-red bow tie and a large Masonic ring.

"Penny Gamesh," she said, giving the hand a quick shake and dropping it so suddenly it fell into the small dish of freshly thawed shrimp cocktail in front of him.

"Not to worry, not to worry," said Haig with a hearty laugh, a laugh that started at his diaphragm and rose to his nose, leaving his baleful eyes strictly alone, large eyes that could water a condominium complex lawn. He licked the cocktail sauce from his ring and sat down abruptly.

"Not to worry," he repeated more softly, weeping sadly into his shrimp. "Not to worry."

Penny felt a twinge. "Uh . . ." She reached out her hand.

"Not to worry," Haig suddenly shouted, galvanized with energy. "Well, well, well, and what is it?"

Penny sat down. "What is what?"

"Your handle."

"Handle?"

"Handle."

"Uh . . ."

"Name."

"Oh. I thought I told you. Penny. Penny Gamesh."

"Breaker, breaker," Mr. Despot leaped again to his feet, curling his hand in front of his mouth, holding an imaginary microphone. "Breaker nineteen, do you copy?" He sat down again.

"I mean," he continued in a quieter though still agitated voice, "what're you here for? What'd you do, how'd you end, why're you here, Holiday Inn Deathwest, Iowa, they tell me, though that frog over there at Table Five told me it looked like somewhere outside of Lyon to him. He told me that yesterday, he's here because of the Gauloises, he tells me."

"Gauloises?"

"Frog cigarettes."

"You mean he had some kind of disgusting cancer?"

Penny thought she was going to retch.

"No, no, no. Not like that at all. He fell into a rolling machine. Industrial accident, he says, but he probably jumped. What're you here for? Breaker, breaker," he shouted. "Do you copy?"

"Hum," Penny grunted, watching Haig Despot's bow tie bob over his adam's apple.

"No, really," Haig said, winking at her, the bottom half of his face wreathed in goofy smiles, the top half wreathed in funeral bleak.

"Jeeps," Penny said. She tried her shrimp cocktail. It was terrible.

"No. Really," Mr. Despot repeated with an identical wink, more ghastly twitch than friendly gesture, mouth all asmile still. Penny noticed the teeth were fakes, too white, too even, unreal. Not even good fakes.

"Oh, suicide," she whispered.

"Breaker, breaker. What's that you say?"

"I said suicide."

"Aha!" he shouted. "Do you copy? Suicide, she said. Of course," he looked at her. "Oh, of course. And how?" He gave his full attention, interest, concern.

"Microwave oven," she answered as soft as the shrimp in her bowl.

"Eh?"

"Microwave oven." A little louder.

"Fantastic!" Despot shouted, leaping to his feet again. "I want you to know," he whispered, sitting as suddenly as he had risen, "I cornered the market on forty-channel CB radios, me and my partner A. Spencer Sparling. Cornered. Had a warehouse full. Then they went to sixty-two channels and I couldn't give 'em away. Ruined. Rats! So I poured a gin and tonic into my SuperScope stereo and dialed in God! A million volts! It was electrifying! Get it? Electrifying? A joke. Oh, my."

Mr. Despot began once more to cry, large, slow tears.

"You mean you killed yourself?" Oh, why did I ask that? Penny kicked herself on the left shin with the heel of her right foot, but it didn't hurt.

"What'll it be?" The lady from the Department of Motor Vehicles was standing by with a pad in her hand.

"We don't have any menus," Penny complained. Mr. Despot continued to cry.

"Don't need 'em," said DMV. "KC, New York or Delmonico?"

"Hah?"

"KC, New York or Delmonico. Ya deaf?"

"Oh. Steaks. But wait a minute, I don't understand. Why do we have to eat? I mean, we're dead, aren't we? So why do we have to eat? I mean, if we're dead?"

"New Yorks for the two of you then." DMV turned away.

"Wait a damn minute," Penny shouted, loud enough to startle Haig into looking up through his tears. "I want to know why we have to eat."

"You'll learn, dearie," DMV answered crossly. "Rules." She went away.

The steaks were terrible too. "This must be hell," Penny said, and Haig just sniffed.

Barney's sunken eyes crossed over his throbbing nose. He sniffed once, and a stab of pain zigzagged across his frontal lobes and fled. His vision cleared and he saw, when he lifted his head, the three final random numbers on the screen, winking on and off, on and off. With his head off the keyboard the program stopped:

800 269 1559.

Pain, haze and dim red tide flowed in and out through his bloodshot vision, and through it all the neon numbers winked, on and off, on and off. A toll-free number, Barney thought, and, bleakly tired, he reached around to his timeshare telephone and punched his Touchtones 800 269 1559.

He cupped his bristled chin in his right hand, elbow on the escritoire top, and closed his eyes. The throbbing redness did not stop, but he could hear a little more clearly the receiver clicking, beeping, switching, and at last ringing in his left ear. It was a real number, thrown up random on his desolate beach, driftwood to a drowning man, a cup of water for his thirst.

Why am I doing this? he asked himself. Oh, why. A toll-free number, given free.

"Data-link Deathwest," said an impersonal androgynous voice. "Place your receiver in your modem and set transmission to forty-eight-hundred band. You have twenty seconds." The voice was replaced by a dry throat-clearing noise, the sounds of high-speed data.

Barney did as he was told, thinking, Deathwest? What is this?

The screen queried: Code and user name?

"Well, it was a nice try," Barney said aloud, and, typing at random, he wrote, "Penny: Barney Gamesh."

"Stand by," the screen told him.

Barney sank down into both his cupped palms now, distracted by the lump of his damaged nose. To the left, he thought. It's swollen to the left. Sinister. And the great red tide rolled in again, curling over his nose, his eyes.

The tide rolled out again, and the screen appeared.

"Code word irregular but acceptable," it told him. "What do you want to know, Barney?"

What do I want to know? I don't know. "Is this time share?" he asked, and the screen said "Yes," so he typed in his own "Stand by" and went to take a bath and shave.

While he was shaving the phone rang, and his double-edged Teflon-coated blade skidded across the right-hand corner of his chin, tearing a nasty gash, so he left a rusty trail to the bedroom phone, Noxzema shave cream drying stiffly on his cheek.

"Good morning, Mr. Gamesh, and how are we today?"

We? Barney cupped his palm under his chin to catch the drops of blood. We? "Who is this?"

"Oh. I am indeed sorry, Mr. Gamesh. Of course. Pete Boggs here. Boggs and Boggs Funeral Home. Calling about the interment."

A small pool formed in the cupped hand. Barney stared. "Boggs?"

"Boggs and Boggs Funeral Home. The late Mrs. Gamesh, Mr. Gamesh. I am calling about the interment." Pete's voice was smooth castor oil flowing into the bowels of Barney's shock.

"Oh, my God!" he shouted, clapping his hand to his forehead. It was the hand that held the small pool of fresh blood. "I forgot!"

"My dear Mr. Gamesh, you are not to worry about a thing. Of course you cannot be expected to think of everything in your moment of grief. That's what Boggs and Boggs is for. You've suffered a severe loss and mustn't worry. No. However, some three weeks have passed since your wife passed on, and while we have been keeping her in storage pending a decision, we can't continue to do so for very much longer without some instructions from you, you understand. You see, Mr. Gamesh, the funeral business being what it is, there are pressing demands upon our space here at Boggs and Boggs. There is, if I may phrase it this way, a waiting list, so to speak. Yes, a waiting list for Boggs and Boggs' services, and your wife is taking up space that could go to someone who has been more, ahem, recently graduated . . ."

"Graduated?"

"Deceased, Mr. Gamesh. Passed on."

"What are you talking about, graduated? What kind of talk is that?"

"You must forgive our little ways of speaking here, Mr. Gamesh. Many people do not like to hear the harsher language we in the profession use among ourselves. What I mean to say is that we've got your stiff down here in cold storage and you've got to tell us what to do with it or we'll throw it away. It's taking up space."

"Is this a joke? Who is this, anyway?" Barney allowed his hand to drop away from his forehead with a slight sticky sucking sound where the blood had dried. His nose throbbed.

"Perhaps it would be best if I came out to your house to talk to you, Mr. Gamesh," Boggs was saying, his voice once more warm oil soothing its way through the twists of Barney's ear, anesthetizing his jumpy nerves, coiling deep into his fear and pain, a syrup of reassurance. Nothing to worry about. "Five o'clock?" Pete asked.

"Oh, all right." Barney sagged into acceptance, hung up, and returned to the bathroom mirror. His forehead was a bright mottled red, his cheeks a crusty white, his nose a purple fig swollen to the left. He stared dumbly for a very long time, and slowly his fear coiled upward out of the darkness, its fin cutting the surface of his awareness, circling closer and closer.

He went back to the living room and sat on the couch. The phone rang again.

"Yes?" he said wearily.

"Congratulations, Mr. Gamesh. This is Willy Apple here, your Bunker Hill Insurance agent. You are, as I'm sure you know, the beneficiary of your late wife's life insurance policy. But your luck doesn't stop there. The late chairman of the board of Bunker Hill Insurance, Mr. Luther Hadley McWhirter — a very great man, I don't mind telling you — instituted a policy of giving a bonus to every ten-thousandth beneficiary of one of our policies. I'm proud and happy to say, Mr. Gamesh, that you are one of the lucky ones. This may alleviate the old grief a little bit, eh, Mr. Gamesh? This is the Luther Hadley McWhirter Memorial Life Insurance Bonus, an extra *five hundred dollars,* to spend just as you please. Isn't that wonderful, Mr. Gamesh? Isn't that simply wonderful?"

Barney hung up.

Behind him his computer screen blinked and blinked. "Stand by," it said. "Stand by. Stand by. Stand by . . ."

2

Pete Boggs rocked back and forth on his deep maroon pile carpet at the window to his office. His lips, the same rich tan as his face, were thinned in thought, and he stared sight-lessly past the lifted curtain at the traffic passing on El Ca-mino. Absently he fingered the four thin gold chains around his neck where they nestled in the luxurious black chest hair. His violet satin shirt was open to the base of his ster-num, and the remaining buttons marched down to the gold design of his belt buckle. The belt, a woven elastic pattern of red, orange and green, held up creamy white pants that flared widely over Wellington boots. The texture of the car-pet was reflected in the shine of the shoes and slid minutely up and down the polish as he rocked.

Pete was pondering his problem. It was bothering him more than most problems because it was *his;* he had no one to share it with.

If only I had a partner. Oh, why did I ever call this place Boggs and Boggs? Because, he knew, funeral homes *always* had two directors. At least two directors. That's what he had learned at Central Oklahoma State College School of Funeral Management, where he had also studied embalming and floral arrangement and cosmetic science and bookkeep-ing and the psychology of grief.

His problem was the Gamesh case, of course. Mrs. Ga-mesh was downstairs in the freezer. He only had room for one in his freezer, which had been fine until this morning because there had been no other customers. But now he had another stiff and no room on ice for it. He had finally gotten through to Mr. Gamesh, at any rate, but Mr. Gamesh had sounded distracted, as though he really didn't care what happened, and people like that were poor risks. They sometimes didn't pay their bills. And Pete had the lease on the building to worry about. At the moment, he was thinking, the funeral business was dead.

The phone rang. "Yes, Miss MacHunt?"

"A Mr. Arkwright, Mr. Boggs. He's very insistent. Says it's important."

A customer? "Oh, all right. Put him on." Pete fingered his small gold ankh while he waited.

"Mr. Boggs?"

"Yes, this is Peter Boggs speaking. Mr. Arkwright?"

"Right. Junior Arkwright here, Mr. Boggs. I'm with the federal government, Mr. Boggs, and I wondered if I might have a few minutes of your time."

Government? Not a customer then. What could the government want with him? "What do you want with me, Mr. Arkwright?"

"Just routine, Mr. Boggs. Just routine. Please, a few moments only. You have a client there, a Mrs. Gamesh, I believe. I need to ask a few questions, is all."

"Oh. Very well, Mr. Arkwright, come on over. I suppose I can fit you in, say, this afternoon at one?"

"Fine."

"Miss MacHunt!" Pete called after he had hung up. "Could you come in here now?"

"I'm coming, Peter. I'm coming," she shouted, crashing through his office door. She hurled herself at his gold-worked belt buckle and began to tug.

"Not now," he said sternly. "We have work to do."

"Work?" She looked up at him, her blue eyes brimming. "Work? Since when we got work?" Her plump lower lip trembled, and Pete almost yielded.

"Work," he repeated. "So not now," he said softly, stroking her golden hair. "Not now."

"Oh." Miss MacHunt's voice was a timid baby rabbit trembling at its burrow entrance. "You're sure?"

"My resolve is firm," he said. "We have work to do."

"Firm," she repeated, patting the front of his trousers. "Stiff, even. Well, let's get it over with. What work?"

"We have to check the stock. That Arkwright is with the federal government and he'll be over here at one o'clock."

"Check the stock?" Her long blond hair fell across her eyes and she shook it back. "Right. Check the stock."

They went down to the showroom, where the coffins gleamed in muted light, rich woods stained dark, polished brass winking highlights at them as they walked down the rows, rich satin linings glowing softly from the depths, the wealthy aristocratic odors of fresh hothouse flowers and furniture polish. Pete trailed his thin, tanned fingers along the closed lids, feeling the smoothness, the glistening oiled textures of oak, of mahogony and teak, cherry and elm. All these containers, waiting to be filled. There should be no shortage of customers, but for some reason there was a lull.

"Miss MacHunt."

"Caroline."

"Caroline. Do you know where these coffins come from?" His voice had the cheesy insinuations so effective at singles bars.

"Yes, Peter."

"Mr. Boggs. This is business."

"Mr. Boggs. Yes, I know where they come from."

"And where do they come from, Caroline?"

"They come from Hong Kong, Mr. Boggs."

"And do you know why they come all the way to California from Hong Kong, Caroline?"

"Not really," she answered. Her eyes gleamed in the discrete twilight of the showroom. "Cheaper there, I suppose."

"Yes, that will do, Caroline. But as far as you are concerned, Caroline, these coffins are made in Pittsburgh. Do you understand? Pittsburgh."

"Yes, sir. Pittsburgh."

"Very good, Caroline."

"May I ask why they come from Pittsburgh, Mr. Boggs?"

"No, Caroline, you may not. Now, shall we have some lunch before Mr. Arkwright gets here?"

Miss MacHunt spread a lace tablecloth over a lovely early American maplewood coffin at the end of the row, opened a split of Almaden chablis, and they dined quite well on take-out chicken tacos and chocolate mousse. "Ahhh," Pete sighed, leaning back in his imitation Louis Quatorze chair and patting his lean, tan, well-muscled stomach. "That was quite good, Caroline. And now" — he glanced at his 18-karat digital watch — "we have twenty minutes before Mr. Arkwright arrives . . ."

"Oh, God, yes, Peter." Miss MacHunt dropped her napkin, sprinted around the coffin, and knocked Pete off his chair onto the deep blue carpet. She squirmed down her panties and hiked her miniskirt and clawed at his elastic belt all at once, jerking down his creamy white pants, tearing at his violet satin shirt, and just as she was "burying his stiff," as they called it, their private joke, the front doorbell chimed to announce a customer.

"Damn," she muttered, pulling off him with a pop, wrestling up her panties, wrapping the remains of the lunch in the lace tablecloth as Pete leisurely replaced himself and buckled his belt. She stuffed the wadded cloth with taco, wine and mousse remains into an open coffin, slammed the lid, and rushed from the room.

"Right this way, Mr. Arkwright," Pete heard her saying. "Mr. Boggs is in the showroom. He's expecting you." She ushered Junior Arkwright into the serene aquamarine showroom gloom.

"Ah, Mr. Arkwright," Pete said, the cheese back in his tone. His voice put its arms around Junior Arkwright's narrow shoulders and gave him a California hug, filled with love and warmth. "Welcome to Boggs and Boggs Funeral

Home. How may we assist you?" The voice was somber, sympathetic, sincere. It held Arkwright's bony hirsute fingers and looked straight into his pale bulging eyes. It gave his skinny upper arm a squeeze of shared tenderness, but at the same time it did not fail to take in the shabby quality of Arkwright's suit (light red plaid), the blue plaid shirt with the silver-gray tie with diagonal purple stripes. The voice on "assist you?" gave another gentle squeeze to Arkwright's badly assembled body and stepped back.

"Well, Mr. Boggs, we are running a routine security check on Mr. Gamesh, whose late wife you have here." He squinted at a note card in his hand. "That's right, his late wife. You do have his late wife here?"

"We do," Peter answered cautiously.

"Well, uh." Arkwright's marbled eyes shifted to Miss MacHunt, who was standing quietly beside a gleaming dark cherrywood French Provincial coffin with baroque brass handles. His eyes drifted downward to her feet, delicate and very bare on the deep blue rug. A faint film of perspiration developed across his acne-scarred upper lip. "Uh," he said again and stopped.

"Mrs. Gamesh," Pete urged.

"Oh. Yes." The eyes snapped back to the card in his hand. "Well, her husband is an engineer. That is . . ." The pale aggies of his eyes rolled back toward Caroline's toes, where they luxuriated in the deep pile.

"An engineer," Pete urged again, giving Arkwright a reassuring pat on the ridges of his shoulder blades with his tone.

"Right. An engineer. He works in" — squinting at the card — "computers . . ." His voice trailed off again, lost in the woods. It gave up and sat on a stump, allowing the eyes to rove back toward Miss MacHunt's pink toes writhing in the carpet. His forehead began to shine as well, lip and forehead forming glistening horizontal brackets for his narrow lumpy nose and furtive eyes.

"You'll have to excuse me," he said suddenly with a gulp that sent his Adam's apple shooting up his scrawny neck to ring the bell in his chin. "I haven't been with the government very long."

"You're with the FBI?" Pete suggested, his voice now wavering with uncertainty. Was this guy trying to trick him? He had taken all the Hong Kong labels off his coffins.

Arkwright pulled himself together with an effort. "Something like that," he said vaguely.

"Quite," Pete said with a gracious smile. "Miss Mac-Hunt, could I have a word with you, please." He led her to one side and hissed in her ear, still smiling for Arkwright, "Put on your shoes, for God's sake! He's staring."

Arkwright's eyes flashed a neon DISAPPOINTMENT as Caroline slipped her dainty feet into her oxblood platform shoes, but he ahem-ed and said, "Your secretary certainly has lovely feet, Mr. Boggs." He smiled wanly. "I used to be a podiatrist. Before I went to work for the government." He was jittering on his own feet, Bo Jangles without taps, eyes still rolling a strange sideways loop to her feet and back to Pete's face somewhere below the nose.

"Yes," said Pete. "And about Mr. Gamesh?"

"Right. Sorry, Mr. Boggs, I guess I'm a little off my feed today." His eyes arced back to Caroline's oxblood platform shoes. "Well, we, that is, the department, feels that Mr. Gamesh, who is an expert on microprocessor design, is privy, yes, privy to some highly sensitive material, classified information. The company he works for has just taken on a large and, well, secret government project, you see, and" — his tongue darted wetly through his purple lips — "well, the department is afraid that he might, well, you know, in this, his moment of grief and all, he might as it were let slippers" — his eyes back to her feet — "that is, might let *slip*. Some information, that is. He might be *vulnerable*." He stared down at the card in his hand.

"Yes, Mr. Arkwright. I understand that. But how does

this affect us. How does Mr. Gamesh's classified information concern Boggs and Boggs? After all, our business is really with his wife."

"Mmmm-hmmm. Right. Good question, Mr. Biggs."

"Boggs."

"Boggs. Good question. Well, it concerns you because
. . ." He ran his finger down the side of his note card.

"Mr. Arkwright, meaning no disrespect or anything, but what is it you really want with me?" Pete had taken the full two-week course of Sparling Unified Meditation and had learned how to be direct.

"Want with you?" Arkwright floundered through his swamp of dismay, keeping, with an effort, his eyes away from Miss MacHunt, who now leaned against the French Provincial coffin, her lips glistening with amusement, her right knee notched inside her left. "Want with you?" His voice rose and broke, the two halves falling into defeat and relief. "I want help," he said dolefully. "I can't really tell you where I'm from. Not allowed, you see. This is new to me, really. But I *am* with the government. And what we want you to do is help us. Me. Yes. Help."

Pete sighed. So it was probably CIA. The FBI had little badges they showed you. Worse and worse, but perhaps they were really interested in Gamesh and not in his Hong Kong coffins.

"Help you how?" he asked.

"Oh, you know." Arkwright waved his hand vaguely toward Miss MacHunt, his eyes followed his hand, and he saw that she had slipped her right foot out of its shoe and was scratching her left calf with her big toe.

"Kazoo!" Arkwright shouted and doubled over, clutching his groin. He hobbled awkwardly from the room, knees together. "Kazoo!" he shouted again as he went through the door. Pete heard him crash against furniture in the reception room. The antique hat rack fell over with a thump. Heavy breathing slowly subsided.

"What made him do that?" Miss MacHunt asked, idly scratching her calf.

"He used to be a podiatrist," Pete explained.

"Oh."

"I'm terribly sorry," Arkwright said, walking stiff-legged into the room. "Terribly sorry. I don't know what came over me." He mopped his face with a large lavender handkerchief.

"Not to worry," Pete told him, and his voice reached over to give Arkwright a reassuring pat on his ridged spine.

"Thank you, thank you." Gratitude beamed forth from the marbled eyes. "Oh, my."

"And now, how can I help?"

"Well," Arkwright checked his note card again, then stuffed it into his jacket pocket. "We'd like you to befriend Mr. Gamesh. Befriend him. Keep an eye on him. We feel you are in an excellent position to be his friend right now. His trusted adviser, as it were. You are experienced with people; you could, perhaps, see that he is, uh, reliable."

"And what would I do after I befriended him?"

"Why, report to me."

"I see." Pete's lower lip pursed out in thought. Arkwright continued to mop at his face, which was quite dry by now, and refused to look at Miss MacHunt at all. The silence deepened in the gloom of the showroom, the floral arrangements banked before the windows loaded the air with their heady scents, and Miss MacHunt slid her pink scratching toe back into its shoe.

"Why should I do this?" Pete asked suddenly.

"Huh? Oh, of course. Why, indeed? Well, to serve your country?" Hopefully.

Pete smiled.

"No, huh?" Arkwright began to jiggle again, picking up a conga beat, tum-tum-tum pause tum-tum. "Well, perhaps we could make it worth your while?" he finished brightly.

Pete kept his warm, sincere, sympathetic smile on his face.

"Money?" Arkwright spoke into his lavender handkerchief.

"Now you're talking," Pete said, and waited.

Arkwright sighed. "We'll have to negotiate." He replaced his handkerchief in his coat pocket, glanced at Miss Mac-Hunt, and sighed again.

"My office," Pete said, showing the way.

After they were gone, Miss MacHunt strolled around the room, pausing now and then to stroke a silver candlestick or to squeeze her lovely thighs together. Finally she climbed into a lovely Japanese coffin of red lacquer, lay down in the lush silk brocade lining, and slid her right hand into her panties.

She was aleep there when Pete Boggs came back into the showroom, her fingers curled delicately over her lovely mound.

"Caroline. Miss MacHunt." Pete shook her shoulder. "Wake up."

She smiled sleepily. "What is it?" she murmured, her upper lip rising plumply over prominent white front teeth.

"Miss MacHunt, why are you smiling?"

She yawned.

"Oh, never mind." Pete wasn't paying attention. "Listen, we can now afford to computerize the crematorium. Or at least we will soon be able to afford it."

"Computerize the crematorium?" She stretched lazily, swung out of the coffin, and smoothed her skirt over her thighs.

"Right. From stiff to stuff, untouched by human hands. Something like that. And I've thought of a new advertising slogan. Get this: We Take the Sting out of Death! How do you like it?"

"Nice," she murmured, moving toward the door.

She was barefoot again when she entered the reception

area and saw Junior Arkwright sitting dejectedly on the couch, his pointed chin settled firmly into his left palm. He was staring at the floor just in front of the doorway, and her pink toes marched, one, two, into view, followed by her delicately arched feet.

"Your fourth metatarsals," he said softly.

"What?"

"Your fourth metatarsals," he repeated, his voice drowned in a honey of depression. "They are apparently the same size as the thirds. Most unusual. And a slight ridge formation there, where they join the cuboid and third cuneiforms." He uncupped his chin to wave at her feet. "It gives your feet a most, uh, distinctive look. A most, uh, desirable" — his voice sank to a whisper — "look."

"Oh, right. You were a podiatrist." She renewed her progress across the room.

"Like my mom's feet. Kazoo!" This time there was no energy in the word, a perfunctory ritual. He squeezed his hands together between his knees, his lip and forehead once again frosted with perspiration. "May I lick your foot?" he asked, words throttled by his lips.

"May you what?" Miss MacHunt's wandering attention was attracted this time. "May you what?"

"Lick. Foot. Footy foot. Your fourth metatarsals, your calcaneus and talus. Oh, God, Kazoo!" He crossed his legs over his clenched hands. He looked up at her at last. "There *is* a Kazooland," he said.

"Mmm-hmm," she answered. "Right. A Kazooland."

He dropped to his knees at her feet. "Listen," he begged in a rush. "I could just give you a, uh, an *examination*. That is look your feet over, just press, here, for instance." He seized her right foot, her scratching foot, with such sudden fervor that she toppled backward softly into the deep carpeting. By the time she had lifted her head, he was engaged profoundly in caressing her toes with his liver-colored tongue. She tried to jerk her foot away from him, but his grip only tightened and his tongue slithered along the sole. "Quadratus plantae," he murmured. And after he had licked her ankle, "Synovial sheath."

Caroline realized that her thighs were open, her skirt draped carelessly over her iliac crests, but Junior was paying no attention to those secret parts. From behind she heard, "My, my, my. What could this be?" She tilted her head back to see Pete Boggs upside down.

"Examination," she said. Arkwright continued without dropping a beat to lap at her foot. "Abductor digiti quinti," he said. "Metatarsophalangeal articulation of the central plantar aponeurosis." He dropped his right hand to his lap and she took that opportunity to tear her foot away from his grip, realizing at the same time that the attentions he had been paying her were not altogether unpleasant. But her boss was there.

This time Arkwright did notice. He blushed a violent crimson, a crimson that clashed brutally with the pale red checks of his suit.

"I'm, uh, oh!" He hobbled back to the couch, knees together. "Terribly sorry. I don't know what comes over me." The honey of depression congealed into murky amber and embalmed him.

"Oh, that's all right," Pete said breezily with a quick motion of his hand. He didn't want to jeopardize his new computerized crematorium. Not when it was just within his grasp. "I'll be going over to Mr. Gamesh's house in a couple of hours," he said. "I'll get in touch with you tonight. Leave Caroline your number."

"Huh?" Arkwright was still panting painfully, blushing and murky and confused.

"I said, 'I'll contact you tonight.'"

"Oh." Junior stood unsteadily, plucked a beaten felt hat from the toppled hat rack, put it on, and walked crookedly out the pneumatic front door. He stopped a moment to shout a number at Miss MacHunt, the door still hissing. The door sighed shut behind him.

"He seems to be a fairly strange man," she said. She had gone back into the showroom to jot down the number and retrieve her shoes and was now slipping into them.

"He does seem to like feet," Pete said.

"He certainly knows a lot about them." She looked at her boss, her eyes glistening with a new kind of excitement.

Pete recognized that look. "Not now, Caroline. Not now. Later maybe. Call my wife and tell her I won't be home for dinner. Business meeting. And call my lawyer. I've got to find out about these CIA payments. Just in case."

Her face fell, a failed angel food cake. "Yes, sir."

Pete went to his desk and began to doodle. He drew a stylized coffin with rococo curlicues around it. Inside he wrote, "We Take the Sting out of Death!" No, he thought, a coffin won't do. Too morbid. Has to be something with a sting. A bee? Jellyfish?

His intercom buzzed. "Your attorney," Miss MacHunt told him. "Line two."

"Hello," he said to line two.

"Prue Nisenvy here, attorney at law." It was a throaty voice that reeked of musk, a feline, female, predatory voice.

"Hi, Prue. Listen, I've got a couple of things I want to discuss with you. Can we meet, say, later this evening?"

"Sure, Peter." Oh, that voice could give a vibrantly obscene inflection to his name, it could. "How about the Ceramic Lobster? Drinks and dinner? A *working* dinner?" Such lurid invitation in that voice.

"Fine, fine," he said heartily, fingering his ankh. "Seven o'clock? I've got an appointment at five."

"Dandy, Peter." Almost, there was no comma between the two words.

He leaned back in his chair, clasped his hands behind his head, and thought: a cartoon bee looking back at its tail where the stinger is missing. We Take the Sting out of Death. I like it.

His intercom buzzed again. "Four-thirty, Mr. Boggs. You have to be at Mr. Gamesh's house at five."

"Right."

Pete Boggs wheeled his rebuilt 1910 Hispano-Suiza 4-cylinder, 2.7-liter, side-pushrod automobile with the semi-elliptic front and rear suspension down El Camino, turned right on Avenida de los Pechos toward the hills, and gunned his powerful engine. It was, as usual, a sunny afternoon; the sky overhead was cobalt blue shading gradually to copper brown near the horizon. Sunnyvale basked in the early fall sun, and the sycamore leaves curled in the drought, withholding from Avenida de los Pechos their ordinary shade.

The breeze of his passage ruffled Pete's fashionable hair; the violet satin collar fluttered at his neck, the Hispano-Suiza's four cylinders purred. Pete steered left-handed and fingered the golden ankh at his throat. He had a double mission now: to befriend Barney Gamesh and to settle the disposition of his late wife, still taking up space in cold storage.

Avenida de los Pechos was a quiet road, well away from the better-traveled byways of Sunnyvale. It wound up the foothills of the Santa Cruz Mountains to a sign that read: Los Cojones de Santa Teresa. An arrow pointed: Model Home.

He turned, winding slowly down the twisting oak-shaded streets, looking for Puerco de Esmeralda Lane. He passed Simpático Drive, Sangre de María Way, Sombrero de Arboles Mews. He passed Lotus Lane and Pear White Drive and Knulla Road. He drove gently down a hill and gently up another, two perfect mounds at the edge of the mountains. The Los Cojones de Santa Teresa subdivision was built on two of the largest and best-preserved, most complete Indian shell mounds in California. Los Cojones de Santa Teresa subdivision was built on well over a thousand years of garbage.

At last Pete spotted Puerco de Esmeralda Lane on the left. He turned and drove down, squinting at the house numbers against the late afternoon sunlight that slanted into his face. Number 34½ was the largest, most pretentious and worst maintained of all the new ranch-style homes that settled irregularly into the shifting adobe soil of the area. The lawn had gone to seed, the tattered tops of the grass bent and brown. The landscaped grounds to the side of the house had dried up completely, leaving only the husks of philodendron and nandina. The azalea bushes were dead, and huge cracks had opened up in the dusty earth between them.

The Hispano-Suiza sputtered to a stop and Pete climbed out. As he walked up the cement drive to the front door, he could see through the large picture window, which in turn looked out at downtown Sunnyvale, ignoring the magnificent view of the hills behind the house, where Pete was sure there would be no windows. Barney Gamesh was sitting on the couch, his head thrown back, mouth open, eyes closed. He appeared to be asleep.

Pete would see — after he rang the bell, woke Barney, and was ushered into the living room — the computer terminal still winking its invitation, and he would wonder what it meant: "Stand by. Stand by. Stand by."

3

"Listen, Prue." Pete gently waved his tequila sunrise at her across the table and a dollop of liquid spilled over the edge, wetting his bronzed knuckles. He patted at them with a cocktail napkin: Courtesy of the Ceramic Lobster Lounge.

The room was large, the decor Olde New England Whaling Port: nets and lobster traps hung on the walls, harpoons supporting the door lintels, and a huge painting of Gregory Peck entangled in the harpoon lines on the side of a huge rubber whale hung over the bar. Pete Boggs and his lawyer, Prudence Nisenvy, sat in a corner. Over Prue's head swooped the nude torso of a mermaid figurehead, hard oak breasts forming an umlaut over the lawyer's round gray coiffure.

She nodded and sipped her own straight tequila.

"Listen," he repeated, "I've got a problem or two for you."

"What, Peter?" Her husky voice seemed to reach inside his shirt and ripple up his chest.

"I had a visit today from a somewhat strange man from the government, CIA, I think — he wouldn't say. He wanted me to befriend the husband of a client of mine, an engineer who has access to secrets, that kind of thing. For national security reasons, he said."

"So?" She finished her tequila and sucked thoughtfully on a wedge of lemon.

"So we came to an agreement, a fee structure. Now I wonder about a couple of things. For instance, is this money taxable? After all, it's from the CIA, and they're secret and all that." He sipped carefully at his tequila sunrise.

"I'll have to look into it, Peter. Usually they arrange some kind of cover for those things, so it looks like legitimate income and would be taxable; but perhaps there's a way around it. What else?" She slid her shoeless foot around Pete's ankle.

"I was wondering if there would be a way I could use this as leverage to get some kind of government contract out of the CIA."

"Hmm," she said, working her toes under his trouser legs. "That is certainly a possibility. Meanwhile, it might be a good idea if I drew up a contract with this man, something binding that would keep the IRS off your back. There are angles, of course." Her toes inched up Pete's calf, but at that moment the waitress, a former communarde and sixties revolutionary named Nina Choklat, who was working at the Ceramic Lobster to put her three bastards through school, their fathers to a man being in prison, appeared at the table with her order pad. She was dressed in early American Pilgrim, high hat and buckle boots.

"What'll it be?" she asked, thinking, Bourgeois fascist pigs.

"I'll have another tequila, straight," Prue told her in a voice that was shaking a pan of sand and water, looking for nuggets.

"Uh," Pete muttered, looking down at the menu. "She'll have the Gloucester Lobster Tails with clam sauce, and I'll have the Whalers' Steak."

"Right," Nina Choklat said. "Steak and tail. Anything to drink?" Thinking, Sexist asshole.

"Oh, I'll have another sunrise."

"OK. Another sunrise," thinking, I hope you never have another sunrise, Redneck Turkey. Nina had a gift for mixing her epithets. She folded her pad and went away.

"Where were we?" Prue asked, her smile sending a shower of wrinkles away from her lips and her toes scurrying for refuge once more under his trousers.

"IRS."

"Right. I'll work up a contract that will tie them up, maybe find a way to deduct the income. What's the man's name?"

"Arkwright. Junior Arkwright."

"Is Junior his real name? Weird. Find out if that's a nickname or what — we'll need his real name for the contract. I'll work it out, don't worry. I'm very good at this sort of thing."

"What sort of thing is that?" Pete asked with a smile. Her other foot was encircling his calf.

"Screwing people," Prue said. "Now, what kind of a government contract were you thinking of landing through this man?"

"Oh, I thought maybe I could help them get rid of their stiffs. The government, especially the CIA, must have plenty of them around that might be embarrassing. You know, assassinations, terminations — whatever the term is now. I could offer them a reduced rate for employees or for bulk orders, that kind of thing. I thought we could work out something that would be mutually agreeable. You know, ever since I went to Oklahoma to study funeral management on a Luther Hadley McWhirter scholarship I've wanted to land the really big one. Luther Hadley McWhirter himself always talked about how important it was to land the big one." Pete was beginning to respond to the feet on his leg.

"Never heard of him," Prue said. "Who was he?"

"I'm not really sure. But he was very important, a kind and generous man, a philanthropist. Scholarships, charity, that sort of thing. A great man. Everyone said so."

"Mmm." Prue lost interest. "Tell me about this man you are supposed to befriend. Have you managed it?" She smiled again, and there was something hideous about that smile, something repulsive, yet at the same time something hypnotic and fascinating about the way the wrinkles rippled away from her mouth, a stone dropped in a stagnant pond. Pete couldn't tear his eyes away.

"He was my five o'clock appointment." Pete clutched her feet between his thighs. "He looked awful — the bereaved often do, of course, but it's been three weeks. He had a bloody nose and a cut on his chin, dried shaving cream on his cheek, one side of his face shaved, circles under his eyes. He said he'd been watching television. Continuously, since his wife died."

"Mmm," Prue said. Pete laced his fingers through her toes. "And this man from the CIA thinks he might be a security risk of some kind?"

"Yeah. I must say I thought the man, Barney Gamesh his name is, was pretty nice in an ineffectual sort of way. You know, kind of soft. Mild. Scientists, I gather, are often like that — very distracted, not all there, if you know what I mean."

"I know what you mean," Prue said, wiggling her toes in his lap. "Do you think he's a security risk?"

"How could I know? He's certainly got a house full of electronic stuff, computers and so on. He probably knows a lot of secrets, but he seems so diffident and absent-minded I'm not sure he would knowingly give any of them away. Hard to tell." Pete shrugged his chair a little closer to the table to give Prue access to his "stiff." Prue called it his "tort," however. "You got a nice tort, Peter," she told him.

"Whalers' Steak!" Nina Choklat dropped the huge oval plate in front of Pete. Monopolistic imperialist running dog.

"Gloucester Tails." She dropped the plate in front of Prue. Fascist bitch.

Prue wasn't really a fascist. She was too self-centered for that. But she did have an authoritarian streak, which appeared particularly in her relationship with her ward, a seventeen-year-old myopic particle physics genius named Josh MacIntosh, who at that moment was sitting in Prue's kitchen absently chewing on a frozen beef pie. Josh had been her ward for three years, ever since his parents had surrendered to a violent dysentery while tiger hunting in northern India and Prue had won him in a difficult custody case. Prue didn't like him, but he was necessary to her self-esteem. He was someone to give orders to; and somehow Josh was gratified to have someone give him orders. His parents had always been away hunting things.

"He sounds like my boy Josh," Prue said. "Your Mr. Gamesh. Head in the clouds all the time, always daydreaming about electronic nonsense. The kid is practically useless."

"Yeah, this Gamesh was like that," Pete said.

Josh, at that moment, was staring into his frozen beef pie, his mind a soup of printed circuits, subatomic particles and computer program fragments. Prue had promised to drive him to his computer club meeting tonight, but he knew she would forget. Deliberately. He would have to take the bus. He was used to that, used to her cruelty, though it always made him suffer. He stirred his suffering into the frozen beef pie with the bits of potato and peas, the carrots and lumps of meat. He stirred in silicon chips, algorithms, pain and rage, and swirled them with his spoon, a thick, mucousy goo in his bowl, in Prue's spotless white kitchen.

"Well, to hell with him," Prue was saying.

"Yeah," Pete answered. "That reminds me, I want to computerize the crematorium."

"Mmm," she said. "That would be nice."

"Yeah," said Pete. He glanced over at the piano, where Mel Mellows, owner of the Ceramic Lobster Lounge and locally known entertainer, was just sitting down. Pete winked, and Mel winked back. Hiya, he mouthed.

"People are probably *dying* to get into your profession, eh, Mr. Boggs?" Mel had said to Pete one evening at the bar.

"Yah," Pete had told him.

"Probably a pretty *deadly* business, eh, Mr. Boggs? Eh? Eh?"

"Yah."

"You probably charge some pretty *stiff* fees, hah?"

"Yah."

Junior Arkwright was there also, hiding behind his menu, keeping an eye on Pete Boggs and Prue Nisenvy.

"The whole process under computer control: temperature, time, packaging, even outlets for the ashes. There's some demand for ashes, you know. Hong Kong, for instance." Pete sighed and waved his fork. "I could let people go from my staff, three people. Imagine. You wouldn't believe the union problems I have with those three — furnace operators, they are. It's as though they just don't believe that people die all the time, not just during business hours. It's incredible."

"Couldn't you cremate just during business hours?" Prue asked around a mouthful of tender white lobster. "I mean, you don't have to overdo it."

"Oh, that's a good one," Pete responded without smiling. "That's a good one. Overdo. Good, ha-ha. Of course not. But when there's a rush on it's more economical to keep the furnaces going full time, to avoid the start-up expense. And those bastards want double time for working at night. Imagine that. Though I must say there's no rush on right now. It seems as though nobody's dying these days."

"Terrible," she agreed, spearing another chunk of lobster. The tails came with claws and legs, but no body.

"Damn right it's terrible." Pete slashed savagely at his steak, and the red innards reminded him of Barney Gamesh's cut chin, a raw slash open to the air. He put his knife down.

"Do you know what that fellow said to me?" he asked Prue.

"Wha' fellow?" She was dipping a hunk of lobster in the thick clam butter and chewing another hunk at the same time.

"Gamesh. The fellow whose wife I've got on ice."

"Uh-uh."

"He said he wanted her back. That's what he said." Pete stared, repelled and fascinated, as the chewing wrinkles washed away from Prue's pursed lips with each ferocious chomp of her teeth on the soft lobster.

"So?" She swallowed and put down her fork to wipe her chin. "They all must say that."

"Yah. But he meant it. He said he was going to get her back. At first I thought he meant he wanted someone else to handle the funeral. You know, he wanted her body back. But no, he wanted her back really. After all, she's been in my basement for three weeks now, in cold storage while he's been making up his goddam mind — I told you he was kind of indecisive. He says he's going to get her back alive. A real screwball, you know?"

Junior Arkwright made a note. Screwball.

Prue split open a leg and pulled out the string of muscle from it. Pete thought idly of his crematorium furnace as the long white flesh was sucked lengthways into her mouth. "I was worried, I tell you," he said.

"But you're not worried now?" Her eyes glittered as she cracked another leg without looking at it.

"Mmm."

"Any idea how he's going to do it? Get her back, I mean." The leg was gone, only empty shell left.

Pete sensed, somewhere under the table, her foot beginning to stir again.

"Nah. He was a little incoherent. Something about using the computer; he was in contact with someplace called Deathwest. Couldn't really follow him. He was a little sheepish about it all. And he didn't seem to care about the funeral. Told me to keep his wife on ice a little longer, he might need the body. Whew. He really could use a course in SUM, you know? He's so *fuzzy*, so indecisive."

"SUM? What the hell is SUM?" She was sopping up the remains of the sauce with a final chunk of lobster.

"Sparling Unified Meditation. It's the latest thing; everyone's doing it. Weekend seminars to make you more assertive. SUM. It means 'I am' in Latin or something. I took it last year."

"You need to be more assertive?" She smiled and her wrinkles flowed on her face.

"Well, to tell you the truth, I was trying to land the Big One then. Luther Hadley McWhirter would have approved, I'm sure. I was trying to get a military contract — the war in Brazil — and all the military brass were being sent through SUM by the Pentagon. So I went through it too to make contacts."

"Did you get the contract out of it?" Prue hadn't been Pete's lawyer then.

"Nah. The colonel in charge of the body disposal program got so assertive himself that he decided to start his own funeral business on the side. *He* landed the Big One then and is now making a fucking fortune. He probably knew Luther Hadley McWhirter, the way he pulled that off."

"Well, it's probably more efficient that way. Keep all the military business inside the military."

"Well, it pissed me off, I'll tell you." Pete bent savagely to his Whalers' Steak and finished it swiftly under pressure from Prue's naked foot stalking his leg.

Junior Arkwright made a note: the Big One.

Nina Choklat whisked their plates away. "Anything else?" she asked. Fornicating Birchite perverts.

"Brandy," Pete told her with his most winning singles-bar smile.

"Right. Two brandies," Nina said. Reactionary capitalist

pigfuckers. She went away, her buckle boots clacking on the imitation oak decking.

"Anyway," Pete continued, "I told him he ought to do the SUM course. It's only a couple of weekends, and it could really help him to make decisions. Especially now, when he's under some strain from grief. Make him take responsibility and all . . ."

A piano arpeggio interrupted the conversation. The lights dimmed and a spotlight snapped on, illuminating Mel Mellows where he sat at the end of the bar at a large Formica piano. A few people sat on stools around the piano, leaning over drinks — two dental assistants from Mountain View and a married insurance agent named Willy Apple. Willy, who had a wife and three kids at home in Santa Clara, was trying, so far without success, to score with the dental assistants.

Pete turned to watch Mel, remembered the fly-blown sign at the entrance: MEL MELLOWS' MELLIFLUOUS MELODIES. APPEARING NIGHTLY.

"Why 'The Ceramic Lobster'?" Pete had asked Mel one evening, the evening Mel had made the string of ancient funeral business jokes.

"Mom's idea," Mel had answered. "She was very influenced by *The Glass Menagerie*. A play. Used to collect little ceramic knickknacks. Her favorite was a ceramic lobster. She said to me, when I was opening this place, 'Mel, why don't you call your place the Ceramic Lobster.' Mom always has good ideas."

"Oh," Pete had said.

Mel was speaking over his opening chords. "I'd like to render for you — that's a little whaling joke. Render, they used to render blubber on the whaling boats, get it? And this is, after all, the Ceramic Lobster, so whaling jokes are in here, or at least almost in, ha-ha. No, I don't mean my own blubber." He patted the bulge around his middle where it settled toward the piano stool. "I mean whale blubber. So,

I'd like to render for you a little song of my own composition, 'Sunnyvale-by-the-Sea.' Well" — he was playing random chords all this time — "here goes:

> Well, it's just you and me
> And the computer fac-to-ry
> In Sunnyvale-by-the-sea."

Mel's piano style was as anonymous as his voice. He belonged, as did so many other singers, to what Nina Choklat, at that moment carrying brandies over to Prue and Pete's table, referred to as the Voice Bank. Pigfucker belongs to the Voice Bank, she was thinking. She had the same thought every night when Mel began to sing. She hated Mel.

The Voice Bank was a joint account for all nightclub and cocktail lounge singers. Steve Lawrence and Buddy Grecco and Mel Tormé and Tony Bennett belonged to the Voice Bank. There were thousands of depositors in the account, and whenever one of them wanted to sing, all he had to do was make a withdrawal. That was why they sounded the same, at least to Nina Choklat, who only liked vintage Stones. There was a Voice Bank for women, too. Nina started making a list in her head as she marched with the brandies to the corner table.

> When there were shellfish in the bay,
> They might have had their say,
> But now we make them pay
> To live near Sunnyvale-by-the-sea.

As Nina served the brandies, she noticed that the woman had settled lower in her seat, withdrawing, as it were, from the nurturing breasts of the oak figurehead that flew out into the room, arms at her sides, with what Nina thought of as a pre-orgasmic expression on her face.

"Two brandies," she said sweetly. Bourgeois pleasure-seeking enemies of the people. Carrion-eating pox-riddled mongrel overlords, your day is at hand.

Nina had been thinking that way for seventeen years, ever since she dropped out as a domestic science major at Michigan State to become a pipefitter for the Weather Underground bomb squad.

> It just is not my fault,
> When I bought that chocolate malt,
> That I won you by default
> In Sunnyvale-by-the-sea.

At home, Josh MacIntosh was listening to Prue's Mel Mellows album, and it was during the rendering of "Sunnyvale-by-the-Sea" that the word "fault" triggered something in his dream-fevered brain. The word "fault" triggered the phrase "in the nick of time," and that led in turn to "in a fault in time." Soon Josh had forgotten the cold beef pie in front of him and conjured up, instead, a Feynman diagram, arrows pointing up (forward in time) and arrows pointing down (backward in time). Subatomic particles moved along those arrows, up and down: photons, pions, positrons. It was all in how you considered it.

Junior Arkwright paid no attention to Mel's song. He was picking at a crab salad and wondering what was happening under Pete's table. His new agent's dinner partner was slumped deeply into her chair. She had an expression of intense concentration on her face, as though she were doing something with her *feet*.

> When you gave me the boot,
> Well, I didn't give a hoot,
> I just held you by the foot
> In Sunnyvale-by-the-sea.

"Foot" did it for Junior. His chin bobbed for his Adam's apple, up and down like Halloween.

> You said I was a heel,
> That I'd lost my sex appeal
> But nothing seemed that real
> In Sunnyvale-by-the-sea.

She was doing something with her feet under the corner table. Junior was sure of that.

> My toe is on the line
> My heart pickled in brine,
> My soul no longer mine
> In Sunnyvale-by-the-sea.

Toe. Oh, God. Sole. Heel. Foot. He clutched spasmodically at the linen tablecloth.

Sunnyvale isn't even by the sea, Nina thought. It's by the bay. This revisionist creep can't even get his geography straight. She passed Junior's table. "Sir? Are you all right?" she asked.

Her buckle boots were in clear view over the edge of his table. The light winking off the silver buckle somehow sent him back into the Einsteinian universe. "Oh, sure, I'm fine. Why do you ask?" His bulging eyes rose to her face, challenging her.

"You looked a little peaked. Maybe the crab salad isn't good?" Her voice registered concern, warmth, love. Degenerate bourgeois glutton.

He glanced down at her boots again. "No, I'm fine," he mumbled.

> Well, it's just you and me,
> Two bushes and a tree,
> My hand upon your knee,
> My kitty cat's pedigree —
> Yes, one big jubilee
> In Sunnyvale-by-the-sea.

Mel finished his song with a flourish and settled back onto his piano stool for a moment, as though exhausted by the effort of rendering.

"Sunnyvale isn't even by the sea," Nina hissed at him on her way back to the kitchen with Junior's crab salad remains. "It's by the bay."

"I know," Mel said with a smile. "But Mom liked it this way. Poetic license, she says."

She would, Voice Bank pigfucker.

Prue's feet stroked Pete's rigid "tort," and his eyes of Paul Newman blue rolled upward in contemplation of the lugubrious puritan brown ceiling as if it were the Sistine ceiling itself. "I want to plumb your depths," she croaked at him over the edge of the table. "The depths of your soul!"

When she felt through her wrinkled soles Pete's answering thrusts and noticed that his eyes had rolled on past the Sistine to gaze at the glorious frescoes painted in lurid colors on the ceiling of his skull, she sat upright, took a deep drink of her brandy, and smiled at Pete. "Drink your brandy, Peter," she commanded sternly.

"Uh."

Junior was just congratulating himself on a narrow escape, seeing Prue and Pete sitting upright like ordinary people, sipping their drinks, when she began to slide once more. Uh-oh. Down again.

In Josh's mind the pions were flowing down, colliding, splitting, recombining. The Feynman diagram grew in complexity, the quantum field theory blending with the general theory of relativity into a partial unified field theory. Time and space pulsated like an electric orange in his head, rotating slowly, glowing, a great navel orange, each segment of the natural universe unified under the glowing orange skin. Josh felt his fever, delirium. The Josephson Effect floated through the orange; electron probabilities dictate that any particular electron could be anywhere, even over there. Or — and here he slapped his hand to his forehead in a gesture very similar to Barney's bloody slap earlier that day — or anywhen! That is, if $\bar{e}$, no, if $\phi = (\vec{k} - \vec{K'}) \cdot (\vec{r} - \vec{r'}) - (\omega - \Omega') \tau$ . . . Josh was lost into his timeless fault.

Mel Mellows launched himself then, a pasta rocket, into a

spirited if lusterless rendition of "Cocktails for Two," apparently under the impression that it might increase customer consumption. He didn't notice Prue's slow subsidence into her chair, but had he noticed, it might have appeared as it she were being born of the oaken figurehead that soared over her head, dropped, as it were, into her aqueous night.

The birth was not, of course, traumatic for Prue. Not at all. Her papery soles rubbed briskly once more, preparing a doughy surprise for Pete's habeous corpus, to release him, perhaps, from unlawful restraint. Meantime, Prue wondered if Barney Gamesh's wife had prepared a will. There could be a fault in the system somewhere that would allow a smart lawyer to intervene.

This wasn't the last time the word "fault" would echo in Sunnyvale. Exactly 9.6 miles to the northwest of the Ceramic Lobster, two vast plates of subterranean rock were distressing one another toward divorce, two members of the earth household having a domestic spat. One was about to pack up and leave — the one to the west. At exactly eight forty-six in the evening the San Andreas fault fractured to the tune of 6.3 on the Richter scale. Not really enough to do a reprise of the 1906 quake, but more than adequate to shake the flying mermaid over Prue's head off the wall and onto the table, narrowly missing her and toppling Pete's brandy into his throbbing lap, thereby disinfecting Prue's leathery feet.

There was some panic in the room. Dishes rattled together, silver clattered. A retired laundry products district manager from Palo Alto dropped his bridge into his butterscotch pudding. Willy Apple sold two Luther Hadley McWhirter Memorial Earthquake Protection policies and scored big with the dental assistants.

Nina Choklat forgot her revolution and clutched at Mel Mellows, who sat stupefied at the piano in the middle of the third chorus of "Cocktails for Two."

"Do something," she shouted into his ear. He jumped to his feet, spread his arms out wide, and in his most mellifluous voice said, "Stand by, everyone. Do not panic. Please. Stand by."

4

The earthquake rattled Barney awake from his post-television stupor on the couch, dried blood and shaving cream still smeared around his face or printed on the couch pillows, a runic inscription of his woe.

"Wha?" he said to the darkened room, glaring wildly. The dream was strange, and he felt the disorientation of the dreamer. He'd been walking across sun-cracked earth in a day that shimmered with heat through a landscape of lifeless vegetation. He met a man with huge eyes and no hands who waved his stumps toward the city, baked brown on the horizon. Then he was climbing some stairs along the outside of a building, up one wall, across a terrace, up another wall, across another terrace, endlessly. Then he saw Penny, her head veiled, her body naked. "Why did you ruin the microwave oven?" he asked her petulantly. She said something he couldn't understand, though he knew he should, and suddenly the building began to shake. "What?" he shouted. "What did you say?" "I said, 'Is it hot enough for you?'" she shouted back.

He sat up, stared around the room, his face slick with sweat. "Wha?" he repeated.

The only thing visible in the darkness was the CRT screen of his computer, glowing across the room, flashing on and off its endless "Stand by." Under it another line of print had appeared. He climbed painfully from the couch and limped over to the escritoire to read it.

"Data link Deathwest terminates in five minutes unless acknowledged: 8:46 P.M."

My God, the timeshare phone has been connected all day. Ah, but it's on them. And he wondered, for the first time that day, who *they* were.

"Who are you?" he typed.

"Holiday Inn."

"Holiday Inn?"

"Holiday Inn."

"This is a Holiday Inn computer link?"

"In a manner of speaking."

"Do I make a reservation?" Even in his present mood it seemed to Barney a whimsical conversation.

"No. There will be a room for you when you arrive."

Barney walked once around the living room. He turned on the table lamp beside the couch. He turned on the standing lamp beside the recliner. He turned off the table lamp beside the couch. He walked into the kitchen. He walked out of the kitchen and back to the keyboard.

"You mean people who die go to the Holiday Inn?" he asked.

"Yes."

"I don't believe it."

The computer didn't answer that. It's not a question, Barney realized. But what can I ask it?

"Is my wife there?"

"Penelope Gamesh." The cursor blinked for a moment and raced on, printing out a date, the date of her death three weeks before. "She is here."

"How can I get her back?"

"Please stand by." The cursor blinked, then vanished, indicating incoming data.

Barney paced again, his eyes riveted to the screen. He made a small arc to the left edge of the escritoire, then to the right edge. He went through the arc again, widened it, from recliner to couch and back. His eyes were unblinkingly connected to the screen.

He made his round of the lights again, touching familiar

things in the living room, keeping contact with his real world, the world of objects and texture, the world of matter, the world of unwhimsical everyday. His mind was refusing to work, so that instead of wondering about his strange contact with the Holiday Inn of Death, he noted under his hand the rough texture of the couch arm, the parchment feel of the lampshade, the cold plastic of the light switch, the metal of the doorknob. His eyes, wired to the screen, saw nothing until the cursor reappeared and printed a swift line across the screen.

His hand trailed down the lampshade and he walked stiff-legged over to the computer.

"Deathwest control says 'Gilgamesh.' "

The words had no particular meaning. Barney flicked idly at the dried blood pooled in the pad of the CHARACTER DE-LETE key as the sentence swam across his mind. Gilgamesh?

"What?" he typed.

"Deathwest control says 'Gilgamesh.' "

Barney backed away. His knees hit the recliner and he sat. Gil. Ga. Mesh. Gil Gamesh. A relative? Barney could recall no relative named Gilbert. He returned to the keyboard. "What is Gilgamesh?"

"Deathwest control informs data link to be terminated. Further contact terminated. 800 269 2559 no longer operative. Codes altered. Deathwest control will no longer accept contact from user. Thank you for calling." The cursor reappeared, blinking at the lower left of the screen. Barney tried commands, but he was no longer in contact with Deathwest.

He tried redialing the number but got a recording. No longer in service.

Just then his own phone rang. "Damn," Barney said. "Damn."

Penny had trouble believing the Holiday Inn Deathwest. She had been there for three weeks now, and they still had not given her any word on the disposition of her case. She swam in the pool, ate her meals with Haig Despot, drank grasshoppers in the bar (the Karnak Room, frescoes of palms and ibises, jackal gods and water plants, borders of hieroglyphics). She watched television, a lot of television. There was nothing much else to do.

Her favorite show was the Keb Tefnut show, called *This Was Your Death*. It was always on in the morning, before breakfast, though it was difficult to determine the time of day here since the sky was always such a dismal and lowering gray.

"Today," Keb was saying in high-resolution color on her room set, "we have a special guest, a Mr. Otto Flink of Coos Bay, Oregon. Mr. Flink, who drove his Chrysler Monte Cristo into the ocean one night — driving while intoxicated is what they call it there — Mr. Flink has put in a request for his next life that we found somewhat unusual. Please give a great big Deathwest welcome to Mr. Otto Flink."

The studio audience went wild. Penny wondered how you got to be a member of the studio audience. So far as she knew, there was nowhere to go from the Holiday Inn.

Otto Flink appeared, a ruddy, powerful man with thick fingers and gaps in his teeth. He shook hands with Keb Tefnut and sat down.

"Cripes," said Penny, turning off her set. The whole thing must be a setup for the guests here. She went to the dining room for breakfast.

"You're late," the woman from the DMV informed her. She sniffed and led Penny to her table. Haig Despot was just patting his mouth with his napkin. A smear of Spanish omelet littered his plate.

He jumped to his feet when Penny appeared. "Breaker; breaker nineteen, this is Wooden Nickel, do you copy?" His mouth was wreathed in a smile, a happy, happy smile, but his eyes were, as usual, bleak.

"We copy, Wooden Nickel," Penny answered gently. She smiled back and sat down.

"You know," Haig said to her in a confidential whisper, "I think they're getting ready to classify me."

"Oh," said Penny, tapping her spoon impatiently on the white linen tablecloth. When were they going to classify her?

"Yeah. I have this feeling."

"You have a feeling?"

"Yeah. Like an itch. Actually, I'm a little worried. Because of, you know, the stereo and all. The gin and tonic, electrifying, ha-ha." There was no laughter in his face. Only his bow tie looked perky and pleased, a pair of scarlet arrows pointing at each other.

"Why should you worry about that?"

"Well, some people around here say you get sent back as a clam or something. If you kill yourself."

"A clam? Were you watching Keb Tefnut this morning?"

"No. Why?"

"Some man *asked* to go back as a clam. Oh, never mind. You were here eating breakfast. I can't imagine it, though; it sounds so silly. I'm not sure I want to go back at all."

"Oh, you must go back. I'm sure of that. Everyone here goes back, one way or another."

"That sounds ominous," Penny said, putting down her spoon. "How do you know?"

"Frankly," Haig lowered his voice again, "the manager told me."

"You mean that guy with the tulip-shaped translation thing? Isn't he the desk clerk?"

"He is. *And* the manager. He said everyone's gotta go back."

"Hmph." Penny's Spanish omelet arrived. "Well, we'll see about that," she said after the DMV had left.

*

"Good evening, Mr. Gamesh," the voice on the phone said. "Sorry to trouble you at this hour."

Barney waited, but that seemed to be it. "Who is this?" he asked, finally.

"Oh. Sorry. This is the Sunnyvale Police Department, Sergeant Masterbrook."

"Oh. What can I do for you, Sergeant?"

"What we want is, Mr. Gamesh, do you drive a late-model Chevrolet Silver Sword? Of course you do." The sergeant went on without waiting for a reply. "The car is registered to you."

"Yes. And . . . ?"

But the sergeant seemed to be finished.

"Well?" Barney asked at last.

"Yes," the sergeant said briskly. "We have a complaint here. From a Mrs. Lotte Bunyon. Blue Ox Drive?"

"Mmm." Barney was confused.

"Tell me, Mr. Gamesh. Do you know where your car is right now."

"Of course. It's parked in front of my house."

"Mmm-hmm. And tell me this, Mr. Gamesh, if you don't mind. I'm sorry, as I said, to trouble you at this hour, but we do have this call from Mrs. Bunyon, and you understand we do have to follow it up. Tell me this, exactly where do you live?"

"Thirty-four and a half Puerco de Esmeralda Lane."

"That's in the Cojones de Santa Teresa subdivision?"

"Yes. Why? What's this all about?"

"Did you notice the earthquake we had a while ago, Mr. Gamesh?"

"Earthquake? What are you talking about? What earthquake? What is this?" A wisp of fear threaded through Barney's confusion, weaving an uncomfortable blanket.

"We just had an earthquake, Mr. Gamesh," the sergeant said reasonably. "I'm surprised you didn't notice it. It was quite a jolt, really. Knocked a pistol off the table down here at headquarters. Pistol went off, too. Surprised a lot of us down here, I'll tell you. Six point three on the Rutter scale, they tell me."

"Richter," Barney corrected absently.

"Right, Mr. Gamesh. Six point three on the Ritter scale. Are you quite sure you didn't notice it?"

"Well, I was asleep on the couch at the time, and something woke me up, but I thought it was a dream. I suppose it could have been a tremor of some kind . . ."

"Aha!" Sergeant Masterbrook had clearly solved that mystery. "You were asleep. Well, that explains it, then. Dreaming too. Mmmm. Well. Then you weren't driving your car?"

"What?"

"I said, 'Then you weren't driving your car?' During the earthquake."

"Driving my car? Are you crazy? I just told you I was asleep here on my couch. My car is parked right outside on the street, in front of the house. At least it was three weeks ago, which was the last time I drove it. I've been inside since then. I've been, I've been sick. You see, my wife . . . died, and I . . ."

"There, there, Mr. Gamesh. No need to get distraught," the sergeant soothed. "This is a purely routine investigation, you know. Purely routine. We had a call from Mrs. Bunyon, Mrs. Lotte Bunyon. Of course, we've had calls from her before, and always we have to investigate. Often it's nothing, fears, noises in the night, that sort of thing. She's an elderly person, and you know how *they* are sometimes. But I would appreciate it, Mr. Gamesh, if you could do one simple little favor for me. Just a small favor, to help me in this investigation."

"Oh, all right, Sergeant . . . uh . . . ?"

"Masterbrook. Sergeant Gary Masterbrook."

"Sergeant Masterbrook. What is it?"

"It's really very small, Mr. Gamesh, but it would help so much. Would you take a tiny peek outside your house and tell me if your late-model Silver Sword is still parked in front?"

"Oh, all right."

There was no car parked in front of Barney's house.

"My car is not in front of my house," Barney said. "It's been stolen. How did you know it was stolen?"

"No, no. Not really stolen, Mr. Gamesh. Not really stolen at all. Your car is in Mrs. Bunyon's living room, Mr. Gamesh. The earthquake probably jarred it loose. I wonder if I could come on out to your house now and get a statement from you? I realize it's late, but there you are. The Sunnyvale Police never rest; around the clock, as it were. Not like some people."

A lance of guilt fixed Barney to his chair. Sergeant Masterbrook had to work around the clock! "Of course," he said weakly.

"Now see here," Penny was saying. "I must get this straight. What if I don't want to go back? What if I want to go somewhere else?"

She had buttonholed the desk clerk–manager outside his office. He was wearing a paisley-patterned crêpe de Chine shirt with puff sleeves and a baroque, carved, wooden mandala around his neck — and, of course, the translator on its lanyard.

"Gnkaah?" he said. The tone was interrogative.

"Gah." Penny twisted her fingers together. "Look, just what is the disposition of my case?"

"Now, now, Mrs. Gamesh. You must understand these things take time. We cannot rush, especially in your case, which, I must say, is presenting us with certain difficulties we do not ordinarily meet. And where else could you go?"

"What do you mean? What difficulties?"

"Oh, you know . . . things . . ." The manager waved his hand at the walnut door of his office.

"But there must be a way not to go back? I mean, I didn't really want to stay. That's obvious, isn't it? I diddled with the microwave oven, didn't I? Though now I can't seem to remember why." Her tone faltered. "But," she went on brightly, "there must be other places to go, mustn't there?"

"Of course, Mrs. Gamesh. But not for you. Not for people like you. Really, I'm surprised your case hasn't already been decided. You took a step backward when you did that with the oven. I can't understand it myself. There seem to be several complicating factors, some *pull* on you. But things are proceeding. You will hear soon. I'm sure of that. There will be something very special in store for you. After all, you were suicide of the year. It says so right outside." The mouth was moving and smiling, but the translator had stopped, a problem with the computer. Then it said, "Understand?"

"No." Penny stifled the urge to tear at that smiling face with her fingernails. "Can I put in to stay? Or go somewhere else? Can I file a request somewhere?"

"Certainly, Mrs. Gamesh. But I would suggest you be a bit patient. Just a little while longer. Until your case is decided finally. Believe me, the computers are working on it right now. Day and night, around the clock. Meantime, I suggest you read the book in your dresser drawer. A free service for all our guests." He smiled widely and dropped his electronic tulip. The interview was over. The tulip swung at the end of its lanyard as he walked away. Penny watched as he went to the entrance of the dining room and spoke at length with the woman from the DMV. Every now and then he nodded in Penny's direction, waving his hands. Penny noticed that he was not speaking through his tulip. The staff could dispense with it.

Penny turned away and went into the gloom of the Kar-

nak Room for a grasshopper. Two stools away Haig Despot
drooped mournfully over a gin and tonic. At last he looked
up.

"Breaker, breaker," he said weakly, and fell silent.

"Hullo, Wooden Nickel," Penny said. They stared into
their drinks for a while.

Haig came over and sat beside her. "Didja find out anything?"

"Not much. He told me to read a book."

"What book?" His voice was as flat as the tonic in his
drink.

"I dunno. One in the room, in the dresser drawer."

"Oh. Probably a Bible. You know, those Gideon people
put Bibles in all the motel rooms. I know, I used to be a
salesman. Gideon people are probably here too."

"Maybe." Penny finished her drink.

"Next time," Haig said sadly, "I think I'd like to be a librarian. Peace and quiet. Yeah, a librarian."

"Mmmm," Penny responded. "Peace and quiet."

Sergeant Masterbrook was a large, pear-shaped man with
a friendly nose and sweet, crinkled eyes. His gunbelt was
slung low over his belly, the holster hitched forward at an
angle. He liked to hook his thumb in the belt and lean
against things. At the moment he was leaning against Barney's escritoire. Barney found it unsettling to be shown such
deference in such an imposing form.

"I'm sorry to disturb you at such a late hour," the
sergeant had said. "I realize it's late, especially in view of
your recent tragedy and all, but I'm afraid I must. I'm on
the swing shift this evening and must work till midnight.
I'm sure you wouldn't like to work those kind of hours,
would you? Of course you wouldn't. A policeman's lot is
not an easy one. No, sir. Now about your car. If you'll just
give me a statement acknowledging your guilt in the matter,

why, I'll be on my way, and won't trouble you further. To-night."

"Guilt?" Barney felt faint. Had he committed a crime?

"Well, certainly. Of course, you have a right to remain silent. And you have a right to legal counsel. You have many rights in this great country of ours, Mr. Gamesh. And the Sunnyvale Police Department will do everything in its power to protect those rights. It's our sworn duty, after all. And we never sleep. Never sleep." Sergeant Masterbrook yawned widely with a flash of golden fillings.

"I'm sure you work very hard, Sergeant. But am I being charged with a crime?" Barney sat abruptly. The table lamp beside the couch appeared to be expanding and contracting, brightening and darkening. Fluctuations in the voltage, probably. What did I do?

"Crime?" Sergeant Masterbrook was astounded. "Crime? No crime, Mr. Gamesh. I'm sorry if I gave that impression. You can't be responsible for an earthquake, can you?"

"No, I . . ."

"But you are responsible for your automobile. It is, after all, registered in your name. And you paid for it. And it is at this minute in Mrs. Lotte Bunyon's living room. Her picture window is ruined, her sofa is ruined. And her new Quasar console television, for which she says she has not yet paid. So you see?"

"No, I . . ."

"Of course, of course. Do you suppose I could have a glass of water?" Masterbrook gave Barney a friendly pat on the shoulder. Buddies. We understand each other, that pat said. We don't really need to talk a lot because we *understand*. "A glass of water? Sure." Barney waved toward the kitchen.

"Boy, this room sure is a mess," Sergeant Masterbrook shouted over the sound of running water. "What happened to your oven?"

"It was . . ." Barney started to tell him, then fell silent. The running water stopped and the sounds of drinking came from the other room. Running water again, and more drinking.

"Ahhh," the sergeant sighed as he re-entered the living room. "In this drought it seems water tastes better than ever, don't you think?" He settled his bulk against the escritoire again.

"Oh, yes," Barney answered eagerly, looking up at the massive figure towering over him.

"You some kind of scientist?" Barney's best friend Sergeant Masterbrook asked him.

"Engineer."

"Right. Choo-choo, woo-woo." The sergeant pulled an imaginary whistle cord. He laughed. "No, but seriously," he said.

"Computers," Barney said.

"Ah. That must be what this is." The seventeenth-century escritoire creaked dangerously as the ponderous officer shifted his bulk.

"Uh-huh," Barney said. "About my car . . ."

Penny pulled the leatherbound book from her dresser drawer. Inside the cover, in gold lettering, she found: THE GIDEON SOCIETY. OK, she thought. A Bible. Wooden Nickel was right.

The Tibetan Book of the Dead. She read, "To the Divine Body of Truth, the Incomprehensible, Boundless Light."

What is this? she thought. She opened it at random. "Thereupon, because of the power of bad karma," she read, "the glorious blue light of the Wisdom of the *Dharma-Dhātu* will produce in thee fear and terror, and thou wilt wish to flee from it."

The phone beside the bed rang.

"Yes?"

"Mrs. Gamesh, would you report to the manager's office, please. The manager wishes to speak with you." The line went dead.

Penny replaced *The Tibetan Book of the Dead* in her dresser drawer and went to the manager's office, and for the first time since she had arrived at the Holiday Inn Deathwest she felt fear. It's that book, she thought. It's got me spooked.

As she walked through the dim corridors it came to her that she was dead. Really dead. Funny, she thought. I hadn't considered it before. I'm really dead.

The dark green doors of the rooms she passed suddenly seemed to be hiding something, concealing the bodies of the dead, the dusty skeletons, the rotting flesh. The carpeting of the corridor dragged at her feet like cobwebs, soft but somehow sticky, and she felt a dusty panic rising in her throat. She passed a fire extinguisher on the wall, and a shadow seemed to loom from it, threatening. She would suffocate in carbon dioxide foam; she would die. No, she was already dead. Dead. And now she was walking through the corridors of death to talk to the manager. The manager of death. He was going to tell her what would become of her.

Suddenly she had changed her mind. She wanted to go back. She wanted to be alive. Bad karma.

Sergeant Masterbrook left with a signed statement in which Barney took full responsibility for the damage to Mrs. Bunyon's living room, her sofa and television, her window, even the withered shrubs in her front yard.

Barney knew the insurance wouldn't even cover it. Oh, Penny, why aren't you here to handle all this? Penny always took care of the insurance. She always balanced the checkbook and made the investments. She always knew how to handle people. It was occurring to Barney that Penny was gone, that the hole in the kitchen Sergeant Masterbrook had so vocally noted was all that remained to remind him of her presence.

"Penny," he said to the escritoire where he had spent so much of their married life. "Oh, Penny, what is a Gilgamesh?"

Maybe, Barney thought, sinking back into the recliner, maybe Pete Boggs knows who, or what, this Gilgamesh is. He's in the funeral business, after all.

For the third time that day, Barney fell asleep.

Penny dragged her leaden feet through the final few yards of corridor and into the fluorescent light of the lobby. She pushed through the glue of panic across the open space, a space wide and clear and lighted and so remote that she failed to acknowledge Haig Despot's "Breaker, breaker" from across the vast emptiness of the room.

They're going to do something terrible to me. I won't see the glorious blue light of the Wisdom of *Dharma-Dhātu.* I'm dead.

The manager's receptionist smiled brightly and meaninglessly at her. "Yes?"

"The manager called. I'm Penny Gamesh." Her voice was very far away. It sounded normal but far, far away.

The receptionist nodded and spoke into her phone. "The manager will see you in a moment," she informed Penny. "Please stand by."

5

"All right, buttbrains." A. Spencer Sparling paced the dais at the front of the room in which seventy-five SUM trainees were lying face down on the floor. He was dressed in a two-tone morocco leather suit, six-inch suede platform shoes of a deep blood red and a crimson formal shirt with an aquamarine tie.

But to Barney, watching the founder of SUM through slitted eyes, his still-aching nose pressed into the rough, durable hotel carpet, the remarkable thing about A. Spencer Sparling was his extraordinary stature. It was clearly not simply that he was not tall nor simply that he was below average height. No, he was *short* in some kind of absolute sense, and his platform shoes only served to emphasize that shortness.

And then — Barney swiveled his eyes slightly — there was Sparling's assistant, who stood gracefully to one side. She was well over six feet tall and had the brightest, whitest, cleanest blond hair he had ever seen.

Spencer paced back and forth, scanning the trainees for any deviation from his instruction to lie face down with eyes closed. Thirty-seven of those on the floor were trying to be inconspicuous about watching the leader. "All right, buttbrains," he repeated. "My assistant, Snow, is going to walk through the room. From time to time she will kick one of you. If there is any flinching or other sign that you realize what is going to happen to you, we will know you are cheating and you will be thrown out. Without a refund. Right, Snow?"

"Oh, yes, Spence," she breathed. Her voice was a whisper

of offshore Pago Pago breezes, an aromatic breath of adoration. Had he been standing closer to her, it might have ruffled the exquisitely cut hairs that waved on top of Spencer's shapely autocratic head.

"OK, Snow honey, you go on and walk among these buttbrains. If any one of them so much as twitches, you sing out and the proctors will toss the scum right out of this room. We have neither time nor room for vermin who cannot follow instructions when it's for their own good." Spencer's voice was even, smooth, reasonable, infinitely persuasive. Barney thought, even as he wondered what the hell he was doing there, lying face down on the Milpitas Holiday Inn conference room carpet, that he would be willing to buy anything from A. Spencer Sparling.

Sparling had a lot to sell. One of his sidelines was trafficking in gurus, organizing public and private audiences with various members of his stable. He already had signed up for tours of the United States, besides the usual complement of Indian mystics and spiritual luminaries, three Chinese, twelve Japanese, a Korean, two Tibetans, a well-known Sufi with a speech impediment, an illiterate Lithuanian peasant with blue-light visions and several South Americans with high-altitude drug habits. He was about to add a filthy Turkish idiot who smiled and drooled. This latter was to prove one of the most popular of Spencer's imports; pilgrims granted an audience with him would come away shaking their heads and saying, over and over, "I get it, I get it," softly to themselves. After paying $300 for the privilege, Spencer told Snow they ought to get it, whatever "it" was. His cut was 75 percent, the rest going into a trust for the Turk's family. Spencer really knew how to make a profit.

An avid reader of *Psychology Today* and other journals of the trendy self market, as he called it, Spencer could foresee what was coming, which was why technology was about to funnel enormous funds into his empire's coffers through the medium of MOM, Multiple Orgasms for Men, the very vanguard of growth and self-improvement, the frontier of truth, of unisex equality (if women can have them, why not men?), the cutting edge, as he called it, the blade of the plow that turned the fertile soil of money into Spencer's cupped hands. "I think of myself as a farmer," he told Snow, "tilling, planting, and reaping. Especially reaping."

At the moment he was reaping Barney for $375 for this weekend session in Milpitas, across the bottom of the bay from Sunnyvale. Barney had bought, for his $375, a better attitude toward life, greater peace of mind, coming to terms with his inadequacies, taking responsibility for his actions, learning that he got what he wanted, no matter how bad it was, and not taking any shit from anybody.

At the moment he was taking a lot of shit from A. Spencer Sparling. So far this morning he had shouted loudly, all by himself (one by one all the trainees had had to shout it), "I am a flaming asshole. I am a snot-filled buttbrain."

Barney was so anxious in anticipation of shouting it and so embarrassed afterward that he noticed no one in the room except the overweight woman who shouted before him and the skinny kid who shouted after.

"Where are you going, buttbrain?" Spencer suddenly shrieked. Barney tried to peek without moving.

"I gotta go to the bathroom," a timid voice offered.

"You gotta go to the bathroom," Spencer mimicked nastily. "Lie down, buttbrain," he thundered. "I'll tell you when you can go to the bathroom. I'll tell you when you can eat, when you can get up, sit down, speak. I'll tell you when you can fucking *breathe,* so get it straight, buttbrain. In here I am your god. Out there I am your god. I watch everything you do, buttbrain, and if you get out of line one inch, you're *out.* Understand, buttbrain: *out!*"

"But . . ."

"Throw that fucker out," Spencer screamed, his voice

purple with rage, all his smoothness, evenness, reason-
ableness gone. Barney heard a body hit the floor.

"All right," Spencer said, "he can stay. But the next buttbrain that tries something like that leaves. OK, Snow,
honey."

Silence fell over the room. No one wanted to be *out;* no
one wanted to be rejected by A. Spencer Sparling, who was
God.

Soft steps sounded on the carpet. Every so often Barney
heard a thump and a grunt. The steps seemed to come
closer. Another thump. Another grunt.

Barney could see the tips of Snow's hiking boots poking
out from under the hem of her floor-lenth djellaba. Hiking
boots? They were coming his way, the brown toes rustling
under the white linen, emerging and retreating, small, blunt,
brown animals aimed at him. He closed his eyes.

Thump. He gasped, his eyes watered, his bloodied nose
throbbed again, but he did not complain. No one else had
complained.

The feet whispered on.

What am I doing here? Barney asked himself for the thousandth time that morning. What? Pete Boggs suggests it, and
here I am. I do whatever anyone suggests. But I don't like
this. And then he remembered the $375 he would lose if he
left, and decided to stay. After all, SUM would teach him
not to take any shit from anyone, not even Pete Boggs,
even — and here the vast, deferential and humiliating bulk
passed across his inner eyelids — even Sergeant Masterbrook, who also had a gentle, humble, reassuring voice
and the knack of turning Barney's bowels to watery broth.
A. Spencer Sparling certainly wouldn't take it from Sergenat
Masterbrook. Even Penny wouldn't have.

"All right, buttbrains, sit up," Spencer ordered.

Seventy-five people sat up, blinking. Spencer leaned
against the lectern, hands deep in his leather jacket pockets,
smiling at the buttbrains. Snow stood deferentially to one

side, a white votive candle with a very pale flame burning at the altar of the god of good behavior.

"And now, buttbrains, it's time to sink in. You are going to sink into yourselves and find the buttbrained asshole in there. You will remember the most embarrassing, stupid humiliating asshole thing you've ever done or thought, and you are going to sing it out right here in this room. Every one of you will sing it out.

"No one will eat any lunch until every buttbrain here has spoken up. Asshole buttbrains."

The seventy-five sat in uneasy silence. Barney glanced hastily around the room, avoiding eyes. Everybody else was glancing around the room, avoiding eyes. Especially A. Spencer Sparling's eyes. Spencer glared from the dais, pinning them in place with an entomologist's stare.

Barney's mind was blank. There must be some humiliating incident he could come up with, some peccadillo or deviant act, some nasty sin he could dredge up and safely present to the group, something that would satisfy that all-powerful god on the dais. But blankness spread across the acreage of his memory, a wide, deep, somehow seething blankness in which nothing stirred but a feeling of vague wistfulness.

"Uh, I have something." It was the timid voice that earlier had wanted to go to the bathroom.

"And what might that be?" Spencer asked.

"I, uh, well, I've wet my pants."

"Terrific." Spencer curled his upper lip into his neatly trimmed mustache, a curl of such devastating sarcasm that the room, which had begun to stir with excitement, fell silent again, aghast.

Minutes went by. Stomachs began to rumble. Pressure was building in the seventy-four remaining full bladders in the room. Barney felt a faintness coming on, a faintness mingled with fear. Pretty soon, he figured, everyone there was going to wet his pants.

There was a loud, throat-clearing sound. "I can't control my need for Boston cream pie." It was the overweight woman.

"Go on," Spencer prodded, almost gently.

"Well, I once had sex with a Boston cream pie."

"You had sex with a Boston cream pie?" Spencer's voice was a caress.

"That's right." Her words began to tumble over one another in her eagerness to divulge all. "I took a Boston cream pie, fresh from the bakery, home with me. I took off all my clothes — I don't understand what made me do this — and I dipped my hands in the Boston cream pie." She was beginning to pant as she recounted the episode, her hands moving in vague dipping motions. "And then I smeared the Boston cream pie all over myself." Every repetition of "Boston cream pie" acquired more emphasis, more excitement. "And then I licked the Boston cream pie off every part of my body I could reach with my tongue."

"Yes?" Spencer encouraged her as she faltered.

"Then I, well, I started to, you know, excite myself. With the Boston cream pie."

"And this was humiliating?" Spencer cajoled.

"Oh, no. It was exciting. It wasn't humiliating at all. What was humiliating was that I got caught. My husband came home. Now he asks me to do it all the time; he wants to watch me with the Boston cream pie."

"I see," said Spencer. "Next!"

The floodgates were opened, and a deluge of minor sins, embarrassing fetishes — handkerchiefs, shoes, velvet, food cravings, bathroom behavior — came gushing from the group. Volunteers for confession stumbled over one another's words to expose their most sweaty secret and nauseating little acts, and as the voices spilled this garbage into the room, Barney began to free-associate such an overwhelming list of terrors of his own that he didn't know where to begin. Finally, though, it was his turn.

"I confessed to a policeman that I was guilty of an accident even though it wasn't my fault. I was so scared and guilty when he asked me that I just automatically confessed, and now it seems humiliating to me."

"OK," Spencer said. He seemed less interested in Barney's sin than in some of the others, and Barney found himself feeling very hurt and left out.

"You buttbrains are doing fairly well, but there is still one of you in the back of the room who has not spoken up yet. No one goes to lunch until every one here has confessed something. So you there, let's hear it." Spencer pointed.

"You there" was the skinny kid next to Barney. The kid was staring into space and did not appear to be paying attention. Barney nudged him with his elbow.

"Huh?"

"You haven't confessed yet," Barney whispered. "No one can eat until you do." The kid stared at him uncomprehendingly.

"Confessed what?" He pulled at his earlobe and frowned.

"Some secret humiliation or something. Everyone else has already confessed."

"Oh. Uh."

"Speak up," Spencer shouted from the dais.

"I said, 'Uh.' I don't have any special humiliation."

"Well, well. And what do you buttbrains think of that? This skinny asshole doesn't have any special shame —"

The skinny kid interrupted him. "In a way everything is shameful to me. I'm very easily embarrassed and humiliated. Everything I do, the way I daydream all the time and don't hear people, the way I blush easily. Everything that's done to me."

Spencer glowered at him. "You're going to learn, buttbrain, in this one short weekend, that nothing is *done* to you. You are going to learn that you are responsible for everything that happens."

"Oh, you don't understand," said the skinny kid. "I don't mind it at all. I like it."

"What?"

"I like it. I like being humiliated and embarrassed. See, lots of times I get caught sort of thinking of things, day-dreaming, like now. It embarrasses me. And I like it. It makes me know I'm alive, that people see me, know I'm real." He stopped tugging at his earlobe and folded his hands in his lap.

Spencer was leaning over his lectern, staring down at the skinny kid. Two or three times he started to open his mouth, to say something. Finally he announced, "Lunch. You have twenty minutes. If you're not back in this room, lying in place, at the end of twenty minutes with your faces in the rug, that's just too bad. The doors will be locked and you might as well go home. Permanently. And continue being the silly, out-of-control, asshole buttbrain you've always been."

There were thirty-seven men waiting in line at the men's room door, thirty-eight women waiting at the ladies' room. The crush was terrible: the hopping from foot to foot, the knee-squeezing, the agony. Barney and the skinny kid stood next to each other against the wall outside the men's room waiting their turn. Barney smiled shyly.

"Barney Gamesh," he said.

"Huh?" said the kid, tugging at his earlobe.

"Barney Gamesh. My name. I'm an engineer." He held out his hand.

"Oh." The kid shook Barney's hand. "Josh MacIntosh," he said. "What kind of an engineer?"

"Computers. Mainly processor chips, but I'm moving more into software design. Programming."

The skinny kid blushed. "My hobby is particle physics." His normally pale face now flushed a deep crimson.

"That sounds like an interesting hobby," Barney said skeptically.

"Yeah," Josh said, lapsing into silence and ear-tugging for a time. Then: "I've been thinking about a Feynman diagram. For instance, when a proton and an antiproton collide, they can exchange a virtual neutron, scattering pions in the process. Here, let me show you."

He took a felt-tipped pen from a plastic penholder in his shirt pocket and began to draw on the Milpitas Holiday Inn wall. He drew:

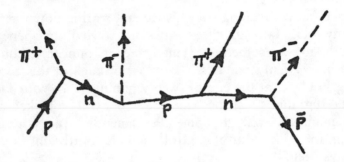

"Now time," he continued, "goes upward in this diagram. You can easily see from the direction of the arrow that this antiproton here on the right is traveling downward. That is, it can be read as backward in time." He glanced at Barney in triumph.

"Your hobby really *is* particle physics," Barney commented.

"Sure. Well, that means that the space-time continuum is one complex pattern, and that there is no such thing as linear time. We could be any time we wanted to. Theoretically, of course."

"You mean travel in time?"

"Yeah. Sort of. I have the theory pretty well worked out. We couldn't use antiprotons, of course. Too heavy and destructive, and the radiation produced would kill. And the particle exchange would be a lot more complicated than this. Probably a positive electron shower would be the method — with the right shielding, of course. I could set the whole thing up at the Positron-Electron Project at the Stanford Linear Accelerator in a couple of weeks! Region Four has the right kind of facilities for the interface."

"You're kidding, Josh." The line edged forward toward the men's room door.

"No, I'm not. It would really be quite simple. Of course, there's no way I could get approval for the project from the Accelerator Programming Committee. Not without being from a university or something, so it will probably never be tested. But it's fun to work it out, anyway."

"I could go back and stop Penny," Barney said to himself.

"Hah?"

"My wife. She died — killed herself in the microwave oven."

"How awful."

"I could go back and stop her."

Josh was dubious. "There is a theoretical limit."

"What do you mean?"

"The minimum jump is somewhere around four thousand years."

"Four thousand years?"

"Yeah. You could go back, say, a little over four thousand years and then jump forward exactly four thousand or whatever. Reappear in the near past. Theoretically. Only two things to stop you."

"They are . . ."

"Well, for one thing you wouldn't have a linear accelerator four thousand years in the past and you couldn't build one. And the Rubber Band Effect."

"Rubber Band Effect?"

"Yes. That's what I call it, anyway." Josh blushed again and stared at his shoes.

"What is it?"

"You would snap back to the moment you left. It's really a kind of particle inertia. Those high-energy particles don't like to be pushed around."

"Amazing," Barney said. It was Josh's turn into the bathroom.

Only seven minutes remained before they were due back in the conference room to have their egos SUMmed. So they rushed for packets of peanut butter crackers from a machine in the lobby. The crackers were stale. Seventy-three people crammed the crackers into their mouths and chewed vigorously before they discovered that the drinking fountain was out of order. There was another mild rush to the restrooms, but by then it was too late. Fifty-nine extremely thirsty people had to rush back and throw themselves on their faces before the doors closed, still trying to gag down dry lumps of peanut butter and cracker. This interfered with the next exercise, a reprise of the morning's "I am a flaming asshole" routine, but A. Spencer Sparling insisted on a spirited performance.

Spencer was very pleased with himself. He could go out to lunch anytime he wanted, leaving Snow in charge of the trainees. In fact, some fifteen minutes after the lunch break he would return to his room, where room service had left him a tray. He had spent his twenty-minute break otherwise engaged with his assistant.

"Ah, Snow, baby, isn't it exciting?" He unzipped his leather pants and allowed Snow to dip her pale golden head to what he called his "fountain of youth." She gobbled on him while he reminisced over the morning's events and related his plans for the future, his schemes for promoting SUM, his guru lecture bureau, recruiting instructors, his nationwide-franchise network, graduate courses for his "clients," as he referred to the trainees.

"Careful not to get the leather wet," he addressed the top of Snow's head as she slopped and licked. "It'll leave spots. I think we could create a whole scale of achievement, a kind of hierarchy. You know, like scientology."

"Mmmph," Snow mumbled.

"Yes, indeed," he went on, patting her long, fine hair with his dainty hand, "next month we will be getting the SUM-mation courses rolling — for graduates of SUM only, of course. I think we could soak four hundred and seventy-five dollars for these graduate courses, since the trainees will then get a certificate stating that they are SUMmed. My accountants tell me we will clear well over eight hundred thousand dollars this year. You hear me, Snow, baby, eight hundred thousand smackeroos. That ought to put a little fire in your lips. Ahhh, nice. Careful of the slobber, though. Don't want spots. This suit cost six hundred dollars. You know, it was the Boston cream pie lady that got me. Yessir, that was the one, when she started smearing it all over her naked body. That reminds me, did I tell you about those guys at the University of Something-or-other who are investigating multiple orgasms for men? It seems to me there is a future in that sort of thing . . . Oh, fuck, Snow, baby, that's nice."

She smiled up at him adoringly, then slowly and gracefully stood as he zipped himself back up. She rose to well over a foot above his head, even though he wore six-inch platform shoes. She smoothed her djellaba with long, pale hands.

"Good work, Snow. No spots."

"I love it, Spence, the fountain of youth."

"Of course you do, baby, of course you do. Now it's time to get back to those buttbrains in there. We'll start them on the Flaming Asshole routine again and then I'm coming back here for lunch. You've had yours." He gave her a chuckle, and they returned to the conference room.

So Spencer was pleased with himself. It was this weekend routine that he liked best. It was never quite as exciting during the week, when he didn't have the trainees around and had to concentrate on paperwork, the tax accountants and lawyers, the advertising agency and insurance executives.

"You wouldn't *believe* the expenses I got, baby," he mentioned more than once. "Reaping is its own reward, but, my God, the overhead!"

The trainees squirmed on through the afternoon. Spence had the heat in the conference room turned up to eighty, so the temperature, the bladder discomfort, the harassment, the exercises, all conspired to help the trainees shed their defenses. "You gotta shed *all* your defenses," Spencer instructed after his lunch. He patted the leather over his stomach, which now contained shrimp Louis, butterscotch pudding and a split of Wente Brothers Riesling. "All your defenses. When you've done that, then you can learn that all the bullshit you buttbrains use to protect yourselves from taking responsibility for everything that happens is useless. Then — " he paused, glaring around the room at the seventy-five buttbrains, bent at the waist, trying to touch the floor with their fingertips. Most could barely reach their knees, but all were presenting themselves as though for a good, old-fashioned caning. Spencer glared down at the sea of hunched bodies, 150 eyes straining to look up at him.

"Then," he repeated, "you will be ready for what we here at Sparling Unified Meditation call SUMUS, which means 'We are' in Latin, although I prefer to think of it as SUM U. S., that is, 'I am the U. S.' When you are SUMUS, you are half way *there,* and *there* is where you want to be. But you will get no further than SUMUS this weekend. If you want to keep advancing, to get *there,* there will be graduate seminars like this open to you. Announcements will be mailed to you at home."

He began to pace back and forth, still glowering at the trainees, whose knees were beginning to tremble. "Now then, there is one thing you must remember above all other things, besides your Word, which you will be given before you leave here. That one thing is that there is no such thing as feeling. All feelings — love, hate, hope, grief, anger and so on — all feelings are bullshit. You just use this kind of bullshit to make yourselves believe that things are *done* to you. But feelings don't exist, and don't you forget it."

"But what about death?" the Boston cream pie lady asked. Her tubular arms barely reached to midthigh as she bent fractionally at her nonexistent waist. "I mean, my sister died and I felt terrible . . ."

"Death?" Spencer thundered down at her, his voice the all-powerful voice of the god of bullshit. "Death?

"Death is a rip-off. Death is a conspiracy. Let me tell you something." Spencer stopped pacing a moment to lean over the lectern; he was about to deliver some Words (not the special Words for the trainees; better, more powerful, more *magnetic* Words, Words from the mouth of A. Spencer Sparling himself). "I often get asked about death. Until recently — quite recently, in fact — I was just a salesman. I sold CB radios. I was driving through Salinas one day, on my way to close a deal for six hundred CB radios, when I suddenly saw a blinding light over the city. I must have blanked out or something, gone blind, because when I recovered I was parked at the side of the road and an officer was writing out a ticket: illegal parking. At first I thought I felt anger; I wanted to protest, to argue with him. And then I realized, as suddenly as that, that it was all bullshit. The anger, the officer, the ticket, CB radios — all bullshit. I saw the word then, SUM, written in letters of fire on that policeman's forehead. SUM — I am. Only I. The policeman didn't exist. CB radios didn't exist. Parking tickets didn't exist. *Death didn't exist!* Only me — SUM, I am. I AM!

"So death is a rip-off. Don't be fooled. My partner in the CB radio business was fooled. He thought CB radios were real. He thought they were *important.* He cornered the forty-channel CB market on the West Coast and the government created the sixty-two-channel CB band. So Haig killed himself — electrocuted himself with his stereo. He thought his stereo was real. He thought electricity was real. He thought that death was real! So now he's dead. Haig Despot, may he rest in peace, is dead, because he *thinks he's dead!* Shows you how much *he* knows.

"When I started SUM, Haig and I parted ways. He went on thinking that things were real, feelings were real, and I went on to bring my vision to the world. I tore up that parking ticket right in front of the policeman and drove back here to San Francisco. Now you know."

He smiled, looking around the room, daring anyone to question him further. It was obvious to them that if they wanted to be SUMmated, to become SUMUS, to achieve SUMmation, they would have to get the idea pretty quickly. The weekend was slipping away, their $375 following minute by minute, although, they now understood, the $375 was all bullshit, not real.

"I got it!" The Boston cream pie lady fell over backward. Her eyes rolled into her head, and she slept, breathing loudly through her mouth.

The man next to her, a burly slab with a flat face and small eyes, stared at the sleeping form. He was a Rumanian named Tiglash Apsu, a strange, sullen man who had proved useful on more than one occasion to his employers, a Las Vegas betting establishment, but who had a tendency to get "out of hand."

As he stared at her, connections were made behind his dim eyes, connections having to do with his profession as much as with the more aberrant aspects of his behavior. He realized that one of his problems was that he became too *involved*. Now he realized, looking at that obese body on the floor, that it was all bullshit, not real. The Boston cream pie lady resembled a corpse. Death was a rip-off.

Tiglash Apsu was filled with a blinding light, and he said, very slowly, picking his way through the vowels and consonants, "SUM, I am, SUM, I am."

Then he sat down heavily and stared at the ceiling, a small smile crusting the lower half of his face. New doors were opening in his mind, new vistas. They would take him far from Las Vegas.

Lights were, in fact, turning on in heads all over the room. Forty-six people were SUMmated that day; thirteen more the next. There were only sixteen left at the end of the weekend who went home with the vague feeling that for $375 they had missed something important. These would be the prime candidates for graduate courses; they were especially useful to the rapidly growing SUM organization because they were the most zealous recruiters. The ones who were actually SUMated recognized that it was all bullshit and went about their business, forgetting about SUM.

Barney was not sure at the moment which category he would belong to, but he knew he was fascinated by Josh MacIntosh's theory. So while mental flashbulbs popped around the room, he wandered among the lines of that simple Feynman diagram, trying to connect those lines with the molecule-thin trails of a silicon chip's printed circuits. He didn't listen to Spencer until suddenly he heard a word he recognized.

"I'll tell you a little story about death," Spencer Sparling said, "and what a rip-off it really is. There was a man, a king in the Middle East a long time ago, named Gilgamesh." Here Barney sat up and attended. "He found the secret of death forty-five hundred years ago, thus being the first man to be SUMmated, and this is how it all happened.

"He wanted the secrets of death because a friend had died, and he was falling apart from grief and all that crap. He was sick with it, Gilgamesh was, so he went on this trip, a really difficult journey up and down mountains and across seas, and through heat and cold and terrible dangers, et cetera, et cetera, and when he arrived he was given the secrets of immortality and death. Well, of course he was overjoyed because he thought he could get his friend back.

"But on the way home he went swimming, leaving this

plant, a sort of shrub, which was the secret, beside the pond. Along comes a snake and eats it all up, making himself immortal, but ripping off Gilgamesh completely. Bye-bye secrets of death and so forth. Some might say this was the biggest rip-off in all history — here he'd landed the Big One and lost it. Well, tough. That's when he took charge of his own life, right then. See?"

And now the light clicked on in Barney's head as well. He realized that there was something mysterious going on, something he didn't quite understand. That had never happened to him before. He always had been able to understand everything — see the diagram, the circuit, the pattern, trace the flow of electrons through the most complex maze and make them do tricks. But now he was being told things he needed to know, names were appearing, Penny had died, and it suddenly struck him that he didn't understand it, any of it.

He had learned two things; there was a way of going back 4000 years or more and Gilgamesh knew about death and had lived 4500 years ago.

"Ahh, just coincidence," he told himself as he made his way to his badly dented Silver Sword that evening.

"What'd you say?" Josh MacIntosh was walking beside him.

"Nothing," Barney said. "Say, can I give you a lift home? I'd like to talk to you."

"Sure," Josh answered. "Prue, Miss Nisenvy, my guardian, is supposed to pick me up, but of course she won't. She never does. We live in Sunnyvale."

"What a coincidence," Barney said.

When they got to Prue's house, Josh asked Barney to wait. "I want to show you something," he said. "Please stand by a minute."

6

Josh returned with a book, *The Joy of Death,* which had resided for the past fifty-seven weeks at the top of the *New York Times* nonfiction best-seller list; it had made its author, a retired stevedore from Brooklyn, a millionaire seven times over. The film rights had sold for $750,000, and 125 million copies had sold so far in paperback. It had already outsold the Bible.

Josh thought it was trash, but Prue liked it and humiliated Josh every chance she got because he didn't. Josh wanted Barney's opinion.

"Thanks for waiting," he said, climbing back into the car. "Have you read this?"

"No." Barney took it and started reading the jacket copy by the light of the street lamp. Josh unfolded the note from Prue he had found on the hall table.

"Dear Joshy, Sorry I couldn't pick you up. Had an appointment with Pete Boggs and couldn't make it. Don't wait up. P."

"This guy thinks death is the only reality," Barney said. "Is he some kind of nut?"

"Well, *I* think so, but it's been on the *New York Times* best-seller list for over a year. Lots of people believe in it. Prue believes in it, but it's weird. He seems to think death is fun!"

"Death is not fun," Barney said. "But I'll read it if you want me to." Barney never read anything except *Computer World* and other professional literature. "But listen," he continued, "I've been thinking about what you were saying during the break today, about time. I'd like to give it a try."

"Give what a try?"

"I'd like to try to go back. Forty-five hundred years. I'd like to talk to Gilgamesh, that hero Sparling was talking about. The problem is, I certainly can't propose a project at the Stanford Accelerator. I don't have that kind of clout."

"Who does?" Josh's polite adolescent face began to glow with excitement. "I'll tell you who does. The government does. That's who does. Ha-ha. And who in the government would be interested in such a project? A project with possible military applications? I'll tell you. The CIA would. And how could we get the CIA interested in such a project?" His face fell. "I don't know."

'Well," Barney said. "I guess that's that. Nice idea. Unless . . . No."

"What? Unless what?"

"Unless we could somehow tap into their computer data lines and put orders into it, creating a front for the project. It would probably never even be noticed if we did it right. Wouldn't have to go through a university or anything. Let's see, I could make myself a CIA agent somehow, have them order me to go back. They have the techniques for getting high priority at the accelerator." Barney sighed and sat back, holding *The Joy of Death* loosely in his lap. "Only one problem."

"What's that?" Josh was gone already, positive electrons buzzing in his head.

"I don't know how to tap into the CIA data lines."

"Oh," said Josh absently, watching pions scatter and alter charge in his head. "That's easy. I used to be a phone freak. Before I got interested in physics. I could get the codes easily enough through the phone freak data network. There are people working on that kind of problem all the time, getting secret phone numbers and all."

"There are?"

"Yeah. Curiosity, you know. If there's something hidden, someone will want to uncover it. I think it's human nature." Josh blushed. "The real problem is, how soon do you want to go? It could take as long as three weeks to organize the equipment at the accelerator."

"Three weeks?" Barney shouted. "Three weeks?"

"Yeah. Is that too long?"

"Are you kidding. That would be perfect. Oh, boy, the CIA . . ."

At that moment the CIA, in the form of Junior Arkwright, who was maintaining surveillance on Barney, was trying to yank his foot out from behind the brake and clutch pedals of his car so he could swing his listening gear into position. He was parked under a locust tree half a block from Prue's house. People talking quietly in cars, Junior had been taught during training, were often engaged in violations of national security. The more he twisted his foot, the more solidly it became wedged. At last it popped free.

He swung his directional mike into position just in time to hear Barney say, "Good night, Josh. See you tomorrow." The gain was up too high, and a high-pitched feedback squeal almost deafened him as Josh slammed the door and Barney started the engine and drove away.

"Damn," Junior muttered, rubbing his ear. He watched Barney's car pull out of sight, noted the address of the foreign agent, and went home. He didn't know that his next orders would come indirectly from Barney himself.

At home, Barney used his modem to connect his terminal with the *Encyclopaedia Britannica* data bank. He wanted to know all about Gilgamesh.

GILGAMESH: HERO OF SUMERIAN EPIC OF THAT NAME. CIRCA 2692 B.C. SON OF GODDESS NINSUN AND A PRIEST OF KULLAB, DISTRICT OF URUK, CITY IN MESOPOTAMIA. GILGAMESH WAS FIFTH KING OF URUK AFTER THE FLOOD. A GREAT BUILDER AND JUDGE OF THE DEAD WHO SOUGHT THE SECRET OF EVERLASTING LIFE WHEN

GRIEF-STRIKEN BY THE DEATH OF HIS FRIEND. SEE CUNEIFORM
WRITING SYSTEM; MESOPOTAMIA; MYTHOLOGY — SUMERIAN;
POETRY-ANCIENT; URUK . . .

The list of citations was long, and Barney cross-checked a
number of them until late into the night. He made a list of
books to buy: Kramer's *The Sumerians, The Epic of Gilgamesh,* texts on religion and archeology. Then he went to
sleep.

He slept well, dreaming the dreams of circuits and gates,
of flow charts and algorithms. He dreamed of the ultimate
program, which he almost understood. When he woke up he
couldn't remember what the program was, but he smiled all
the way to Josh and Prue's house and all the way from there
to the Milpitas Holiday Inn. All day long as A. Spencer
Sparling harangued and harassed, cajoled and insulted the
buttbrains in the room, Barney smiled. At the end of the
day, after falling on his face, leaping to his feet, touching his
toes, curling into a fetal ball, abasing himself and exalting
himself at Spencer's orders, Barney figured he must be
SUMUS.

"You are all SUMUS," Spencer shouted as the seminar
drew to a close. "This means, of course, that you are not
only SUM — U.S., you are also SUM-US; that is, WE are
SUMMED. You belong to a special, select, I might even say
elite, group because you have been through Sparling Unified
Meditation. Bullshit cannot bother you anymore. You will
never be at the mercy of bullshit again. Nothing, I repeat,
nothing is real, everything is bullshit. Except one thing. ME.
I AM. SUM. So let's hear every one of you say it: SUM. I
AM. Shout it out loud."

"SUM I am," the seventy-five shouted. Thirteen more
lights flashed on at that moment, including, as it happened,
Barney and Josh, who realized that A. Spencer Sparling was
dishing out his own particular brand of bullshit. They

promptly forgot him in the glow of their developing comprehension of the nature of the universe.

So while A. Spencer Sparling was commenting to Snow after the seminar, "We have, baby, as old Luther Hadley McWhirter would say, landed the *Big One*," Josh was saying to Barney in the car, "The matter of the universe — the matter *with* the universe — is energy."

And Tiglash Apsu, who had sat cross-legged on the floor of the Milpitas Holiday Inn conference room all night, staring into the darkness toward the ceiling, dim eyes wide in the gloom, Tiglash hallucinated. Corpses danced in his brain. His corpses. Others' corpses. Death was a rip-off. Nothing was real except Tiglash Apsu, Rumanian refugee who always got too involved. He would never again derive pleasure in hurting, in killing. Never again. It wasn't real. It was all bullshit. SUM — I AM, he murmured. When he was finally discovered and thrown out of the Holiday Inn, he noticed a huge billboard going up across the street. WE TAKE THE STING OUT OF DEATH, it read. BOGGS AND BOGGS FUNERAL HOME, SUNNYVALE.

Tiglash Apsu haunted funerals after that and never returned to Las Vegas.

"Sure," Barney replied to Josh's remark. "E equals mc squared and all that."

"Not quite like that," Josh responded. "More like, well, all the subatomic particles down to quarks and antiquarks, strange, up, down, charmed, truth and beauty and their colors; muons and pions and baryons and so forth, they are all *patterns* of energy. Like infinitesimally small whirlpools. You know, vortices. So when you hit one of them with another one, what you get from the collision is not parts of particles, but altered patterns of energy. We are all made of these particles, and the particles are really just energy. In a sense, matter itself doesn't really exist. At least it doesn't matter, hee-hee, so we are really bundles of patterns of energy. But some of them are quite hard, and breakable," he added, bracing himself as Barney swerved around a funeral procession slowly crossing the new Dunbarton Bridge. Barney fleetingly recognized his friend Pete Boggs at the wheel of the hearse and waved as they drove past. Pete didn't respond.

"But Einstein thought they were equivalent, not the same, didn't he?" Barney asked, accelerating smoothly. They left the bridge and turned toward Sunnyvale.

"Right. E equals mc squared. Conservation of energy. But that's a matter, hee-hee, of turning one into the other. Get it, *matter?*"

"I get it," Barney smiled. Josh liked his little matter jokes.

"Anyway, the universe is just a huge dance of energy, always changing form and shape, a pattern constantly shifting, all the time. And time itself is another dimension of the energy dance, so that the antiparticles, about whose existence there is no longer any doubt, are really particles — at least this is one way of looking at them — going backward in time. It's very simple, actually. That's why we ought to be able to send you back in time to whenever it is you want to go." Josh was blushing and tugging at his earlobe at the same time, he was so covered with excitement and embarrassment.

"Somewhere around 2642 B.C., I think. Gilgamesh should have been around fifty then. Will be around fifty? Do I mean was? Anyway, around 4625 years ago."

"We'll get you as close as we can," Josh assured him.

They went to Barney's house, winding up the Avenida de los Pechos toward the Los Cojones de Santa Teresa subdivision. The evening was beginning to cool, though the drought continued unabated. There were forecasts of another two years without rain. The battered Silver Sword glided through the neatly winding streets of the subdivision past lawns parched brown, dead shrubbery, wilted trees, bare magnolias, the withered leaves of locust, sycamore and hawthorne, of linden and plane trees, yew and ash. The brown earth was cracked and shattered by the heat, and here and there the houses themselves showed long jagged cracks, the result of last week's earthquake, which had shaken the sloppy construction slightly apart.

Barney turned up Blue Ox Drive and glanced over at the huge sheet of plywood that was still nailed over Mrs. Bunyon's picture window. He noticed the shadows of the late afternoon sun pooling in the tracks his Silver Sword had made through the dry, friable earth of her front yard. He smiled. All bullshit, he thought. Not real. No more real than Sergeant Masterbrook. Only me. I'm real.

And Penny, he thought. Penny was real. Is real. I'm on my way.

Josh MacIntosh made a few phone calls from Barney's house. "I've got it," he said, hanging up. "The CIA data line number. It's not a public line, of course, but it's leased full-time from the phone company. Supposedly completely secure. Takes two code words, changed every day, and a random number code based on multiples of prime numbers changed every millisecond. That part should be easy, just plugging the same number in every millisecond until it hits our number. They'd be expecting people to try it the other way around, to make a program that would guess their number, but that's silly. Our way may take longer, but I doubt it. And it's a whole lot easier."

"I have a feeling about the code words," Barney said. "I have a feeling that the words A. Spencer Sparling gave us when we left just might be effective. There have been so many coincidences so far that it seems logical, if I can say such a thing, for there to be one more."

"I doubt it." Josh frowned. "But it's a place to start. We can work through the echo effect, put trail words through and see if they bounce back or not."

"Right," Barney said. "That should be safe enough if we do it right. What was your word?"

"Kazoo," Josh told him. "What was yours?"

"Pink."

"You don't suppose we ought to try "pink kazoo," do you?" Josh was smiling.

It wasn't quite that easy. Three hours later the code words they sent through the CIA lines were not bounced back, and contact was established. Then they picked a random prime number multiple and waited. It turned out that the two code words were supposed to be imbedded in a sentence; today the phrase was: Through a kazoo, pinkly.

"Whew." Barney sighed. "What's with those guys at CIA? A strange group."

"Just cautious," Josh answered. "Wouldn't really be any fun if they weren't, would it?"

Junior Arkwright, now convinced that Barney was leaking secrets all over the place, was perched in a shriveled poplar outside 34½ Puerco de Esmeralda Lane tapping into the data-link line instead of the regular phone line, so when he slipped his earphones on to listen, what he heard instead of Barney's voice spilling secrets was an excrutiatingly loud blast of high-speed data. Junior didn't know it, but it was the sound of Barney cutting orders for himself and Josh MacIntosh to begin a secret project at the linear accelerator. Barney would get his positive electron shower. And Junior would be working for him as his CIA liaison officer.

Junior cursed as he climbed awkwardly down the tree after taping the miniature tape recorder to the trunk. At the final branches before the ground he caught his ankle painfully and twisted upside down in a violent rustling of dried leaves.

"What was that?" Barney glanced up from his console, as did Josh, bending over his shoulder.

"I don't know."

Junior hopped to his car, holding his swollen ankle in both hands.

That night Barney developed an itch, but every time he

scratched it, it moved. He could not satisfy that itch. If he scratched his back, it switched to his arm; if he scratched his arm, it moved to his leg. For two days the itch distracted him. He tried reading *The Joy of Death* but found himself time after time staring at the page, where Penny's face floated. She glared accusingly at him through the print, fading in and out.

"Hot enough for you?" she asked him. "Hot enough? Hot enough?" Barney tried to scratch, and the itch jumped from his knee to his neck. "Hot enough?" He was walking across the dream plain that was also the patch of dessicated lawn in front of his house. The gravel hurt his feet, the hot sand dragged at him, and he couldn't reach Penny, waiting on the wide, mud-brick terrace for him. As he came closer he saw that her face was veiled, her head covered. She turned away and went inside. He knew it was Sumer, though it was also Sunnyvale.

"Hot enough for you?"

"What?" Barney sat up abruptly, and *The Joy of Death* slid off his lap. It was ten o'clock in the morning on Tuesday, October 8, twenty-five days since Penny died, and the phone was ringing. Barney slumped in his chair, glancing stupidly at the rumpled book by his feet, a feeling of terrible desolation keening through him, a desolation as vast, dry and empty as the plain in his dream, a desolation without water or hope.

The phone rang five more times. Finally he pulled himself to his feet and answered it.

"Mr. Gamesh?"

"Yes?" The dry wind swirled the choking dust through his throat, so his "Yes?" was a cracked whisper, a parched croak.

"My name is Arkwright. I'm your liaison for Project April Showers."

"Project April Showers?" Barney had no idea what the man was referring to.

"Right. Could we get together for lunch? We have a lot of work to do if we are going to get you away by the thirty-first."

"Away?" The steady winds of desolation blew on and on. Barney wanted nothing more than to get away. He looked out the living room window at the drought-stricken suburb and thought about April showers.

"Right," Arkwright was saying. "Get away. By the thirty-first. That's the target date. Lunch at noon, say? The Ceramic Lobster in Sunnyvale isn't bad."

"At noon." Barney licked his cracked lips. "OK."

"By the way, Mr. Gamesh. I had no idea you were with the Company. Here I've been following . . . Oh, never mind. Some kind of bureaucratic foul-up, no doubt. Noon, eh? Don't forget."

"The Company?" The winds were a hiss in the phone, the wail of distance, dry as a consumptive cough. "Oh, right. The Company. You mean the CIA!" Barney slapped his forehead. "Noon will be fine." The winds receded somewhat, became background noise. Their trick must have worked: through a kazoo, pinkly. Barney smiled a chapped smile. "By the way, how will I know you?"

"Oh, don't worry about that," Junior Arkwright assured him. "I'll know you."

Barney glanced at his clock. The bright red digits changed: 10:13. Less than two hours.

He called Josh. "Contact from someone named Arkwright. CIA. He calls it the Company. Those guys! We're meeting for lunch. This is it!"

He hung up, elated, and paced the living room. As he paced, he slumped, for the keening of dry wind slithered back into his mind, the emptiness, the desolation, the dry, hot surface underfoot. Then he thought of A. Spencer Sparling and the $375 course he had just been through.

"All bullshit," he said aloud, trying it out. His voice was as flat and tasteless as the peanut butter and cracker sandwiches at the Milpitas Holiday Inn. "All bullshit. You know who's all bullshit?" he asked the bright book cover on the floor. "A. Spencer Sparling is all bullshit. That's who. I get it all right. Death is a rip-off and so is life."

The wind began to wail across the barrens, bringing with it a dark cloud of locusts. "But what else is there?" he asked the cover of *The Joy of Death*. "What else is there?" he murmured, scratching at his side. The locusts hummed around his head, an angry whine that ate through everything living, everything green. Locusts.

"What's made me think of locusts?" he asked the book. He felt the pull of the dream, the seductive drag pulling him down. "Well, it suits my mood."

The phone rang.

"Hiya, Barney, how're things?" Pete Boggs, the cheerful mortician. "Hey, didja do SUM like I suggested?"

"Oh, hi, Pete. Yeah, I did SUM."

"Great, Barn. Makes a big difference, hah?"

"Mmm. What can I do for you, Pete?" The hot dry wind blowing. Barney could barely hear Pete's cheerful voice over the howl.

"Well, Barney, I want you to know that I've been keeping your wife here, as a sort of favor, you understand. On ice. I was wondering if you had come to any decision regarding her disposal."

Penny was shaking her head, saying something Barney couldn't make out. The wind blew her words away. "Am I going crazy?"

"What's that, Barney? Crazy?"

"No. No, nothing. Listen, Pete. Could you keep her the way she is? Just for a while longer. Say, about three weeks. Just till the beginning of November."

"That'd be the first, right? You want me to keep her frozen downstairs until the first?"

"I guess so, yes. You could bill me for storage or something."

"Well, I guess I could do that for you, Barney, if it's important."

"It's important. One other thing, Pete. I might need a lawyer, a couple of problems — my car, for instance. And a will. You wouldn't happen to know a good lawyer, would you?"

"Sure, Barney. Sure. Give Prue Nisenvy a call. She's one terrific lawyer. She's in Sunnyvale, in the book. Listen, I gotta go now; my wife's on the other line." Barney could hear Pete Boggs wink at him over the phone.

Two days ago Barney had been SUMUS. He had been in control, taking charge of his life; he had been Number One, the only reality. Now, suddenly, he felt exactly as he had felt the day he stopped watching television, with his half-shaved, cut face and a bloody nose.

He realized with a sudden clarity that he had confessed the wrong thing in the SUM seminar, that his encounter with Sergeant Masterbrook was not his secret shame at all.

His secret shame was that he didn't know who he was. He didn't know who he was, and he didn't know who Penny was. He didn't know why he wanted her back. But somewhere behind the desolation of the wind he knew he had to find out, that the things that had always been most important — designing processor chips, following the circuits, his work — those things meant nothing. A means to an end only. And here was a mystery worth working on.

Lunch with Junior Arkwright was strange.

"You talk too much," Junior told him. "I have your phone tapped. You called a Josh MacIntosh after I talked to you this morning. You mentioned the CIA. You shouldn't mention the Company on a line, especially a public line that hasn't been secured. Sure, you're both in the Company. I know that. I don't understand why my section chief didn't know that, but there you are. Still, you shouldn't be so free with the name. After all, we are supposed to be a secret organization." Junior's Adam's apple bobbed over the downward flow of crab salad. He spoke and ate at the same time as though he had been practicing it all his life.

"Well," Barney responded, "we're really only on board for this one project, April Showers." These guys, he thought. What an imagination! "We're not regulars."

"One thing I don't quite understand." Junior's knobby chin ruminated over his salad. "Why do you want to go to this place, this Sumer, anyway?"

"Intelligence." Barney said. That should be vague enough.

"Ah!" Junior exclaimed. "Right. Intelligence. That's very good, very good." His odd, lumpy hands were two tarantulas working the knife and fork: black-furred, repulsive, fascinating. "You know," he went on, spearing a hunk of crab and transferring it to his mouth, "I don't quite know why I'm in this business. I have a lot of trouble with some things, like remembering the codes. I'm not very good with the gear, the electronic stuff. I imagine you're much better at that sort of thing." He shuffled his crepe-soled shoes under the table. "Ever since I screwed up my first job for the Company I've wondered why they kept me on."

"What was your first job?" Barney didn't care, but something in Junior's tone compelled him to ask, something insistent and desperate.

"I was recruited for an assassination. A foreign leader. You see, I used to be a podiatrist, and this man had foot problems . . ."

"Was it . . ."

"Shhh. Yes, it was who you think. I was to become his doctor, treat him, and rub a poisoned ointment on his feet."

"What happened?" Barney forgot his own meal. The wind of desolation faded for the moment.

"Oh, I cured him." Junior's eyes began to water.

"Cured him?"

"Yeah. For years I got Christmas cards from him. I really screwed up the job. Finally, he slipped in the tub."

"I remember," said Barney.

"Ironic, isn't it?"

"What's that?"

"His feet got him in the end." Junior blinked a few times.

"I guess I'd better report to you," he said. "I called the head of the Stanford Linear Accelerator scheduling yesterday. I talked to him again this morning; he's clearing the time on the accelerator for a super-high-priority MIT project — that's us. They're closing down the strange antiquark experiments to make way for April Showers. They will be ready tomorrow for Dr. MacIntosh's equations."

"He's not a doctor. He's a kid."

"Huh?"

"He's a kid. He's seventeen."

"A kid?"

"Seventeen."

"You're kidding . . ." Junior's marbled eyes popped and crossed. "Oh, but he's one of those geniuses."

"He's one of those geniuses," Barney agreed, feeling a sudden rush of positive affection for Josh. The kid *was* a genius. Barney hoped he was a genius. And Barney prayed in the tiny childhood chapel in his hindbrain: Because if he isn't a genius, April Showers is going to give me nothing but radiation poisoning.

"Why April Showers?" he asked Junior. "It's October."

"Yeah," Junior agreed. "Weird, isn't it?"

"Anything for dessert, gentlemen?" Nina Choklat asked, thinking, ha, a pair of soulless fat-cat pleasure-seekers if ever I saw them.

"No, thanks," Junior said. "Just coffee."

"Right. Two coffees." Come the revolution, you pigs are going to be the first in the pens.

"Well," Junior told Barney, standing to leave. "See you

tomorrow at the linear accelerator. With the kid, eh?"

"Tomorrow," Barney said. He watched Junior Arkwright squeak his crepe soles across the dining room of the Ceramic Lobster and out the door, which opened onto bright October sunshine. The light blasted into the air-conditioned dimness of the restaurant like a death-ray laser, and as the door closed the hot, desolate wind rose again across the emptiness. Barney felt in his stomach the sinking void he might have assumed was hunger if he had not just eaten.

He finished his coffee and followed Junior into the white afternoon heat. Five hundred and thirty-seven straight days without rain. The hills to the northwest were brown, the pine forests tainted with wide tracts of dying oak and bay laurel. Beside the door to the Ceramic Lobster a life-sized carved wooden statue of a New England seaman in a slicker and rain hat leaned against a nor'easter, harpoon in hand. The sun had bleached most of the color from the front of the sculpture, exposing the weathered grain underneath.

There was a parking ticket tucked under the wiper of his Silver Sword. Barney looked at the pink paper, limp in the heat. He looked at the wrinkled fender of his car, the shattered headlight, the dented bumper. He got in and drove home. Once there, he tapped easily into the police department computer and inserted his own program. From that day on, every morning at six, the computer would automatically erase everything in its memory banks. No more parking tickets. It cost the city of Sunnyvale $750,000 to straighten out the mess when it was finally discovered. A strange excitement seized Barney as he worked, and his hands trembled on the keys. He ordered the program to move itself around in the computer's memory so no one could find it and to self-destruct in a month.

Then he threw away his parking ticket.

He called the Stanford Linear Accelerator. A woman answered. "SLAC. Miss Sternwood speaking."

"I'd like to talk to the director of scheduling. This is Barney Gamesh calling. Tell him it's about Project April Showers."

"Just a moment." She put him on Hold, which played for him a spirited rendition of the theme from *Lawrence of Arabia*.

"Dr. Milkworth is coming to the phone. Please stand by," she said.

7

Penny waited a long time in the manager's office, tapping her foot, pacing the small area in front of the receptionist's desk, feeling the flow of desperation and fear move through her. "Please," she said at last, "I've been waiting for a long time."

The secretary smiled professionally. "You're dead, Mrs. Gamesh. You have plenty of time. You have no end of time." The smile snapped off as she bent over her paperwork.

Finally the buzzer sounded. "He'll see you now." The smile was back, as warm, friendly and accepting as a very dear friend's smile should be.

Penny went in, thinking of her body curled in its grave, smothered in its coffin, rotting in the earth. Her feet dragged at the carpet, and it seemed to her that she didn't *feel* dead.

"Good morning, Mrs. Gamesh," the rasping tulip greeted her. The baby face was smiling too, and the smile seemed strangely hideous to her.

"What's going to happen to me?" she wailed impulsively, thinking once more that the glorious blue light of the Wisdom of *Dharma-Dhātu* was never going to be hers. "Oh, what is going to happen to me?"

"Now, now, Mrs. Gamesh." The tulip gave her soothing words. "I have some very good news for you. Very good news indeed. You will be very pleased."

Penny had been sniffing, feeling the fear.

"What is it?" *Dharma-Dhātu?* She was going back? Forward?

"You have been invited" — the manager bubbled with pleasure, as though somehow it was a credit to *him*, as though *he* were responsible for her very good fortune. "You have been invited," he repeated. "I can't tell you how pleased we all are here."

"What is it? Please tell me."

"You have been invited, now get this, to appear on the Keb Tefnut show, on *This Is Your Death*. You will be the guest of honor!"

"No. No." Penny sank into a viscous syrup that closed over her head. "No." She waved her hands in front of her, fending it off.

"Why, yes, Mrs. Gamesh. It's a great honor. You were suicide of the year. You saw your name up on the marquee out front? Well . . ."

"But I didn't mean it," she wailed, and as she spoke a small flame of the opposite of her despair ignited: she felt *flattered*. To be on television, even in death. To be guest of honor! A secret self inside her hungered for that attention.

"Of course, Mrs. Gamesh. Accident. But we know better, don't we?" The baby face above its wide gold-and-orange-striped Banlon shirt smiled widely.

"It was an accident," she said again, but even as she said it she was thinking about appearing on the Keb Tefnut show, the center of all that attention.

"You're on tomorrow morning," the tulip rasped.

Dr. Milkworth was a spry, affable scientist with an ear-cleaning compulsion. A box of Q-tips peeked out of his shirt pocket where the other scientists kept their pens and calculators. He was a terrific administrator.

"We have the strange antiquark experiments completely shut down. We had the strange antiquark pretty well sewed up anyway," he informed Barney, Josh and Junior Arkwright. "Time to move on toward the up, down, truth, beauty and charmed antiquarks. We were hoping to get them next week, but that can wait. Should be easy enough to capture, now that we have the process down. PEP Region Four, meantime, is at your disposal. Would you like a tour?"

"Boy," Josh exclaimed, "would we. I mean I, anyway . . ." He blushed.

"Right. Come this way, please." Dr. Milkworth's fuzzy bald head bobbed as he led them to the two-mile-long klystron gallery above the tunnel where the electron-positron beam was shot. He took them to the beam switchyard, where the electrons or positrons were channeled into the various experiment end stations, the huge concrete buildings, A and B. He showed them the old SPEAR ring and the new, much larger PEP ring, with its stations. Finally he led them into Region 4, where they would be setting up their recording apparatus, the photo cells, the synchrotron radiation monitors, the spectrographic analyzers. Forklifts, cranes, liquid nitrogen tanks, compressors and cooling towers were everywhere, making a deafening symphony of buzzes, hisses, roars and thuds. Scaffolding and metal stairways, loops of cable, connectors, computer sensors, power units, workrooms and storage areas, stacks of concrete or lead shielding blocks, everything appeared haphazard and random, constantly being moved around, altered, rearranged.

The silence in Region 4 was pleasant after the tour. "The accelerator is a gun," Dr. Milkworth commented, "with the longest barrel in the world. And, of course, the smallest bullets."

The target area was surprisingly small, almost cozy. "Normally the target is quite small, the size of a pencil or a soup can. When we want to hit protons or neutrons, that is. Of course, here at PEP we are colliding beams of electrons and positrons mostly. I gather in this instance the target will be the size of a man."

"It *will* be a man," Barney said.

"Really? A live man? I didn't know that. Most of the things we do here would be quite fatal: secondary radiation. There are never any people around when an experiment is on. Everyone is either up at the main control center or the computer facility."

"That won't be necessary this time," Josh assured him. "This will be perfectly safe, and we will need people around in case of emergencies and to kludge up the equipment. There won't be any radiation produced at all, not with this shielding."

"We won't be held liable? I doubt our insurance would cover something like this."

"No. Don't worry," Josh said, tugging at his earlobe. "We'll be using positrons for the most part, pulsed forty-five times a second at thirty-two GeV, but split like this to produce sideblasts of negative pions. Here, let me show you."

Dr. Milkworth expressed no surprise that a seventeen-year-old boy was describing complex high-energy processes to him. That was about Asari's age when he did the work that won him the Nobel Prize. They stopped beside a table where Josh sketched diagrams and made calculations. "Yes, yes, I see." Dr. Milkworth was nodding. "Right. I think we can do that. We'll have to order some equipment from Fermi in Chicago, but that would only take a couple of days. Mmm. I think Augenblaue AeroSpace makes one of those, no problem there, just get it up here from Sunnyvale." Dr. Milkworth nodded his fuzzy pate vigorously.

"OK," he said at last, straightening up and pulling a Q-tip from his pocket. He dug it into his ear. "Let's get those equations over to the computer boys so they can run a couple of simulations for us before we start patching together what we need."

Junior and Barney stood uselessly to one side as the physicists talked. "By the way, Junior," Barney said as they walked back to the computer facility with the equations, "I've been meaning to ask you. What's your first name?"

"Junior. Junior is my first name. It was my father's idea."
Junior's lip curled. "He wanted to call me Junior, so that's
what he named me."

"Oh," Barney said.

Penny was the second guest on the Keb Tefnut show the
next day. She stood in the wings and watched as a thin,
scarred woman preceded her.

"Before we bring out today's special guest," Keb was saying, "let's have a big welcome for Mrs. Elmira Vetch, of —
well, where are you from exactly, Mrs. Vetch?"

"I'm from all over," Mrs. Vetch answered in a strangely
powerful voice for one who seemed so frail. "I moved
around a lot before I died."

"I see," Keb said, waving her to a chair. "And why do
you suppose you were invited on this show, Mrs. Vetch?"

"Why, to talk about my operations. I had seventy-three
operations during my lifetime."

"Seventy-three operations! Now that is something."

The studio audience agreed, with applause, that that was
something.

"Most of them were exploratory," Mrs. Vetch said.

"Exploratory? Amazing."

"Well, seventy-two were exploratory. One was for tonsils,
when I was five."

"Much pain?" Keb's handsome profile, turned toward the
camera, displayed clean interest, sincere concern, honest
wonder.

"Oh, my, yes. Terrible pain."

"Wonderful!" Keb leaned back in his chair, pleased with
this guest. "What were they exploring for, if I may ask?"

"Oh, various things. Mostly bowel complaints. You
know, obstructions." Mrs. Vetch sniffed loudly in approval
of herself.

"The bowel!" Keb was delighted. "Did the explorers ever
find anything in your bowels?"

"No. A bunch of incompetent quacks. Stupid tests always came out negative. But I knew. I knew."

"Really?" Keb's voice was silk unfurling in clear water. "But isn't it true that you also went under the name of Mrs. Sean Reagen during your lifetime?"

"Why . . ."

"And Alvira Delander?"

"But . . ."

"Also Elizabeth Powers and Evelyn Matheson and Esther Fordyce? And that you invented several different social security numbers to go with the names? And that all these names and numbers and symptoms were solely for the purpose of getting yourself into hospitals for spurious and useless 'exploratory' operations? Isn't that true, Mrs. Vetch, or whatever your name is?" Keb folded his arms across his chest and smiled sweetly at her.

She didn't flinch. "I didn't come on this show to be insulted, Mr. Tefnut. I came here to talk about my operations. I had obstructions of the large bowel. Painful obstructions. I was bent over with pain, couldn't walk, couldn't do housework. I went to the hospital on several occasions and was turned away because the doctors were incompetent. Naturally I had to change my name from time to time just to get in. For some reason I became known around the hospitals and would be turned away before I even got to say what was wrong. In terrible pain, I would be turned away!"

"Isn't it true, Mrs. Vetch, that you appeared at hospitals from Virginia to Hawaii, from Montana to Florida. That, in fact, you went from hospital to hospital throughout your entire adult life. That you never had a home of your own at all but *lived* in hospitals?"

"Yes. I had this terrible bowel obstruction and no one would treat it. Why, I talked about this obstruction all the time. I talked about it to everyone. Ask anyone who knew me, they'll tell you how I complained. I was constantly on medication — Probanthine and such. Just look here!"

Mrs. Vetch lifted her blouse to display a crisscrossed network of fine white scars woven across her abdomen. She looked like a screen door.

"Fascinating," Keb said dryly. "However, Mrs. Vetch, I have here a computer printout stating that in fact all you ever had was gas, and that you were diagnosed as having a psychiatric disorder known as Munchausen's Syndrome, which means that you went around from hospital to hospital demanding treatment you did not need. You were a freeloader, were you not?" Keb was beaming.

"Well, all I can say, Mr. Tefnut, is that I died of this Munchausen's Syndrome, or I wouldn't be here now, on your show." Mrs. Vetch smiled in triumph, and the audience expressed tentative approval. She left smiling.

"And now," Keb was saying, "the moment you have been waiting for: our guest of honor, the suicide of the year, Penelope Gamesh, of Sunnyvale, California."

The audience went wild as Penny walked out into the bright lights. She squinted against the brightness, trying to see out into the auditorium, but the heat and light were too intense. She could hear the thunderous applause, the whistles and foot-stamping, though, roaring in on her from the darkness behind the lights.

It felt good to her. Reassuring. A glow of excitement flowed through her. This was almost as good as appearing in *People* magazine.

Keb held up his hand and the applause died away, slowly faded to the rustle of shoes on tile, quiet coughing, throat-clearing, an occasional whisper. She sat in the chair across the little table from Keb and looked at him.

He smiled encouragingly. "Well, how are you?"

"I'm not too sure, Mr. Tefnut. This is all a little new to me. I guess I'm nervous."

"Quite understandable, Mrs. Gamesh. But this is your moment, you know. You are the envy of every person in the studio audience and all the viewers at home. Especially in

98

view of your unusual method of getting here. You used, I understand" — Keb looked up, and Penny followed his gaze to the large electronic cue card he was reading — "a microwave oven! That's simply wonderful! You're the first we've had, though now that it's been done, I'm sure a lot of folks will be following along behind you. You are, in a sense, a trailblazer, eh, Mrs. Gamesh? Technology comes up with something, and soon someone will figure out another way to use it. You broke ground. A novel approach. Tell us, how did you happen to think of it?"

Penny squinted against the light. She couldn't tell if there was anyone out there or not, though the cameras were, red lights winking on top of them. The show was being seen in the rooms at the Holiday Inn. She was in the center.

And she couldn't remember how she had happened to think of it. "It was an accident, sort of."

"An accident. Like all great discoveries, eh?"

"Well, I wasn't exactly sure I wanted to . . . kill myself. I wasn't very happy, I guess, just wandering around that house, Barney always gone working or thinking about his science. What he did was important, but there didn't seem to be *room* for me. I just wanted some attention."

"Some attention," Keb said, encouraging her.

"I thought marriage would be glamorous or something, I don't know, just not the way it was. Barney was famous and all, and I thought . . ." Penny's voice was wistful. "I thought that would make me worth something, I guess."

"I think we can understand that, Mrs. Gamesh. Even though you will not see the blue light of the Wisdom of *Dharma-Dhātu,* at least not this time around, eh? We can understand it, can't we, folks?"

Keb lifted his hands, asking for applause.

It was deafening.

Dr. Milkworth twisted the Q-tip vigorously in his left ear, probing for the elusive itch, the stray wax. He frowned at the same time, staring down at the heap of molten machinery pooled on the cement floor.

"Microwaves," he muttered, twirling the Q-tip.

"What's that?"

"Eh?" He spun around too fast, snapping the Q-tip and painfully jabbing the tender inner end of his auditory canal. "Oh, it's you." He hurriedly pushed the Q-tip into his coat pocket.

"Yep," Barney said cheerfully, "It's me. What's that?" He pointed at the mess on the floor.

"Generator," Dr. Milkworth frowned again. "The Luther Hadley McWhirter Memorial Generator. He was the chairman of the board of Thoth Communications, left us that generator. Damn things keep burning out. We have a dickens of a time keeping them going. It's the microwaves, throws the timing off and they overheat, burn out, and melt like that. Goddam microwaves. Can't control 'em around this place; engineers always playing, no shielding. A real administrative headache, I'll tell you."

Microwaves, thought Barney. A real headache.

Dr. Milkworth caught himself probing another Q-tip from its box in his shirt pocket and pushed it back. "George!" he shouted.

"Yessir."

"Let's get this mess cleaned up and a replacement generator installed. We only have ten days to go before April Showers."

"Yessir." George got right to work.

Barney stared wistfully at the brass plaque set into the floor next to the generator: Luther Hadley McWhirter Memorial Generator.

Dr. Milkworth said, "Come on." Barney looked up, and the scientist's fuzzy head was bobbing again, the generator problem forgotten. "I want to show you the target stage." Dr. Milkworth led him away.

The stage where Barney would be standing when he received his positron shower resembled a phone booth without windows. "Well?" Dr. Milkworth asked. "How do you like it?"

"Looks like a phone booth. Or a coffin. I suppose it'll do, though. I won't be in it very long."

"I gather not. As I understand the equations Josh has given us, you'll be in there about a half-hour while we get the beam up to speed. Then we fire the burst, you go back, return, and we let you out; you get snapped back from wherever you went to the exact moment you left. Right?"

"I hope so."

"You have doubts?"

"Mmmm."

"Well. How long will you be at this place? Sumer? If you don't mind my asking."

"We don't really know. Perhaps a year."

"And why are you going? If you don't mind my asking." The Q-tip impulse overcame Dr. Milkworth, and he was now busily engaged in mining his right ear for new fossil fuels.

"I've got to meet a man named Gilgamesh. An epic hero who tried for the secret of immortality. There's some evidence he may have been on to something."

"Hmmm," Dr. Milkworth murmured as he dug. "How are you going to talk to him?"

"Huh?"

"How are you going to talk to him? This Gilgamesh? I mean, he probably doesn't speak English."

"Oh, no. No English. He speaks Sumerian. I'll be getting RNA injections of a scholar's knowledge, some hypnopaedic learning, that sort of thing. I should be able to speak, read, and write it."

"Really? Interesting." Dr. Milkworth folded the used Q-tip and stuffed it into his white coat pocket, which bulged with used sticks. "Very interesting. I didn't know they even could write that long ago. Forty-five hundred years, I understand."

"Yes. Used a reed stylus on soft clay. Made wedge-shaped ideographs, called cuneiform. Quite attractive, actually." Barney's voice assumed a lecturing tone.

"Mmm." Dr. Milkworth frowned at the tiny phone booth set into the metal mesh platform. "I wonder how we'll know you've gone."

"You're photographing everything, aren't you?" Barney hadn't thought of that.

"Of course. But if you returned the instant you left, there wouldn't be any evidence, would there? Unless you brought something back with you. But as I understand the theory, that would be quite impossible. Temporal inertia or something, Josh called it. Well, I guess that's your problem, eh? We just do our job for the government. Mmm. Very good for the accelerator here. Very good. All those funds coming in." He fingered another Q-tip from the pack.

"Yeah," Barney said.

The show was over. Penny sat for a long time in the easy chair across from Keb's, staring off into the bright television lights, trying to figure what had gone wrong. She was sure being on television was what she would always have wanted, being a celebrity, the center of all that interest. But now it was over; everyone was gone.

Keb was gone. The technicians and cameramen, the stage manager and the man who controlled the electronic cue cards were gone. As far as she knew, the studio audience was gone as well, though she hadn't noticed. The bright lights stayed on, pouring eye-killing dazzle and sweltering heat on her. She felt her upper lip dew with sweat.

She stared so long into the brightness that when at last she glanced down at the set she was sitting in, it appeared washed out, pale, faded, as though the substance of it was beginning to loosen, to dissolve into the air. She still thought of things as material: wood, plastic, air, water. In her retinas the rhodopsin had bleached; her eyes could barely pick out the detail of the table, the chairs, the carpeting. The huge color television cameras loomed in the shadows behind the lights, vague, unreal. It came to her once again that she was really dead, a ghost wandering through the corridors of her life as she had known it, Holiday Inns, Iowa cornfields, TV talk shows, all-electric kitchens; a midwestern girl who had married an engineer and moved to California. Everything around her was bleached, unsure, warped into shapes no longer recognizable.

The lights brightened, stepped up another notch by the stage manager perhaps, and suddenly snapped off with a loud crack, leaving behind a sudden darkness and the smell of ozone, burnt insulation, hot glass, brimstone. Penny blinked rapidly. The room she sat in was small, not much larger really than the area of the set itself. There was no auditorium, no rows of seats. There had been no studio audience at all.

She sighed, got up and walked back to the lobby of the Holiday Inn. She went to the manager's office.

"I'd like to talk to the manager, please," she told the flawless secretary, professional smile in full bloom.

"Of course you would," the secretary responded.

"Ah, Mrs. Gamesh," the tulip was rasping before the secretary could finish her sentence, "you were wonderful. Simply wonderful. Everyone here loved you." Unreality increased every moment; she was beginning to doubt herself, her existence, her life with Barney, her death. Glancing around the office, she felt the faded look, the bleached, washed-out, strained-eye cast of the place increasing, a film over her vision. She remembered a sentence from *The Tibetan Book of the Dead*: "Thou wilt beget a fondness for the dull white light of the *devas.*" She didn't know quite what the *devas* were, but she thought she understood the dull white light.

"And now, Mrs. Gamesh, I'm sure you want to know what is going to happen to you." The manager smiled broadly.

"I suppose so."

"This will interest you. Unlike the staff, who must remain here forever, and unlike the other guests, who will be reborn in the same old cycle, you're slated for something unusual. There are forces at work here, Mrs. Gamesh, that I frankly don't understand. Attractions and the like. Perhaps you will understand them. But we have found a spot for you in Mesopotamia. Does that mean anything to you?" He nodded and smiled at her, his mouth moving strangely out of sync with his words.

"No."

"Mesopotamia. Well, I guess you wouldn't. Anyway, you are going to Mesopotamia, about forty-five hundred years ago. Now it's Iraq. The Tigris and Euphrates. A very nice pair of rivers. You will become a temple prostitute, the temple of Innana in the city of Uruk. A very honorable profession in its time. Well, you'll see, no doubt, though you won't remember anything, of course. It's been wonderful having you here, Mrs. Gamesh. A real privilege."

"Breaker, breaker," Haig Despot greeted her in the lobby. "I hear you're leaving us. Lucky you."

"Good-bye, Wooden Nickel," Penny said to the faint, watery form. "Good-bye."

Most of the staff at the Positron-Electron Project were having a Halloween party the night Barney was scheduled to leave. Josh was as excited as he could be, hopping from foot to foot, blushing violently, tugging at first one earlobe and then at the other. He had been practically living at the accelerator since the project began, so although Barney had hired

Prue as his lawyer, made out his will, and named Josh as his beneficiary, Josh himself had quite forgotten her. And Prue, for that matter, didn't seem to notice his absence.

Dr. Milkworth, in his white coat, wore a plastic Dracula mask pushed up on his forehead. He was not allowing any rum punch to the April Showers team until the experiment was over.

Barney was sweating. Josh had determined Barney would have to travel naked; no twentieth-century clothes would make the transition to 2642 B.C. But Barney was sweating anyway, standing near the tiny upright coffin he would soon enter. "Damn," he said to Josh. "It seems awfully hot."

"Does it?" Josh asked, glancing down at a long computer printout of the simulated particle collisions they were about to attempt in reality.

"Yes," Barney said, holding a towel around his middle while he mopped at his brow with a paper napkin.

"Probably anxiety," Dr. Schmidlapp said. He was an internationally famous neurosurgeon brought on board for this experiment. There was a persistent rumor of an unsuccessful lifesaving transplant he had once attempted, but it was such a difficult attempt, such a remote possibility, that the failure had done nothing to harm his reputation. If anything, in fact, it had increased his prestige.

"What kind of a transplant?" Barney had asked Junior Arkwright, who had recommended Dr. Schmidlapp from CIA files.

"Oh, he tried to do a head transplant," Junior told him. "Some fellow named McWhirter came to him and offered him a lot of money if he would save him — body was going. So he tried to give him a new body. Didn't take."

"Ugh," Barney said. "But I don't quite understand. Would that be a head transplant or a body transplant?"

"Who knows?" Junior asked.

"Right," Barney said to Dr. Schmidlapp. "It's probably anxiety."

A man from outer space wandered unsteadily by, huge green head and bulbous eyes nodding on top of a skinny body covered with a light green chitin, a plastic glass half full of rum punch in his hand, and stopped for a moment in front of Barney, weaving back and forth, to drink. He pushed his glass into the sucker-shaped mouth of his knobby head and made hideous slurping noises. When he brought the plastic glass back out it was empty.

It was a fine film of apprehension Barney was wiping from his face, a gritty, slick, bitter glaze. He was considering the danger he was about to face, the untested and random suggestions of his computer, suggestions that could, in fact, have been nothing but the haphazard dance of stray electrons in his own computer's memory chips, a stray fluctuation in his household current. After all, he had dialed a set of random-generated numbers on impulse and had connected with the Holiday Inn Deathwest data link.

A man in an Edwardian morning coat touched his arm. "It's almost time, Mr. Gamesh. You should be getting on the stage now."

"What?"

"I'm Oscar Wilde. I mean, Dr. Weston . . . in charge of instrumentation. You have to get in the box so we can begin calibrating the telemetry."

"Ah." Barney was covered with sensors, trailing wires.

For once Dr. Milkworth was not probing his ear. He was frowning at the rapidly unfurling paper of an EEG; ten needles danced wavy patterns on the page. Next to him, an assistant with a note pad scribbled figures. Dr. Schmidlapp nodded around his pipe at something the man next to him was saying.

Josh MacIntosh was jiggling from foot to foot. The door swung closed in Barney's face, shutting out the light. He dropped into sudden darkness, a darkness as absolute and deep as the space beyond the edge of the universe. There was no air in there! No air!

"Help!" But of course no one could hear him.

"Now, Mr. Gamesh, it is nearly time." The speaker crackled into life, providing Barney with something to hang on to for the moment. "It is nearly time. We will begin the countdown in fifteen seconds. Please stand by."

FIRST INTERIM REPORT

"Hey, Buddha. Come on."

"Hah?"

"Wake up."

"My foot's asleep." Buddha was surprised. All day, it seemed, he had been sliding his awareness up and down the X-ray spectra, contemplating a Seyfert Galaxy beyond Andromeda. His legs, spanning parsecs, were crossed in the full lotus, making the infinity sign: ∞.

"Never mind the foot; we have a problem. It's earth, still."

"It's always earth. Tell me something new."

"They're messing with time."

"Oh, Allah. What's that got to do with it, time?"

"That's what we'd like to know. Wake up."

"One thing you young fellows don't seem to understand is that I am awake. I happen to be very busy right now; I've got a new double pulsar almost completed, and . . ."

"Please."

"Look. Just give me a call when the situation is a bit more urgent, OK?" Buddha looked at his navel. "I wonder if I should reform that foot now. No, I think I'll wait a bit."

PART II

Yesterday

Cuneiform lesson:

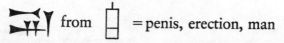 from ⬚ = penis, erection, man

8

At first there was only noise, a crackling white buzz that filled the universe. Barney thought of positrons shunted, of pions deflected, of radiation flashing through his body. He squeezed his eyes tightly shut as the sound grew louder, more penetrating, as it climbed inside his head. Then he opened them.

The light and the heat flattened him. He fell, naked now, to the flat, dry ground, threw his hands over his head, and crawled a yard, screaming in pain. He couldn't hear his screams over the buzz around him, the vast undifferentiated roar of random noise.

Nothing happened. The noise continued, the heat beat down on his back, the sandy ground under his knees and face radiated heat up at him. He turned his head and opened his eyes.

The air was filled with locusts. Not enough to darken the sun, hanging in the empty sky above him, but enough to keep the high decibel level of white noise constant around him. The swarm was two feet above him, heading in the direction he faced, moving fast, their hard bodies dark streaks in the air. There was nothing here for them to eat, so they must be flying toward food. He should follow them, but he couldn't stand up in this swarm, which cast tiny moving shadows on the bare earth as far as he could see. He waited, lying face down on the sand, breathing hard.

Hours passed, and the vast thin cloud of two-inch insects roared on. He began to doubt that they were moving purposefully at all; there were too many of them, they were too loud, the air was too hot. A gray-green insect landed in front of his eyes. He stared at it. It stared back, working its mandibles at the empty air. It was practicing, for the devouring motions never ceased, even when there was nothing to chew. Barney reached out his hand, fisted it, and smashed the bug. When he lifted his hand, the insect was still staring at him, jaws working though its back was crushed. It started to crawl away from him, then spread its translucent wings and buzzed into the air, continuing the erratic flight to food.

The sun moved across the sky behind him, pushing the shadows of the swarm out ahead. Low-flying insects battered at his back and he squirmed, thinking of those jaws. Locusts! He had been reading *The Joy of Death* when he thought of locusts, only a few weeks before. And here he was, in the middle of a swarm of them, like positive electrons, whining, buzzing, violent and sudden, an unpredictable, vicious assault on all his senses.

What was the joy of death? He couldn't recall. Where was he? Sumer. It must be. He looked around again. In every direction, under the black swarm, the earth was perfectly flat, perfectly dry, perfectly barren. There was no sign of either building or man, no living thing but insects and himself. I'm in the wrong place, he thought. They've sent me to the wrong place. A trick, a miscalculation. This is no place I've ever seen, even in a dream. Mojave Desert? With locusts? Certainly not at the end of October.

Barney failed to notice the sound dying away until it was gone, replaced by the thin wail of breeze, hot on his skin.

"Huh?" He spoke aloud, a naked, dirty man with long hair (despite a $17 razor cut only six weeks before). He looked around. The locusts had disappeared. The sun was setting, fat, flattened, an angry boil on the backside of the desert. His shadow stretched out in front, a line pointing east. Small blots of darkness revealed minute variations in the terrain, places where, he now noticed, there were stubs of plants, dry, gray and brittle.

"I'd better move," he said. He began walking into his shadow, thin and straight and so long he could not see the end of it.

The daylight faded as though a fuse had blown in the cosmic basement, and the stars appeared.

"Well, at least there's no pollution," he spoke into the silence, staring up at the blaze. He felt curiously calm now. There was, after all, the Rubber Band Effect. He was in no danger; he would be snapped back to the Stanford Linear Accelerator in time.

Barney was still gazing at the stars when he tripped. "Son of a bitch!" He sprawled across a low wall onto a pile of rotting skins, dirt and decaying leaves. Groping along the wall, he strained to see in the faint light. The wall appeared to form three sides and to be made of dried mud that flaked and crumbled under his touch. Finally he fell asleep. He dreamed of watching reruns of *The Brady Bunch*, *Charlie's Angels*, *Hollywood Squares*. A bronze bust of Farrah Fawcett-Majors spoke to him from a cloud.

". . . placed an evil hand on you . . . is . . . close to you?" she said.

"What?"

". . . carries off? Who are you, that . . . this place?" It wasn't Farrah Fawcett-Majors, it was Henry Fonda, his voice fading in and out so only fragments of words were understandable. Barney shook his head.

"What?" he asked again, opening his eyes to bright sun.

"I said, '. . . carries off? Who are you, that . . . this place?' "

"Penny," Barney mumbled, "ask him what he's saying. I can't understand him."

He sat up, suddenly awake. "Oh, my God!"

"Enlil?" The man standing over him asked, a puzzled

expression on his bearded face, wide eyes squeezed in concentration. He seemed to be listening to something. "Enlil?" he repeated.

"Hey, I must be speaking Sumerian." Barney clapped his hands, delighted. "It worked!" "Sumerian" came out sounding like "Shumerian."

"Shumer? Ah! Enlil. Shumer, yes. Good. Your accent is atrocious."

"What?" Barney decided he hadn't heard right. My accent is atrocious. Oh. The word the man used meant corrupted flesh of a dead camel. As in "eating the corrupted flesh of the dead camel."

"Have some atrocious," the man said, offering Barney a small gobbet.

"No, thank you. Not right now."

". . . yourself," the man said with a shrug, eating some of the atrocious with apparent relish. Then he squatted next to the low wall and fell asleep.

"Hey!" Barney exclaimed, but the man did not stir. He slept, arms folded across his chest, chin down, breathing quietly.

Barney studied him, wondering how he did that trick, going to sleep like that. The man had a short bow, a quiver of arrows, and a cloth sack from which he had taken the food.

The day wore on. Barney began to wish he had eaten some of the "atrocious" the man had offered him. At last he grew so hungry he reached for the sack and rummaged in it. More rotting camel flesh. Some kind of dried meat. A chunk of cheese with a stench that reminded him of bad dreams. Some bread.

He tried the bread. It cracked between his teeth, once. It refused to be chewed or bent. Barney let it lie in his mouth to be moistened by his saliva. At last it softened enough to break up between his teeth. He couldn't really call it chewing, but at least it felt enough like food to keep hunger at bay.

The sun crossed the zenith and began to slide down the western sky, and still the hunter, as Barney had begun to think of him, slept. Barney ate more bread. He found a clay jar in the sack and tried the contents. It was a strange-tasting beer, reminding him of the bread.

It was atrocious. "Guh," he said.

The temperature was clearly going to climb into the nineties if not higher. The dry ground seemed to groan under the heat, and still the hunter slept on. Barney didn't know what else to do but stay where he was and wait for the man to wake up. He had no idea where to go, where to find food, even how to speak very well. Talking to the hunter had been unsatisfactory somehow, the conversation filled with lacunae.

Toward evening the hunter woke at last. "I had a dream," he told Barney without preamble. "Aruru instructed me to talk to the king. You are from the steppe?"

Am I from the steppe? Is that what he asked me? What the hell is the steppe?

"Sort of," Barney answered.

"Sort of?" The hunter was puzzled. "Ah, I see. Sort of. That's good. Very good. Sort of." He turned abruptly and started to walk away.

"Hey! Wait a minute!"

"You wait here," the hunter told him. "I will talk to the king, as Aruru says. There is food in the sack. You talk to Anu." He trudged away from the setting sun. "Sort of," Barney heard him say. "Sort of . . . that's very good, ha-ha.

"Sort of . . . sort of. Sort it out. Sort camels from goats. Not our sort. Oh, this stranger is very good. The king must hear of it. Sort of . . ."

The voice faded away on the air. Barney waited throughout the night for the hunter to return. He waited through the next day, and hunger drove him to try the camel flesh. It was awful, but it was food. The dried meat was also awful. He drank the beer and was almost instantly dizzy from alcohol and hunger. He passed out and awoke the next day as the sun was coming up.

"Oh, my head," he said, holding it. He peered through slitted eyelids at the east, where the yellow-white sun swelled to fill the sky. I've got to move on today. I can't wait any longer for this fellow to come back. He might never come back. A strange man. Who the hell is Aruru?

His head drooped, so he didn't notice the person walking toward him until she was only about twenty yards away and her foot turned a clod of dirt.

"What?" he asked, staring into the shadow approaching him.

"Don't worry," said the woman, stopping at his rude shelter. "Don't worry." Her voice was silk and milk, it was cool water.

And it was Penny's voice.

Barney went numb with shock. "Penny!" His voice was dry like the meat, sour like the beer.

She had black hair, as before, but now it was long, braided into a heavy pigtail that wound around her head. She wore a long shawl that exposed her right arm and shoulder, a gold band around her arm, and her eyelids were painted blue. Now that she was close to him, he could see her smile. It was certainly Penny's smile.

"Don't be alarmed," she said, glancing frankly at his nakedness where he sprawled on the rotted skins.

He grabbed a patchy fragment of what might have once been camel and covered himself. She laughed, silver and silk, bells in a cool garden. She raised her arms over her head and gave a sinuous writhe to her body that seemed to ripple from her feet to her neck. There was something so lascivious about that ripple, something so inviting and urgent and steamy that Barney had to look away. He wasn't sure then that he had really seen it. It couldn't have meant what he thought it meant. No, she was simply stretching.

Penny. But it couldn't be Penny. Penny was dead.

He looked back. She had one hand cupped under her breast, offering it to him. Her huge round eyes were moist, her lips curled into a moist smile. No. He shook his head.

"I don't feel so good," he said, feeling at the same time a twitching turgidity under the camelskin. He groaned as a sudden clamminess crawled over him in spite of the increasing heat of the day. He realized that he had nothing to drink but beer for two days, had eaten nothing but dried meat, rotten camel and bread like shale. He really did not feel so good.

"You need water." She was at his side at once. "You should have some water." She was moving a flat slab of dried clay, revealing a hole in the ground. She lowered a leather sack into the hole and pulled it up, brimming with clear water.

It tasted wonderful, though brackish and hard. It was water, and Barney drank a whole skinful. There was marginal improvement in his hangover, but his other bodily functions began to demand their turn. He looked around, but there was no facility, no Port-a-Potty, no clean, tiled, service station restroom, not even a tree to go behind. Barney began to sweat, a glaze of salt forming over the layer of grime that covered him: cold skin, grime and salt. This was all hallucination, he thought. Some effect of the positron shower. I'm home in Sunnyvale.

Like hell, his body groaned, goading him. "I've got to, uh, go to the, uh (bathroom)," he said, thinking, they don't have bathrooms here; what did I just say?

Her laughed tingled down the scale, a B major descending arpeggio. "Oh," she said. "You've got to . . ."

"I don't know that word," he said, "but, yes."

She laughed again and turned around. One hip tossed itself at him, softness under the shawl. "Dig a hole," she said over her shoulder. He crawled away from the shelter and did.

When he got back she had filled another jug of water.

"You lie down," she told him. He felt too dirty, sick and tired to protest. He tucked feebly at his tattered loincloth, but she laughed again as she pulled it away. Then she gave him a bath.

She pulled clean linen from a sack she carried under her shawl. She dipped the linen in the water and dabbed at his face, cleaning away the desert dust. She scoured his ears. When she washed his neck, he could feel her soft breath on his cheek. He watched in fascination as her round arm moved, the smooth muscle binding and rolling under the delicate skin, the gold band, a coiled lizard, catching the brightness of the sun. She dried his face and neck and began on his chest, and he experienced once more the turgid throbbing in his groin. His mouth went dry.

"Uh," he said.

"Oh, you have a lovely scepter, my lord," she said, and her laughter rippled down his spine, a xylophone arpeggio this time that rolled down his vertebrae and stopped at the lowest note and throbbed. Her soft white hand closed around what was unmistakably *there* and slipped down once. "Like alabaster, so white," she said, and Barney blushed under the feverish glare of the sun. The shadow of her head moved across him, blocking the light and releasing it, a flickering that added to the vertigo he already felt.

"What about the hunter?" he asked, thinking that she must be his woman somehow. His voice was clotted like cream, thick and tasting too sweet to him. The damp linen slithered under his arms and across his belly as the bath continued.

She rinsed the linen again and began to work her way down his thighs. "Hunter?" she asked.

"That fellow who was here a couple of days ago. He went

to talk to the king, he said. Something about Aruru?"

"Oh, him." She dismissed it. "He won't be back. The king gave him a new goat and a bur of land. He's a farmer now." The linen moved between his legs, scrubbing away the griminess, the chill of fever. The scrubbing brought a rush of blood to the area and Barney's toes curled in embarrassment. She finished his feet. "Now stand," she commanded, and he stood.

She washed his back from nape to ankle, neglecting nothing. The dampness dried on his skin in the sun.

"Who are you?" he finally asked her, certain she could not be Penny. Penny had never been like this. Penny had been like him, the product of two thousand years of Christianity and technological sublimation, a furtive groper in darkness, a back-seat lover, a shy beginner and sore ender, a reluctant partner whose sweaty palms wanted only to fend off the need they felt and to feel the need as seldom as possible. At least after marriage. Before, of course, it was another story, a series of auto pit stops, drive-in movies, living room couch sorties into each other's pants, adolescent fumbling.

Barney and Penny got married in college and never recovered. So he knew, as the linen lingered, the soft fingers probed, the warm breath rolled across his skin, that this was not Penny of the tight lips and tensed knees. "Who are you?" he asked again as the air dried his skin under the wide sky.

"I'm a priestess of Inanna, of course." She ran the palms of both hands up the front of his legs, over the swell of his knees, and on into the vertiginous dark. He felt her lips move across the small of his back.

"Inanna?"

"She is my goddess. My name is Punumma. And now, my lord, you will lie with me," she said, clipping him neatly behind the knees so he fell over backward. She was on him instantly, his long-forgotten but now resurrected sex in her soft mouth; her tongue trickled up the bottom of it as her hands fluttered over his stomach and thighs.

"What is Inanna goddess of?" Barney thought he remembered from his reading, if he couldn't by now guess, but he was trying to keep his mind off what was happening.

"Mmmph," Punumma said. She lifted her head a moment and her eyes twinkled at him, two moist stars in a custard cloud. "Love, of course. She is a very powerful goddess." Her forefinger trailed up Barney's steeple, and the middle of his body from navel to knee jumped as though the earth had quaked. "Very powerful," she repeated. Barney's hands flopped at his sides, two pale, soft fish gasping on the bank as she sank down onto him once more, sending small flutters along the length.

"Should a priestess be doing something like this?" Barney gasped. "I mean, it seems sacrilegious or something."

Lifting her head, she reached behind her to loosen her shawl, which fell away a bit; inside, her small breasts lifted as she slipped the smooth material over her left shoulder. She teased him with glimpses, flashes of white skin, the pinkness of nipple. The cloth rustled down her arm, and she reached inside the shawl to caress the softness inside, and now Barney's midsections were twitching without stimulus from her.

"Of course I should be doing this," she said, her breath an evening breeze through the fronds of a palm tree. "What else should a priestess of love do?"

"Oh," he said, his eyes wide as the shawl fell to her waist. She kneeled a moment on it, sliding both hands, palms out to the sides, between the perfect breasts (and they did look like Penny's breasts, as Barney remembered them, though the memory was as dim as their bedroom light). She took his hand and led it to a melon, a hill, a church (he felt), and a watery weakness flowed through him.

"Lust is good, hien?" she asked him, writhing under his

hand. She stroked him some more and swiftly stood out of the shawl, towering naked above him so the triangle of her grotto filled his sky. She had nothing on now but the golden lizard around her arm, and Barney was beginning to feel maddened, a crazed weasel circling in his brain, frantic to escape, so when she sank down to guide his hand into her dampness, the lights went out in his eyes, a bulb burst at the base of his skull, sending waves of juice down the spine to trigger random convulsions in toes and buttocks, ears and elbows, until his center knotted hard and blasted half a million germ cells in a spoonful of goo onto her shawl, leaving him thrashing, a flounder on a spear in the middle of the desert sea.

"Oh, fuck!" he cried, not sure where he got the Sumerian word, but filled nonetheless with humiliation and shame and disappointment. He wanted to crawl away, a failure, but she held him fast and coaxed him back.

"You're damn right," she responded, and the next time around she changed positions so fast, above, below, behind, before, a blur of acrobatics that left Barney's computer circuits fused and blown, that his pelvis collapsed in fatigue, his tongue wrung, eyes red and gritty, fingers wrinkled, toes cramped in a fetal curl, knees scabbed and sore and all his glands drained dry.

When he recovered, the sun was easing down into the white sand, but this time it seemed not so much a boil swelling in pain as the sign for the biggest red light district in the universe. Idly Barney fantasied that this was as wet a dream as ever a repressed and hungry man ever had in the dankness of his thrashing sheets. But by then Punumma had built a tent of felt and made him dinner, and for the next seven days she kept him stripped and working hard, and bit by bit she licked him into shape.

And at last, after his seventh day in the desert, his fourth with this priestess of Inanna, his battered flesh failed, limp under all her ministrations, and a wave of self-loathing and guilt washed over him, an invisible blackness that dimmed the sun. Then she told him that animals would shun him now.

"Huh?" he grunted.

"The animals will shun you now. Not the gazelle of the steppe nor the creeping things, the hyena nor wild dog will come near you. No more will you feed with the beasts on the wild grass . . ."

"Hey, wait a minute. First of all, you look like you're repeating something someone is telling you. And second, I never had any special knack with animals. In fact . . ."

She interrupted him. "Of course I'm repeating what the goddess is telling me. What do you think?" She looked at him, head tilted, eyes smiling, deep pools of darkness glinting highlights that were unbearably wicked to him; they whispered some kind of betrayal he couldn't understand. You are a strange man, they said to him.

"I thought maybe you memorized it," he mumbled. His chin sank to his chest under the burden of misery he was feeling. The animals would shun him. Penny had wanted a dog, had, in fact, brought a playful puppy home to Sunnyvale. Within a day it had eaten a shoe and bitten Barney twice on the hand. They had to give it away; it growled every time he got near it.

"Listen." He heaved himself up to tell her. "Even tame animals hate me. Even puppy dogs. Cute, cuddly little doggies growl and bite me. Kitty cats scratch. Much less the wild beasts and all that. And I don't eat grass. Never have."

"Of course," she said, and cupped his hand around her naked breast. "They will shun you now. But I will not. Inanna is good."

"Oh, never mind." He sank back into his private dark, where he felt obscurely betrayed still. The sun moved minutely across the morning. Punumma stared into the distances, a small lascivious half-smile playing hide-and-seek around her lips, holding his hand against her breast. He didn't notice her even breathing.

"Today we will go to the city," she said at last, looking at him again. He clambered out of his pit.

"The city? What city?" His voice was dull.

"Why, Uruk of the mighty walls, of course. Where have you been? My king, who sent me here to you, will see you now that you are tame." She gave his limpness a playful shake.

"Uruk!" Barney woke up. "But that's where I want to go. I've got to talk to Gilgamesh." His cloud of guilt vanished.

"Oh." She seemed disappointed. "You know."

"You mean he's there? In Uruk? Why, this is terrific. It really worked, I'm here. I can get Penny back."

"Penny?" Her fine brows knitted the question. "You mean Punumma."

"Well, you certainly look like her, but no. She never had your, uh, enthusiasm. In fact, she didn't have many of the qualities you have. Still . . ." He faltered, suddenly unsure. "No, I did something wrong, somewhere. We both did." He was eager to have her understand. "I didn't know who she was, then, when we were married. Ever. Or who I was. Oh, I don't know . . ."

Punumma stared at him, a different look on her ivory face, a look that held some fear, but more concern. "If you didn't know who she was, why do you want her back? What is wrong with me? I know I'm only a priestess and not worth very much, but I am devoted to my goddess and my king, and I'm good at what I do. And now I think I may be devoted to you . . ."

"I know, I know," Barney said absently, patting her hand. "But I don't want a slave . . ."

She was on her feet, trembling in fury. "Slave! How dare you call me a slave. I am no slave, I *own* slaves. I am a woman of Uruk, no crude mountain girl to be a slave. You are an evil man to call me that!"

She tilted her head in that listening manner again. "Really?" she said, but not to him. "No!" she said, and she paused. "Oh, all right. But I don't like it." She turned back to Barney. "The goddess says you are not a bad man, but strange and ignorant, and that your ways are different. She says to be patient with you."

"The goddess talks to you? Just like that?"

"Of course. Doesn't your god talk to you?"

"No. I don't have a god. Not like that."

She was on her knees beside him, her white hands fluttering around his head, patting his hair, touching his ears, his lips, his nose. "Oh, my poor man. No god? Of course you have a god. But perhaps you don't listen to him, or perhaps you never ask him, but he is a very great and good god. Your god is Enki, water and wisdom. You are Enkidu. I know that, for my king, who is a great follower of Inanna, and the goddess herself also, they have told me."

"What? You know me?" Barney was confused, annoyed and pleased at the same time, though the metronome of Penny's death still beat steadily behind his eyes and caused him to squint against the tears he felt there: the hunch that she was Penny fought against the knowledge that she was not. The white hands fluttering around him, her concern, the deep puzzled sorrow in her eyes, all brought back the loss of someone he hadn't suspected he'd ever had. Penny. Penny. Penny. The metronome. And something strange went through him as that puppy, Penny's puppy, ran across his memory, wagging its tail, and he cursed himself for a fool. After all, the dog had bit him, and he had gotten rid of it.

"Back to the pound," he said.

"What?" she asked, the golden lizard flashing in the sun as her arm moved.

"Oh, nothing. Nothing."

"Then come. We must go to the city now."

"Ah." He climbed to his feet and stared to the east. His

first day in the desert — was it really a week ago? — came back to him. "The locusts!" he said.

"What?"

"The locusts. What happened to the locusts? They were heading toward the east, millions of them. They must have eaten everything!"

"Oh, no. We have heard they flew to Shuruppak, to the north. Enlil was angered with the people of Shuruppak; they are stupid and lazy. So Enlil sent the locusts to eat their crops. You see?"

"Oh."

"And now let us go to the city. It's half a day's walk, and it will be hot. But when we get to Uruk, there will be cool trees and water and melons and sherbets cooled with mountain snow. All the good stuff." She winked at him.

"Oh," he said again, and so she led him off to the city of Uruk of the mighty walls beside the shallow, muddy Euphrates, rich with fish.

9

"These are the mighty walls?" Barney placed his palm against the rough, mud-colored surface and looked up. A black-haired man peered back at him over the top of the wall; he held a long reed with a sharp point. The point, aimed at Barney, hovered inches from his eyes.

"Oh, yes. Are they not magnificent?" Punumma asked.

"Mmm, certainly," Barney answered, moving away from that trembling point. "Very magnificent."

The walls were a disappointment. The small hovels they had passed on the way to the city had been a disappointment. The city itself, mighty Uruk, at least from out here, was a disappointment. How could the king of this dump help him get Penny back? The houses were miserable, squalid square mud shelters with rotting reed roofs; pigs and cattle wandered through the yards and into the houses. The fields were patchy oblongs of mud and dust. The canals were crooked troughs of stagnant water. Flies buzzed everywhere.

"These walls," Punumma was saying, "have been most effective in keeping out the Gutians. Nowhere in all Sumer is there a city with walls as mighty as these."

"Is that a fact?" Barney edged toward the gate, which looked more like a place where the wall had collapsed than a formal entrance. A donkey was making an addition to the heap of droppings beside it. "I'd think perhaps it was the flies that kept the Gutians out, whoever the Gutians are."

"The Gutians are Enlil's wrath. A nasty people." Punumma wrinkled her nose.

"Right," Barney said, watching a syphilitic figure with the nose rotted away lurch past with a ragged, jerky gait. "A nasty people."

The city unreeled before his eyes, a nightmare of stink and filth, the river a corrupt, currentless pool of sewage and dead fish. Reed boats with tattered woven sails slurged back and forth, dragging rotted nets behind them. Gap-toothed smiles greeted him derisively as he walked toward the ziggurat in the center of town, through streets almost straight, past buildings almost tall, almost white, almost level. The effect was one of visual cacophony, a cubist hallucination by way of Hieronymous Bosch, a murky depression of heat and smell and ever-present flies hovering over the discarded melon rinds, chicken guts, and donkey droppings in various states of freshness that littered the streets.

"Aha-ha-ha!"

Barney switched his eyes from his feet, whose path through the mire he had been checking attentively, to seek out the source of this strange half-exclamation, half-laugh.

Barney Gamesh was not a big man, as people in his century went, but he towered over the population of Uruk, who seemed to him to be a stunted, gnomish people, with, of course, the dazzling exception of Punumma, who, veiled and shawled, her glistening black hair coiled around her head, stood quietly to one side.

"Aha-ha-ha!" the man repeated. Even his voice was bigger than Barney's. His ham-sized hands were fisted and stuck into his sides; his sturdy legs were spread. He was standing in front of a gate in another wall, this one oddly clean and gorgeously decorated in a geometric mosaic of black, red and blue. The gate behind him was a ten-foot-high double door of cedar, intricately carved. "Aha-ha-ha!" The voice was as hearty and cheerful as a Shriners' convention. "Welcome to my city," he boomed, rollicking back and forth on his feet, his hands clenched at his sides. Copper bracelets at his wrists winked in the sun. "Isn't it a terrific city?" he asked.

"It's very impressive," Barney answered. Doubt chased apprehension through the suburbs of his tone.

"Goddam right it's impressive. You have no idea how I have to drive these oxdung-eating buzzards to get them to build these fantastic walls. No idea. Such a mealy bunch of simpering, weak-minded slaveys the world has never seen before. They drop like flies when they work. No stamina at all! I don't know how many of the pathetic peasants we've had to throw in the river this week alone. You just can't get good help anymore. Not like in my father's day." When the man shook his head, his greasy ringlets swung to and fro across his knotted brow.

"Well, well," he went on brightly. "You didn't come here to listen to my complaints, Enkidu. No, no. Not at all. So come in, come in."

He turned and banged on the carved wooden door with his fist, and the wood gave as though it would collapse under his assault. Before he could smack it a second time it abruptly swung open, and a small man in a floor-length robe bowed profoundly, banging his forehead on the ground before them. Then he ushered the three of them inside.

The contrast with the outer city was stunning. A vast open courtyard spread before them, swept clean and white, flagged with burnt brick. The walls were brightly colored, pleasingly harmonious, beautiful. Above their heads, tier on tier of the ziggurat soared, solid and clean, four levels built one atop the other, each smaller than the one below, but all decorated with the intricate mosaics of round clay cones brilliantly painted. The stairs up the outside of the walls were spotless, though narrow and steep. Men and women dressed in clean linen walked unhurriedly on the terraces or gathered in small groups to talk.

"Aha-ha-ha! Well, I guess you realize that I am Gilgamesh, steward of Inanna in Uruk. You can call me king if you want to, by god." He turned suddenly to Punumma. "He's tame?" he asked her.

"Yes, lord," she smiled. "Quite tame."

"Splendid, splendid. You did a fine job, Punumma. Come and see me later, eh?" He pinched her bottom through the shawl and winked.

"Hey, wait a minute," Barney protested.

"Aha-ha-ha, never mind," Gilgamesh roared. "We're going to have a hell of an orgy a little later, and I'm sure you'll get your spirit back, Enkidu. Get the old god-rod working again, eh? Ha-ha! Of course, nobody here fucks like I do, but then, that's why Inanna made me her steward of this vast city, isn't it? Ha-ha!"

Barney winced and glanced at Punumma, who smiled at him encouragingly. He started to protest again but Gilgamesh was walking toward a door in the opposite wall. There was nothing to do but follow, jogging along in the king's wake, pilot fish to a shark.

When he caught up, Gilgamesh nudged him in the ribs. "Wait'll you see the beauties I've got lined up in here, ha-ha. *Three virgins* among them, by god, if you can imagine that. All due to get married tomorrow. Amazing we could find three virgins in this town in these decadent days. Boys. We got boys, too, if you go in for that sort of thing. Some animals, 'specially trained. Maybe you would prefer a nice ewe, a she-camel? Me, now, I prefer virgins, but Inanna! they're getting scarce, ha-ha!" He nudged Barney again and led him through the sweet-smelling cedar door.

Inside it was cool and dim. "This is the entry hall to the lower temple," Gilgamesh told him, his voice echoing pleasantly in the vast room. "Not a very interesting place, if you ask me, but we have to keep those priests happy with all their oxdung or they get out of hand, if you know what I mean, though probably you don't, being a wild man from the steppe and all that, but Inanna! they are a sniveling, plague-ridden lot of fly-blown mounds of oxdung and atrocious, the way they go on about building this and building that, and we need more clay for the records and more wood for the walls and more stone for the statues and more reeds to write with and boats and sails and more animals and generally more of everything. There's no end to their demands, and they all come indirectly of course from the goddess, so there's nothing I can do about it but try to amass all this stuff they want when really there's nothing I'd rather be doing than sticking it to a nice juicy virgin and listening to her squeak, fear, pain and pleasure. No, there's nothing like it, I tell you, but then you probably know all that, being a wild man from the steppe and all that, and then perhaps you don't, do you? only recently tamed by Punumma here, the prettiest little temple prostitute we have in all Uruk, by Inanna. Ha-ha."

He led them outside again, this time to a small courtyard filled with trees, a small pond, heavy-scented flowers, and a fountain that filled the small space with the sound of flowing water. Gilgamesh sat on a brick bench and sighed, as though exhausted by his speech. "Well, Enkidu, you'd probably like to eat something. Punumma couldn't carry anything very fancy out into the desert with her, and I am told you are a great eater."

"Told?" The change in Gilgamesh's tone was a relief, but puzzling. And when did he have time to talk to anyone?

"Sure. Told. Lugulbanda, my father, told me."

"Your father?"

"Yup. Been dead for a hundred and twenty years, he has."

"Oh."

"He's my personal god, you know, and a good god he is, too. Gives me a lot of good advice. A great one with the virgins he was, too, old Lugulbanda, so the legends say."

"Great."

Food appeared, brought in by a group of clean but servile slaves, who set it down and prostrated themselves at Gilgamesh's feet, covering his hide sandals with sloppy kisses. He accidentally kicked one in the face crossing his legs but didn't notice. Already he was stuffing dried dates, fish sticks, flat bread and beer into his mouth. He was a big eater.

"Mmmph," he said. "Damn, if this isn't good food. Sometimes these carrion-eating lumps of oxdung can really cook up a meal. But then, you wouldn't know that, would you? Being from . . ."

"The steppe." They finished together.

"Aha-ha-ha. Very good. Yes, the steppe, a wild man, ha-ha. But you don't really look so wild, now that I have a good look at you. You're big, I'll say that. Bigger than those swine I have to live among, but not all that strong, I think. A little doughy, eh? Probably all that grass you ate, out there in the . . ."

"Steppe."

"Right. Well, come on, eat up." Gilgamesh downed a jug of beer and belched.

The food was good. Certainly a satisfactory improvement over the atrocious decayed camel. But Barney thought he could use a nice steak, medium rare.

"Well, what city are you from?" Gilgamesh belched and smacked his beer jug down on the little table in front of him. It cracked and fell into pieces, which he threw into the pond.

"Sunnyvale," Barney answered without thinking.

"What's that? Sunny Vale? That's a pleasing name. Isn't that a pleasing name, Punumma? Sunny Vale."

Punumma, seated quietly, hands folded in her lap, nod-ded.

"I've been thinking of a new district for the city. Across the river, next to Kullab. My father was from Kullab, so they say. A priest. But what do they know?" He waved a greasy hand vaguely toward the river, dismissing *them*. "Yup, a new district. Sunny Vale, eh? Very nice. Well," he boomed, thumping the table, "let's get on with it. A bath, perhaps? And then, by Inanna, the orgy!" He stood up abruptly and strode from the garden.

"Is he always like this?" Barney asked Punumma.

"Oh, yes. He is a great fucker. A great wall-builder. A mighty king. Oh, some of the people complained, of course. He insists on having the walls built, then forgets about them and they decay. And he sleeps with the new brides before their husbands, so of course some of the ignorant complained to the goddess. She sent you to be his friend."

"His friend?" Barney was incredulous. "His friend?" he squeaked. "Good god, anything but that."

"You will be his friend," Punumma said quietly. "The goddess has arranged it. So come, you need a bath."

I'll never be his friend, Barney thought. Never.

He did need a bath. Badly. And the water, heated in huge clay pots and tipped into the tub, was warm, if a bit muddy, and Punumma washed him herself as the servant in charge of the hot water stood impassively by, staring at the wall over Barney's head, but Barney still squirmed at the unfamiliar attention and the public nature of the bath.

There was no soap, but the oil she rubbed all over him after he was dry was sweetly scented and felt wonderful, though it failed to arouse any interest in his god-rod, as Gilgamesh had called it. No interest at all. Barney didn't really feel like an orgy. Somehow it seemed unfair. Punumma was gentle and lovely, and she had tamed him in the desert. It didn't seem right to turn his back on her now. (He turned his back to her so she could run her palms down either side of his spine, slick with sweet oil.)

She slapped his bare bottom. "Time to get dressed, Enkidu," she said brightly. She leaned down and breathed in his ear, "You are a big man. I like you."

Barney gulped. His ear twitched, seeking the warm breeze of her breath. He noticed as she pulled away from him that her teeth were perfect, as perfect as Penny's had been, the first good teeth he had seen in Sumer, a land with no dentists or dental floss, dental hygiene or fluoride, Listerine or running water. Why hadn't he noticed her teeth before? She was as clean and well polished as a television ad.

She wrapped around his waist a tan flounced skirt that fell to the floor. "Simple to get under this," she murmured into his ear and giggled. Barney glanced over at the slave beside the water jug, but the slave stared at the wall. Punumma ignored him, as though he were a piece of furniture. She seemed to regard the slaves as no more important than a water tap, part of the plumbing.

She wrapped a brown felt cloak gently over his shoulders, for his sunburn had reached the itching stage. She stroked his freshly shaved cheek with her soft palm, and her hand lingered strangely at the down curve of his jaw. Barney gulped again, and an old hinge suddenly rusted in his neck. It was Penny's gesture, back in college when they were going steady, a lingering touch at the jawline, fingertips trembling a moment on the pink-shaved skin. And Penny was dead, a frozen lump of deadness in Pete Boggs' freezer, a side of meat and bone, gone.

Barney's spine froze too, beyond cold, a zero at his center, a death of flesh and blood, so deep did that touch go, that lingering at the jawline from those trembling fingertips that so suddenly haunted him.

"What?" He shook himself, aware at last that she was talking as she strapped the copper bracelets on his wrists, bracelets chased with lion and deer locked in death together.

She was lecturing him on orgy etiquette. "Let the king lead and take his pick first. He will probably deflower the virgins first. I understand there are three, to be brides soon, so it is his duty to have them first. He may be in a bad mood since there are so few. Lugulbanda is supposed to have taken on fifteen in one day, and Gilgamesh is very sensitive about that — the most he was ever able to manage was nine. It wasn't his fault, of course. The gods only made nine available that day, but still, it is something he worries about.

That's probably why he works so hard on the walls. And it would be a good idea to try to keep up with him; he'll respect the goddess more if you do, since you come from her, and he *must* respect the goddess. You see, sometimes Lugulbanda tells him to do the things the goddess doesn't like, and then we have trouble."

She threaded leather thongs through the holes in the final copper bracelet and tugged them tight. Then she stepped back to look him over.

"I don't quite understand." Barney was worrying about several things. "He has to have the brides? The husbands object, don't they?"

"Well, it makes them unhappy, of course. But they don't object to the king, not directly. He'd have them filleted and made into sausage if they did."

"No! Listen. I don't think I want to go to an orgy. First of all I'm kind of, uh, tired, you know? From the desert. I just don't think I could, well, keep up with him. Besides, you . . . Well, I don't think it's fair!"

"Fair?" Punumma stared at him, her soft lips pursed into a puzzle-knot. "What is fair?"

"Just. You know, *nigsisa*. Justice."

"Oh. That. Well, *nigsisa* is what the gods want, not what we might like. Whatever is, that is just. Don't worry about it. Just tell Gilgamesh what a wonderful fucker he is and try to keep up. No faking, now." She smiled at him and took his hand.

They walked a long time, in and out of courtyards, past buttresses and niches, some containing statues of wood or stone, through carved doors and square-capped arches, passing at times through broad patches of afternoon sunlight, at times through cool shade, and everywhere they went the people made way for them, giving Barney looks that contained either pity, awe, or gratitude. He heard them saying, "Enkidu. The king's friend. The hand of Gilgamesh will lighten." Barney felt like the red cape, there to divert the bull's attention, the expendable decoy. It was a feeling familiar to him from his earliest days of office politics, and he didn't like it, but Punumma was leading him on, and he couldn't just drop her hand and run. There was nowhere to go.

They proceeded down narrow steps and up narrow steps and across broad courts and down steps again, twisting through the maze of the sacred precincts under the ziggurat to arrive at last at a small building just inside the outer walls of the temple. The door was open, and inside, in the cool dimness, Barney glimpsed the flash of bare flesh, woven cloth and small feet.

"We will wait here," Punumma said, "for the king."

The shadow of the wall pooled at their feet as the westering sun slid down. It lapped, a tide of darkness, slowly up his leg, a cool shadow that blended with the fading chill in his heart, the chill touch of her fingers on his jaw. The faint gleam of skin inside the room flowed smoothly here and there in the darkness — liquid, obscene, half-hidden lubrications suggestive of pain, coercion and violation, shameful surrender within the sexual gape of the door. A prickle of sweat ran down Barney's spinal furrow, the beginnings of heat in the stomach pit as he stared at a landscape of violence.

"O, a-wenching we will do, a-wenching we will do, Ú-gul-úl-ulándu, a-wenching we will do!" A hoarse and tone-deaf voice rolled across the empty court, through the reddening sunlight and into the pool of shadow that by this time had risen to Barney's neck.

"Three juicy virgins, and that's a lot. We'll fuck 'em all, willing or not . . ." Gilgamesh staggered around a corner and into the square, swinging his arms at his sides, veering from side to side, straddling an enormous stuffed leather phallus, waving its blunt end before him, a parody of fertility. He was clearly drunk.

"Ú-gul-úl-ulándu, I'll give 'em a good screw . . . Hi, ho,

Enkidu, ready for the screw, aha-ha-ha. Hot damn and here I come," Gilgamesh said. Barney glanced over at Punumma. To him, her smile was a scratch on a perfect mirror.

"Aha-ha-ha," Gilgamesh screeched again. "Well, Enkidu, are you ready? Got the old god-rod limbered up, ha-ha? Let's go!" He threw one arm around Barney's neck and started to drag him toward the yawning door. The thick, sickening exhalations of license and lust gusted into Barney's face.

"No!" he shouted, wrenching himself from under the king's thick arm. "No. You won't go in there!" He turned his back to the door, barring it with his outstretched arms.

"Hah?" Gilgamesh looked puzzled. His ithyphallic prop drooped. He stood still in the sun, swaying slightly, breathing hard, dazed. "Hah?" he said again. "Hah?"

Barney was breathing hard too, accumulated thousands of hours of television reruns unreeling in his head: *Starsky and Hutch, Charlie's Angels, Baretta, Gunn, Kung Fu.*

"I said, 'No!' " His voice slid up the audible range, a recording suddenly speeded up. He was breathing so hard he could barely control his voice enough to articulate. The insouciant image of the Kung Fu master, calm in the eye of danger, wavered in the waves of hot adrenalin that surged through his body, and his plump hands shook against the wooden frame of the door.

"No?" Gilgamesh said. "No? I don't understand." He tilted his head to one side, listening. "Uh-huh," he said. He listened. "Uh-huh. No. All right." His eyes came back into focus and he smiled. "Lugulbanda says to ask you to get out of the way so we can get on with the wenching. Hot juicy virgins waiting in there, you know." He grabbed his leather dingus and gave it a suggestive shake.

A lifetime of television violence exploded in Barney's head. With a terrifying shriek he propelled himself away from the doorway toward Gilgamesh, zero to thirty in 2.6 seconds, his sedentary legs suddenly filled with power. Six feet from the still-smiling king he hurtled his body into the air, twisted sideways, and pointed his feet straight at Gilgamesh's chest. His arms were held lightly in the correct Kung Fu position, hands lightly fisted, ready to gouge and maim, fingers to hook in nostrils and pull, thumbs to flatten eyeballs, heel of hand to splinter the delicate bones in the bridge of the nose, feet to kick and destroy ribs, solar plexus, groin (unfortunately well protected at the moment by the leather apparatus), kneecaps, ankles. Barney's teeth were bared in a snarl of terrifying destruction. He was the Bull of Heaven, the rage of Enlil, the unstoppable power of death itself: plague, flood, locust and drought.

Alas, television reruns and imagined violence are not enough to transform a sedentary and cerebral computer engineer from Sunnyvale, California, into a fighting machine. Barney's judgment was faulty, and his feet, ready though they were to strike fatally, sailed well past Gilgamesh in a harmless trajectory.

He was only lucky enough to be in such an amateurish posture as he flew through the air that his behind, stuck awkwardly out, struck Gilgamesh solidly on the shoulder. Both king and wild man from the steppe fell in a tangle of limbs, leather prick, felt capes, sandals and dust.

There was, as well, just enough air resistance to Barney's graceless flight to flutter his flounced skirt up over his face, both exposing his naked shame to the open air and covering his eyes, blinding him. "Oh, shit!" he exclaimed in English, struggling with the linen, which was richly entangled and caught.

"Hah?" he heard, somewhere to his left and above. He swung his free left fist toward the voice and cracked his knuckles on what could only have been Gilgamesh's sandal heel.

"Aaah," he moaned, but the moan turned into a thick deflating sound, a *pooh* as the heavy king landed on his back. The darkness under his skirt turned a dim red. When

Barney shook his head to clear it, his skull connected solidly with the king's royal chin, stunning him. He stood and wandered in vague circles long enough for Barney to yank his skirt down and clear his vision.

They were by now thirty or forty yards from the orgy room and the other participants — the virgins, the ewe, the she-camel (my god, Barney thought, he really meant it about the camel!), the boys and the priestesses — and Punumma had formed a circle around the battling pair, a circle that swelled rapidly with new additions as priests and scribes, masons and tax collectors, doctors and teachers, prostitutes and landowners, serfs and slaves, all rushed to see, as the king and the friend-who-would-distract-him fought in the dust.

Gilgamesh recovered enough to realize that the leather tool between his legs was something of a hindrance, so he began tugging at the buckle to shed it and continue the fight. Thus occupied, he forgot Barney, who hurled himself onto his back with a bloodcurdling "Haaaaiii" karate shout. Fortunately for the king, he had chosen that moment to bend down for a closer look at the buckle, and Barney glanced off the rounded back presented to him, toppling over the top of the king's head and landing heavily at his feet. At that moment the buckle gave way, and Gilgamesh swung the leather down at Barney's head.

It was filled with dried wool and was quite light, so there was no pain. But a seam gave way with a small ripping sound, spilling wool into Barney's eyes, so as he lunged once more at Gilgamesh his vision was blocked and his aim went astray. His head hit the king's stomach, which was as hard as a burnt-brick wall.

Both men were panting wildly now, gasping for breath, throwing leaden arms at each other but rarely connecting, while the enormous crowd cheered and wagered. Finally Gilgamesh tottered toward Barney, gave him a feeble shove, and staggered past him.

Barney fell over, exhausted and feeling quite sick. The crowd cheered. Monetary units changed hands; in one instance a slave changed owners four times.

The next thing Barney knew he was on his feet, and Gilgamesh, king of Uruk, steward of Enlil and Inanna, son of Lugulbanda, was embracing him and weeping drunkenly for joy and calling him friend.

10

"I'm pregnant."

"What?"

"I'm pregnant."

"How do you know?" Barney and Punumma were sitting in the garden courtyard, which was refreshingly cool though the days were getting hotter. Barney had learned that it was spring in Mesopotamia, though he had left in October. He didn't understand why, but he suspected that it had something to do with the fact that Sumer was on the opposite side of the world from Sunnyvale. He'd have to ask Josh about it when he returned.

"I had a visit from the goddess last night. From Inanna. She told me."

"Oh." Barney was getting used to everyone communicating with the gods and goddesses. It felt as if he were in a room while someone was on the telephone: He could only hear half the conversation.

It was especially disconcerting when Punumma received a call while they were making love. "What did you say?" he asked.

"She said I was pregnant. She said the child was yours, from the desert." Punumma laughed. "She said it would be a boy, a mighty warrior and a great king. Things like that."

"She said it was mine?" Barney was lying on the brick bench eating dates, his head in Punumma's lap. He felt extraordinarily comfortable and totally unreal. The place was unreal. The light was unreal. The air was unreal. His life with Punumma and his growing friendship with Gilgamesh were all unreal.

"Oh, yes. It's yours all right. Our son will be almost a god. Partly a god, at least."

"How do you mean?" Barney ate another date.

"No one has ever come so close to beating Gilgamesh in a fight, and he is two thirds a god. So you must be at least a third god yourself. Maybe a half. So our son will be part god. That's very good."

"Well, I suppose it would give him a little head start in life," Barney said, thinking. This is unreal, a computer simulation, a movie. And Gilgamesh is Anthony Quinn.

The king had sent the virgins, undeflowered, back to their grooms the day of the fight. "I have a friend," he had announced to the crowd once he regained his breath. "This is my friend Enkidu. In honor of my new friend, Lugulbanda has decreed that there shall be no orgy today; the virgins may go home to their grooms. There will be no work on the walls for two weeks in honor of my friend Enkidu. I, Gilgamesh, steward of Enlil, son of Lugulbanda, say it shall be so, and so it shall be. In honor of my friend."

The crowd cheered wildly and carried Gilgamesh and Barney around on their shoulders and roasted a flock of goats and camels and baked 14,560 loaves of thick, chewy, tasteless bread with grain from the public storehouses, and the city of Uruk and all the towns under its dominion had a wonderful party and stayed up late and got very drunk, and there was a baby boom in Uruk nine months later.

"You have no idea," Gilgamesh confessed to his new friend later that night, as the torches flowed in rivers through the city and the fires burned late roasting animals and the crescent moon harvested stars in the fields of heaven, "you have no idea what a strain it is to be a king."

Gilgamesh was even drunker than he had been when he arrived at the orgy. "All those virgins," he went on. "Keeping up appearances. I tell you, I get very tired sometimes, and frankly I feel sorry for them. But it's expected. It's what kings do. Part of the job. And the biggest problem, my friend, is that there's no giving it up; you can't resign. You get famous, get a reputation for this or that — you know, building walls or fucking virgins — and you're stuck with it. You have to keep doing it forever or some wise-ass clump of oxdung will come along and try to kill you to make a reputation for himself."

"Sort of like a gunfighter," Barney mumbled, staring pensively at the thousands of winking torchfires in the city. They were seated on a bench in the third tier of the ziggurat, facing south. To their left was the river and the town of Kullab and the vast open space where Gilgamesh planned to locate his new district of Sunny Vale. Before them and to their right the city spread out. It didn't spread very far, but it was definitely urban. It looked rather pretty at night.

"Gun? What's a gun?" Gilgamesh asked.

"A kind of bow and arrow."

"Aha-ha-ha, right! A bow and arrow. Yes, that's very good, my friend. A gunfighter. You get a reputation as a gunfighter, ha-ha, and the punks come along and try to kill you. Yeah, being a king is like that. And frankly, the virgins are almost always lousy lays. No enthusiasm."

"The husbands probably don't think that."

"No, I suppose they don't. Still the god says build a wall, you build a wall. The god says screw all the virgins, and by god, you screw all the virgins. Otherwise you get the pox and have to go to a doctor, and there's nothing worse than that."

"The god gives you the pox for not screwing virgins?" Barney wondered how these people could get things so mixed up.

"Naturally." Gilgamesh was surprised. "The god gets pissed off, and that's it. Believe me, there's nothing worse than having to go to a doctor. I know. I've been." The king poured them both another cupful of the thick, sour beer. "I get so tired of it. So tired," he murmured.

Barney's thoughts were wandering too. "Oh, you're not so bad," he said. "Everybody gets tired."

"The worst of it is," Gilgamesh continued, draining his cup and wiping his mouth with the back of his hand, catching his lip painfully on the edge of his copper bracelet, "the worst of it is," he repeated, patting his torn lip with his finger, "that with a god like Lugulbanda for a father, and a reputation like his to live up to, and the shortage of virgins and all, it's damn frustrating. You know, he was supposed to have had fifteen virgins in one day! Fifteen! I can't even find that many! Of course, the parents lie all the time, talk about how their daughters are all sluts, screwing since they were six and all that. I can't test them all. These peasants, how they lie." He sighed as he poured another cup. "The most I could ever collect was nine, and I was lucky to get that many. And honestly, I'm not even sure I could manage it even if I could find enough. The poor old god-rod is getting battered. I wish there was some way of finding something else to do with my time." His sigh turned into a snore. Barney glanced over, and the king was sound asleep, slumped on the bench.

Yes, he was Anthony Quinn, gusty and lusty and pure pudding underneath.

"So we have to go to the doctors," Punumma was saying.

"Huh?"

"We have to go to the doctors. Weren't you listening?"

Barney blinked himself back to the garden court, his head on Punumma's lap. "Hey!" he suddenly shouted. "You're pregnant!"

"That's what I've been saying, stupid." Her mouth in a pretty pout.

"And it's mine! Really mine!"

"Of course. You've kept me busy." She was smiling.

Jumping to his feet, he grabbed her hands and swung her around in a dizzy waltz until they tripped and tumbled into the ornamental fountain, scaring the catfish and dousing themselves, laughing.

"Oh. Oh, I'm sorry," he gasped, pulling her out gently. "You should be careful. I mean, I should be careful." He kissed her eyes.

"Don't be silly," she told him. "I'm not made of pottery. I happen to be a very tough loaf."

"Of course you are," he laughed. Then he sobered. "But what's this about going to the doctors? I mean, I heard that the doctors are, well, a little *strange*."

"Of course they're strange. They're doctors. It's a very important but uncertain profession."

As they wandered through the precinct, Barney was amazed anew at the complexity of the courts and chambers, the fountains, the intricate mosaics, the priests' quarters and royal palace, the schools and temples, the sculptures of gods and goddesses, and especially the stairs: On three sides of the ziggurat stairways ran up the outer walls, and on the fourth side a long, very steep stair had been built at right angles. It had 360 steps, which Barney, one morning before the heat had slammed down on the city (which it did every day without fail), had climbed and counted.

They arrived at what Barney thought of as the hospital, where maimed or diseased members of the ruling class came for treatment. Punumma introduced Barney to a gnomish, clean-shaven man in a floor-length gown, who bowed without removing his hands from his sleeves.

"This is Lugglanu, director of the medical school," she said.

"We have a pox case going on right now," the doctor told them. "Perhaps you'd like to watch." He turned and led the way, though Barney had begun to decline the invitation.

He wished he had been more vigorous declining. "He has, as you can see, a disease of the tun; this comes of disobeying the goddess." Barney could see; but it was the combination of odors that was most troublesome. Barney couldn't tell which was worse, the disease or the medicines.

"First," the doctor continued, "the attendant anoints the opening with crushed turtleshell and oil."

Barney had to watch; after all, he was Enkidu, the king's friend, part god. But the sight was not pretty, and the patient was grimacing in agony.

"Next," the doctor went on, "he rubs it with beer, washes it, and fills it with crushed fir wood. The fir wood is, of course, imported from the mountains and very valuable. And expensive."

"And painful," Barney added.

"Well," said the doctor, waving his arm at the patient, "pain is from the gods."

It was then that Barney noticed that the doctor had no hand.

"What happened to your . . . ?" he blurted, not stopping himself in time.

"What? Oh, that." The doctor looked down casually at the stump. "I lost a patient. That's the penalty, I fear."

"They cut off your hand?"

"Hands." The doctor waved his other stump at Barney. "That's why I teach here — can't practice anymore. We recruit all our faculty that way. Those who can't practice, teach."

"I see," Barney said, feeling faint. Lugglanu led them on, leaving the patient's hideous screams behind.

"Here is your doctor." He introduced them. "His name is Urlugaledinna. He is a great water-knower, a great doctor. His specialty is women." Lugglanu winked and left.

Urlugaledinna had hands, so Barney presumed he had not lost any patients. Not yet.

"Indeed," Urlugaledinna said, "the god has been with me so far. Besides, I only take cases that will present no problems. No sense tempting a god. Punumma here will be no problem, I'm sure. The goddess loves her; she is a tough loaf and in terrific shape. Altogether a pleasure to work with." He turned to her. "I gather you're pregnant?"

"The goddess told me in a dream last night." She smiled.

"Mmm-hmm. Any other evidence?"

"I'm six weeks late."

"I see. Well, that should take care of that. I conclude that you are pregnant. Tentatively. I will send Lord Enkidu my bill. Good day." He walked them to the hospital entrance and smiled them out.

"That's all he does?"

"Oh, yes. He is a great water-knower."

"Doctors haven't changed much."

"What?"

"I said doctors haven't changed much. In my time . . . Oh, never mind." Barney was thinking about Gilgamesh. The two-week festival was long over and the king was back to building walls. The brick ovens blazed day and night, and with the temperatures climbing well into the nineties, Barney judged, during the day, it was miserable in town. Peasants were still dying all over the place of heat stroke, though not, Punumma told Barney, in the numbers they had been before he arrived. The mud walls did not last very long, and large stretches of them were crumbling. Gilgamesh had ordered burnt bricks made; they were stronger and lasted much longer but were hard to make. Also, the king had gotten some grand ideas about height; nine or ten feet wasn't enough. They had to be thirty or forty feet high, with towers and slots for archers. They had to be pretty. There was a rumor that Lagash, fifty miles to the northeast, was building twenty-foot walls, and Gilgamesh was afraid Uruk's reputation would be damaged.

"It's an open invitation to the Gutians," he told Barney. "They hear about a city with weak walls and pow! here they come. Then we have to raise an army, train it, feed it, equip it, and lead it out to fight. That's a terrible drag on the treasury. So it's preferable to have a reputation for walls. Also, they are useful during floods. Five kings ago we suffered from a terrible flood that wiped out a lot of cities — Ur, Uruk, Shuruppak. No walls."

Barney was looking out over the dry, baked land, broken only by the thin lines of the stagnant canals and the wide, shallow, chocolate-colored Euphrates. "Bad trouble with floods, eh?" he asked absently.

"Yup. That was the worst, though. Really wiped out the whole country. Only one man, a fellow named Utnapishtim, was spared. The god told him to build a big boat and fill it with pairs of all the animals . . ."

"I think I know that story," Barney told him.

"Well. *That* was a flood, I guess. Lately, though, we've been having the other problem."

"What's that?"

"Drought."

"It certainly hasn't rained since I've been here."

"Oh, of course not. It never rains this time of year. But the river is low, lower than anyone can remember. And fish are getting scarce. Enlil must be angry; he wants bigger walls." Gilgamesh sniffed at the air — the scent of fires, bricks drying, dead fish and rotted garbage.

Barney had gotten used to the smells. But the gray-green of the plowed fields bothered him; the grain looked weak and dry. "You ought to irrigate more," he suggested.

"Sure, but I'd have to take people off the walls to dig canals. We can't afford that, not now. This is Gutian season."

"I see. Nomads, eh? Probably come down from the mountains when the grain is ripe."

"Sent by Enlil."

"Everybody's sent by Enlil. Listen, *I* was sent by Enlil. I think you ought to irrigate more. Without food, there won't be much left to defend against these Gutians."

"Oh." Gilgamesh laughed. "*We* won't be bothered by not

enough food. Just the peasants, ha-ha!" It seemed to be a very good joke.

"Yeah. Ha. Ha. I think you ought to irrigate more. Or dig wells."

"Wells? What's wells?"

"Holes in the ground."

Gilgamesh cocked his head, listening to the other end of the phone conversation. "Ah, dig wells. I get it. A very good idea, won't take so many people off the walls. Right. You know, Enkidu, Lugulbanda thinks you have a touch of brains. Just a touch. You have a good god." He hurried off to see about digging wells.

"I've got to figure out something to distract him," Barney said.

"What's that?" Punumma asked, her hand on his arm. They were walking through the vast court in front of the ziggurat, the sun directly overhead.

Barney squinted up at the sky. "I've got to think of something for Gilgamesh to do. He's driving the people too hard; too many of them are dying on these stupid walls."

"What's *think?*"

"It's, uh, figuring things, getting answers, working on a problem, you know?" He saw her puzzled look. "No? Oh, never mind. It's getting a message from the god telling you what to do."

"Oh," she said, satisfied. "Like this." She was patting her stomach. "A message. From the god."

"That's right." Barney smiled. His baby. He and Penny had never had any children, never seemed to get around to discussing it. First there was his job, his promotion to head of the research team, his patents, his growing reputation as a computer circuit designer. There was the model home in Sunnyvale and staying late at the office, or returning only to work at his home terminal. He seemed to remember Penny bringing it up once or twice, but he was too busy. Too busy. So she raised rabbits for a time, until the health department objected. No children, no responsibilities. It had seemed like a good thing to him. No children.

He glanced at Punumma, the harsh light striking her glistening black hair, the bridge of her nose, her shoulders. Her eyelashes caught a brightness as she returned his gaze, quizzical again, sensing something in his mood. She was so much like Penny. A strange drain opened in his stomach, and his preoccupations with Gilgamesh, his reveries about his marriage, the unreality of Sumer, all a fragile underwater structure, dissolved and swirled down that drain, leaving a catch in his throat and a welling in his eyes.

Because sometime, and he had no idea when, he would be snatched back to the Stanford Linear Accelerator by the Rubber Band Effect, back to a Halloween party and a positron shower. Back to the pathetic towel from the Holiday Inn. Back to Josh MacIntosh and his empty model home in Sunnyvale. Back to his automobile problem with Sergeant Masterbrook and the dilemma of Penny's body, frozen in the Boggs and Boggs basement.

"Many are cold, but few are frozen," he said to himself without a smile. "Many are cold . . ." He felt cold and shivered in the terrible noon sun. He would be snatched away from Punumma, from his son, and from Gilgamesh, his friend.

"A god is jealous," Punumma said, watching him. "Inanna does not like to see her priestess' husband frown. She does not like to see him unhappy. Especially when he is going to have a son." Taking his hand, she led him away from the courtyard and the terrible sun and the shadow it cast over him.

They strolled to the temple room where nearly two months ago Gilgamesh had planned the orgy. Now it was a reception room, a cool place accessible to the outer city where the king listened to petitioners.

Gilgamesh was alone when they arrived. The king sat glumly in his chair, his chin cupped in his hand. The scribes had gone home for lunch and a siesta; even the petitioners were hiding from the heat.

"Well, well, oxdung and camelflops, if it isn't Enkidu and Punumma, welcome faces on a day like this," Gilgamesh said tonelessly, his chin still cupped, his elbow on the table among the shards of shattered clay tablets.

"You look glum," Barney said.

"I look glum, huh? Well, I am glum. You got me started on this damn recordkeeping and filing and listening to complaints and all the rest of this stuff, and frankly, I'm going nuts. The gods hate me and won't talk to me anymore. I haven't heard a thing from Lugulbanda since last week. I spend all my time reading these damn reports. So much barley here, so much wheat there, so many *es* of walls built, so many *es* fallen down, so many *iku* of grain planted, so many harvested, so many spears and bows and arrows and helmets in the warehouses, so many *es* of canals broken down and not repaired, so much grain eaten by rats. And now a messenger brings some tablets that tell me there's a plague broken out in Kish, up north. It's the goddam gods quarreling with each other again, and the people get all the fallout. It's not fair. I know, I know, what *is* is fair, but by god, I think it's not fair. It's a miserable, rotten life we have to lead down here — the immortal gods screw around all year long while we do all the dungwork — and you say I'm glum. Well, you're damn right I'm glum. The whole world is falling apart, we have a drought on our hands, and if it doesn't rain next winter we won't have any peasants left to plant crops for the following year and we will be reduced to acting just like the plague-ridden, pox-riddled Gutians, grabbing everybody else's food, instead of being civilized city people enjoying a few comforts. We'll be as bad as those Gutians, raping and pillaging and picking our noses. Of course I'm glum." He closed his eyes.

"I'm sorry." Barney wasn't prepared for this outburst and began feeling glum himself.

"Sorry, he says!" Gilgamesh rolled his eyes. "Sorry! Do you realize that the food reserves are dangerously low, there are probably a billion refugees headed this way, all purple and swollen with plague. Since we started this record-keeping, the scribes have filled four huge rooms with clay tablets, and that's this month alone. And here" — he waved his elbow at the litter on the table. "Notes! I use up tons of clay just taking notes. I've got people digging the river for clay twelve watches a day, sunup to sunup, and we still can't seem to collect enough clay. It's awful. Ouch!" He had put his elbow down on a jagged piece of clay.

"I haven't had an orgy in days." he went on, his litany seemingly endless. "The last one I had wasn't any fun. The virgin complained and I felt awful. I sent her home without doing it. I make her promise not to tell anyone, but I know they're all talking about it behind my back. 'Gilgamesh doesn't have it in him anymore,' they're saying. 'Gilgamesh can't even deflower one virgin anymore.' Oxdung! It's no wonder I get depressed. I sit here all day listening to complaints: 'Gilgamesh, my canal has gone dry, my grain is drying,' 'Gilgamesh, my daughter can't find a husband, do you think I should sell her?' 'Gilgamesh, my wife has gone dry,' 'Gilgamesh, gimme gimme gimme!' On and on it goes, complain, complain, complain. You'd think these oxdung-eating peasants would have something better to do with their time than crab at me all the time. I wish I'd never opened this office, Enkidu, really I do."

"But . . ."

"I know, I know. Now the people have a place to go to air their grievances. They are happier, knowing that. I know, I know. Well, I'm not happier. And I don't have to like it, do I?" His voice was querulous, in need of a new valve job, fresh oil.

"No," sighed Barney. "You don't have to like it."

"Dammit," Gilgamesh shouted, banging his fist on the table, cutting his hand on the shards, "I am a man of action.

Always have been. My father Lugulbanda doesn't want me to sit around like a scribe. I gotta be building walls or fucking virgins or something. I'm going across the river to see how Sunny Vale is coming along. Will you come?" He was up abruptly and headed toward the door, his mood completely changed, his face smiling now, affable and gracious.

Punumma hugged Barney's arm and nodded. He said, "OK, let's go."

Barney wasn't sure that he cared to see another Sunnyvale in the world. One seemed more than enough.

The boat was made of reeds. Reeds were one thing that grew all over the place. There were no trees, and the grain was nearly dead, but everywhere there was water, there were reeds. Everything from cloth to boats was made of them. Houses were roofed with them. Styluses were made from them. Sails and pipes, spear shafts, sandals and potholders, rugs and drugs, everything that could be was made from reeds. Barney was very sick of reeds.

He didn't trust the boats, either, reed canoes with two prows paddled by rotten-toothed men with terrible breath.

Today, though, they had Gilgamesh's royal boatman, whose general health and muscle tone were a notch above the norm for his class and profession. He actually had seven visible teeth when he smiled, and he had been doused with a perfume of some kind that partially masked his aroma. "To Kullab, O my Gilgamesh?" he asked.

"To Sunny Vale," the king replied.

The frail boat settled turgidly under their weight, and the boatman paddled furiously, as though anxious to reach the other bank before his boat sank beneath him. Barney, holding tightly to the gunwale, realized that his fingers were sinking into the logy reeds. He found himself silently urging the paddler on.

They made it and climbed out onto the shore. But not a moment too soon, as it turned out, for the boat began to settle gently under the boatman. "Damn," he muttered, climbing into the water just as the craft hit bottom. Only the two high prows remained above the waterline. The man pulled a copper knife from his belt and began to hack at some reeds on shore. "I'll have another boat built by the time you wish to return, O my Gilgamesh," he said, sweat pouring off his face as he slashed away.

"Right-o," the king said with a jaunty tone. "Well, let's go look at Sunny Vale." They walked across the soft silt of the shore to the slightly higher and firmer ground where the new district was being built.

"Main Street," Gilgamesh said, pacing down the outlined road between two strings. "This is the first time a town has been drawn out in advance, before the buildings went up. A good idea your god had there, Enkidu." He nodded. The only building standing so far was the meeting hall. "Here is where the council of freemen will meet. And, of course, where orgies will be." The king tried hard to leer, but his heart didn't seem to be in it. He was very proud of Sunny Vale, however.

"I'm going to be remembered a long time for this," he told Barney and Punumma, "a long time. 'Gilgamesh, builder of cities,' they will say. 'Founder of Sunny Vale.' It makes it all seem worthwhile. I'm even having a song written about it."

"You seem to have cheered up," Punumma observed.

"Cheered up? Of course I've cheered up. Isn't this magnificent?" He waved at the dusty desolation surrounding them — the one building, the stacks of bricks, the stringlines (made of reeds) marking streets, building walls, canals. "We will have lunch." He clapped his hands, and four gaunt slaves appeared out of the rubble bearing a picnic for the king, his friend and Punumma.

"We're going to have a baby," Barney said, wiping his mouth after eating the last date. "A boy, Punumma says." He was feeling better himself, the shadow having passed.

"The goddess says," Punumma corrected.

"Enkidu!" Gilgamesh beamed more broadly than he had over the new city, even. "That's wonderful news. Wonderful! A boy, you say! And it reminds me, I have news for you, too, news from Lugulbanda, from the boat ride over."

"Oh?"

"Yes. We're going away, you and I. On a trip. To the mountains. To get wood. Oh, it will be great, believe me! Very, very dangerous. We're going to be famous, Enkidu!"

11

"But I don't want to go," Barney said for the two hundred and forty-seventh time that day. "I just don't want to go."

"It'll only be for a month or two," Gilgamesh reiterated. They were seated in the royal court under a pair of ancient palm trees. Reeds and lilies grew in the pond. The full moon was just making its appearance over the edge of the wall, and the sky was a splendor of stars.

"I don't even want to go for a month or two." Barney was petulant, his voice a sagging taffy on a hot day. "I don't want to do anything dangerous. I don't want to have a big reputation, I don't want to be famous, and especially I don't want to be away from Punumma while she's pregnant. Maybe after the child is born, hah?"

"We have to go now. Summer's almost here, and believe me, summer in Sumer is hell. Try to think of this as a nice trip to the mountains. Cool air, cedar trees pouring out their fragrance, no flies or mosquitoes. Think of it as a vacation."

"I don't need a vacation. *This* is a vacation; besides, I like it here." He slapped at a mosquito. "And you said the Hu-wawa are unfriendly. They won't like us cutting down their trees. They probably *like* their trees. They'll get mad. They might even attack us."

"That is a possibility, I admit. But they're just barbarians, foreigners. They don't even have the bow and arrow. At least, that's what I've heard."

"You mean you don't *know*? No, thanks, I don't want to go." Number 249.

A three-piece band was warming up — drum, lyre and

reed flute. Tootle-tootle. Drrrump-drrrump. Plink-plink. The noise — Barney didn't consider it music — was not un-pleasant.

"Hello." Punumma appeared out of the darkness with a slave carrying a torch. After she sat down, he moved off to one side and held it out so the smoke would drive the mosquitoes away. It also made Barney's eyes water.

"The king insists I go," he told her, waving his hand in front of his face. The thick, greasy smoke parted sluggishly. "But I don't want to go." Number 250.

"Oh, it's all right. You should go. Actually, I had another dream last night that I must tell you about. The goddess' older sister, Erishkigal, came to me."

"Oh, no," Barney groaned. Everyone was against him. "Not another dream. I can't stand it."

"Oh, yes. A very important dream. Enkidu should go with Gilgamesh, she told me. Really, Enkidu, it will give you a very big reputation, make you very important. Especially because of the danger."

"So it *will* be dangerous! I knew it!"

"Oh, yes, very dangerous. You could even be killed. But gloriously. That part was not too clear. About dying, I mean."

"I don't want to die. Not even gloriously. I want to stay right here in Uruk with you. Gilgamesh can go."

"The goddess has spoken. You must go. Besides, we need the trees." She folded her hands in her lap; the matter was settled.

Barney, despairing, appealed to Gilgamesh. "What do we need trees for? We don't really need trees, do we?"

"Aha-ha-ha, of course we do. For Sunny Vale. The new district is going to smell very good. Lots of cedar in it." Gilgamesh gestured to the three-piece combo, and they launched into a vigorous tune, a sprightly melody that set the blood to singing and thoughts of glory spinning in the mind.

Barney's fluency in Sumerian was good by now, but since he was sunk in gloom and the singing style was odd, he didn't hear the words for a while. The song sounded more or less like:

Ú-da kúr-se dú-na-mú-de
Án du-dú-dam gár-gar-má-ni-ib
És-gu-én-na túku-a-má-ni-ib
E-dingír-ri-e-né-ke nigín-na-má-ni-ib

Rhythmic nonsense from the lyre player, pulsing beats, pleasant to the ear but meaningless until he began to recognize the words. Then he listened:

Oh, it's just you and me
Feeling glad and free
Filled with joy and glee
In Sunny Vale-by-the-sea . . .

"Oh, no," he groaned again as the unreality stirred into the turgid soup of his gloom, for the *plink-plink* of the melody had coalesced into a familiar series: Mel Mellows at the piano of the Ceramic Lobster Lounge, the anonymous voice, the smooth syrup, the bland words, the cloying banality. "I can't stand it."

"Terrific, isn't it?" Gilgamesh leaned back in his seat, banging his fist against his iron stomach in time. "It's the new song, written just for the new district. You know" —he nudged Barney's ribs — "the one we're going to get the cedars for, ha-ha." He turned back to the band in time for the next verse:

We're sure you all agree
It's a Gilgamesh jubilee
That our kingly king did decree
Our Sunny Vale-by-the-sea . . .

"Dammit," Barney said. "It's not even by the sea. It's by the river. The river is not the sea."

"Really? I hadn't thought of that. Perhaps I should have the author thrown in the river." It seemed a pretty fair criticism suddenly.

"No, no," Barney said hastily. "It just seems a little strange. Why do you suppose he wrote it that way?"

"Let's ask him." Gilgamesh beckoned to the darkness. A cowering figure scurried and slavered to the king's feet. "Why did you write it that way?" Gilgamesh demanded.

"Poets, O king, have the liberty to shape words to fit the song, and my mother liked it that way. Besides, the sea used to come all the way up here to Uruk before Enlil defeated Tiamut and cut her in half —"

Barney interrupted what promised to be a long dissertation. "All right, never mind." Gilgamesh beckoned the cowering poet back into the darkness. "It's just that it sounded so familiar," Barney finished.

"It's familiar," Punumma said, "because it's the same tune as 'Inanna and the Snake' and 'The Worm and the Toothache.' You remember, when you went to the tooth water-knower because your tooth hurt and he sang it: 'After Anu created heaven, heaven created earth, earth created rivers, rivers created canals, canals created swamps, swamps created the worm, and the worm went weeping before Utu,' and so on. Utu gives the tooth to the worm finally, and it's the doctor's job to pull it out. Remember?"

Barney touched his jaw. "I remember." It *was* the same tune. But the words were different.

The band staggered to a halt at the end of the song, and Gilgamesh waved them away. "Another thing," he said. "The refugees from Kish will be arriving soon. They will probably bring a bit of plague with them. It's a very good time to be away from the city."

"Then Punumma had better come with us." Barney turned to her. "I don't want you around here if that's going to happen, the plague and all."

Punumma smiled, her hands crossed on her belly. "You

don't have to worry about me," she said. "I'll be fine. The goddess Erishkigal says so, and she ought to know."

"Why? Why should she know?"

"Well, she's the goddess of death. And gloom. She knows all about it."

"Also," Gilgamesh added, "Punumma will be up in the temple. No refugees allowed up there. Only the peasants will suffer."

"Only the peasants will suffer! I don't like to see anyone suffer."

"I don't either, I don't either. But it is the fate of man to suffer, to be a slave to the gods." The king shrugged.

"And besides, if you don't obey," Punumma said, "you'll get the pox. Remember what you saw at the hospital."

"I remember," Barney said again. "All right, you win. I'll go. But I don't want to go." Number 251.

"I don't want to go." Barney was lying on his back, staring through the open hole that served as a window to the stars; they were so bright they seemed to drip in the sky. He couldn't see the moon, but a shaft of its light lapped at Punumma's toes, silvering the nails.

She stirred and sighed, and he felt her cool tapering fingers on his rib. Her palm slid, fingers in the rib grooves, up his side and across his belly. "People can't do what they want," she whispered, her hand whispering too across the tan softness of his stomach. "People are slaves . . ."

"To the gods. I know. And I'm going. But I don't want to. Frankly, I'm scared. What if I get hurt? The doctors here in Uruk aren't even as good as the ones where I come from. Not quite. But they're better than no doctors at all. What if I get killed? I'm four thousand years from home . . ."

Her hand continued a descent, a long, lingering glide from altitude, smoothly down toward Enkidu International. "But Gilgamesh says it's almost like the steppes up there in the mountains. It'll be almost like home."

"Gilgamesh has never been there. He's never been to the steppes, either. He's making it all up."

"Oh, no," she answered, her long fingers closing around Barney's stiffening god-rod. "The goddess told him."

"The goddess told him! Oh! Well, that makes a difference." Barney tore his eyes away from the window to see what she was doing. His feet curled, and he rolled toward her. "Ouch!" he said when his hipbone smacked into her head.

Her laughter, the laughter he remembered from the desert, the laughter of his early marriage to Penny, liquid and warm, bathed him.

The moonlight moved slowly up their bodies, now legs, now trunks, now arms, as they twinned and twined in the litter of soft skins, the smells of wool and lust, the tastes of dew and love. Her fingers found him out, his fingers walked her back and stroked her breasts and wove themselves into hair here and there, and he forgot that he didn't want to go.

She sat on his chest and painted his face. His hands cupped the swell of her bottom. She ground her knuckles into the soft undersides of his feet, and he lapped with his tongue at the insides of her knees. She found ridges and folds, creases and lumps, soft parts and hard parts, and she breathed the breath of life into them. His mouth sought out the honey of her hive, sweet nectar of the blossom, and the moonlight blurred them both, two kinds of oil shimmering one into the other, hands, fingers, tongues, secret and scepter all together.

"Oh, Enkidu," she cried, riding him. "Oh. I. Had. A. Dream. Oh, goddess." She toppled forward to his face and lapped at his chin, shivering him with the shaft of memory, Penny's touch again, that special place on the jawline, and he popped into a fierce red light where 4500 years vanished in an instant.

"I've got to tell you about the dream," she said, squishing

in the slickness, trailing fingernails through the snailtracks and glister of their lust.

"Mmmm." The moon had moved on, a brightness on the rough wall over his head; his fingers twined through the nape hair on her fragile neck.

"It was from Erishkigal." Punumma spoke softly into the hollow of his collarbone. "She was tall and thin and bony, and she pointed me into a large room, an eating place. I met a man who was like Lugglanu at the medical school, a small man who smiled and smiled. He kept jumping up and down, trying to tell me something, but I couldn't understand him. Then you were there, but like on the other side of the Great Swamp, very far away. I called to you, but you were busy doing something, writing on a clay tablet or drawing. I tried to get you to listen, to hear me, because I was afraid; it was so strange, the smell of the swamp, the damp. And the cold. I was getting colder, I wanted you to help me, to warm me. But you still didn't hear, you were preoccupied. Finally I froze, like the ice that is brought down from the mountains by traders. I was in a box, clay or wood, and colder than a winter night. So cold." Her small, white hand closed on his pectoral, crying silently for help, for warmth, but Barney was cold now himself, as cold as she was in the dream, for Penny frozen in the cellar of Boggs and Boggs.

Her voice fell so low he could scarcely hear her. "From very far away the goddess, Erishkigal the terrible, spoke to me. She told me to let you go, you must go to the mountains. If you went to the mountains, she said, the child would be healthy, and would be a great man, but I was afraid. I knew, she made me *feel,* that there was danger for you. I thought it might have something to do with the small man in the eating place, what he was trying to say. But I don't know."

She tilted her head back to look at him, her eyes large and glistening in the darkness. "I only know you must go with

Gilgamesh. Something terrible will happen if you don't."

He didn't answer, staring blindly into the dark — where the model home in Sunnyvale ticked to itself, the automatic sprinklers silent, the clocks humming quietly, the red digits on the panel of his computer bright in the night — and the galactic cold seeped into his bone; Penny frozen, dead, and this dream. He no longer felt SUMmated, in control, but led, pushed, prodded. The cold he felt was the cold of fear, because he recognized that this woman beside him, who had taken him so thoroughly into herself, was Penny, his wife, and he was feeling something he couldn't name, though much of it was loss and grief. For he would leave for the mountains as he used to leave for the office, and he would not return the same.

He touched the bridge of his nose, suddenly uncertain who he was. He remembered it bloody, and the knot of bone there, the slight bend to the left that disturbed the regularity of his features. Faint glimmers of moonlight vanished from the room then, and he could no longer see Punumma in their pale reflections.

He cried out in the night, a wordless shriek, and it took the pain of her hand clutching at his pectorals to bring him back. "I don't want to go," he whispered, but she put her finger to his lips.

"Come with me," Gilgamesh said, leading the way. They climbed the long stair toward the second level of the ziggurat, and Barney marveled again at the intricate mosaic designs set into the walls, hundreds of thousands of three-inch clay cones glazed red, black or buff and shoved point first into wet mud plaster, creating zigzags and chevrons and diamond patterns, polychrome lozenge shapes, triangles and spirals, a visual harmony that covered the exterior walls. Though Gilgamesh had sent someone for Barney at dawn and it was still early morning (so the sun's beams were rosy as they slanted across the wall before them), Barney had begun to sweat, and only partially from exertion and heat. The stairs were endless, and Punumma's dream haunted him.

"Where are we going?" He presumed they would stop at one of the lower temples.

"To talk to Inanna," the king answered, bounding with exhausting enthusiasm up the stairs two at a time.

"Isn't she" — puff puff — "at the top?" Puff puff. Barney craned his head, calculating another fifty feet of stairway at least. From there he couldn't see the small shrine that crowned the ziggurat.

"Aha-ha-ha, yes, indeed, my friend. All the way, hey, to the top! Come on, Enkidu, put a bit of energy into it. We've got a long trip ahead of us to the mountains. Fight some Huwawa, cut some trees, build Sunny Vale, hey? Gotta get in shape." He slapped his solid stomach and grinned at Barney over his shoulder.

On the terrace of the third level, a priest presented Gilgamesh with a light wooden tray laden with bread, a cup of beer, goat cheese, a spray of barley, a dried fish. "Here," Gilgamesh said, passing the tray to Barney, "you carry this."

The two of them went on, up the final stairway to the top. Gilgamesh was singing under his breath:

> It's a Gilgamesh jubilee
> Our kingly king did decree
> Mmm, mmmm, Sunny Vale-by-the-sea . . .

Barney was wilted by the time they reached the summit, his linen cloak and skirt clinging to his back and legs, his arches aching, his palms slick with sweat at the edges of the wooden tray. A bit of beer had slopped out of the cup and was drying stickily with a pungent odor.

"Here we go," Gilgamesh said as they stepped off the final stair onto the small terrace. Barney could see farther than he had ever been able to before, the endless desert to the west and north, the now-dry Great Swamp to the south, the sluggish river winding gently into the distance.

The terrace was empty, a flat platter of heat. In the exact center of this pale brown plain, a building of blue glazed brick waited, its door a rectangle of blackness, a mouth that drank the light.

At least it looked cool, but Gilgamesh sat suddenly cross-legged on the hot ground and waved Barney down beside him.

"What do we do now?" Barney asked, glancing with longing and apprehension at the darkness of the shrine.

"We eat. Then we wait."

"You mean this food is for us?" Queasiness peeked its rodent nose out of Barney's exhaustion and twitched. He looked with distaste at the hard bread, the sticky beer, the melting, pungent cheese.

"Aha-ha-ha, you're making a joke! That's what I like about you, Enkidu. You never take anything too seriously." Gilgamesh broke the loaf in half, passing Barney his share. His face fell into its listening pose, and his hands proceeded, now assured of the ritual they were performing. His smile was gone, and his eyes focused on something beyond the horizon to the east. He slowly swallowed half the beer, then handed the cup to Barney, who was still struggling to break the bread into manageable pieces with his teeth. He gulped it down, gagging on beer and bread.

Next they had to eat the fish.

Waves of nausea, chill and fever swept over Barney. Sweat broke on his forehead and as swiftly dried. His throat went numb and he couldn't speak; his eyes also lost their focus, and the horizon undulated in the rising heat.

Gilgamesh sat motionless and waited. Barney kept still.

The sun climbed, dragging the heat up with it. Barney's hands and feet fell asleep; his nausea faded. The brightness of the day, a brightness that washed everything out, faded the brown of the desert, the pathetic patches of gray-green barley and date palm, even the blue of the temple. It all began to pulse, washed out and overexposed, then suddenly color so vivid it hurt his eyes sprang at him, in and out, in and out. And then, as though the god had set the focus, everything appeared in the sharpest relief. The blue temple glowed from within, filled with life and light.

What did you put in the bread, Barney tried to ask, but there was no sound on the terrace; his mouth and throat failed to move. What did you put in the bread? He stared straight ahead at the vision that filled him, the muscles of his head and throat paralyzed.

"Now!"

What? Barney thought at Gilgamesh, but the king was rising to his feet, eyes still unfocused, and Barney realized dimly that he had heard a woman's voice say "Now!"

Who's up here with us?

Gilgamesh led him into the yawning blackness, though a terrible reluctance dragged at his feet. He wanted to turn and run, but his feet carried him, slowly and solemnly, toward the door. He noticed with dazzling clarity the embroidered collar of Gilgamesh's cloak, the individual hairs on the back of his neck, the puckered depressions in the flesh around the king's elbows where the corded muscles came together.

The darkness swallowed them, and Barney's fear dissolved into the glory. Inanna stood against the far wall, looking down at the stone table before her. The ceiling was open beamwork, so squares of sunlight fell into the room, checkerboarding them in light where they stopped. One broad shaft shone full on the goddess herself, setting fire to the gems in her cloak, the gems in her girdle, the crown on her head, her earrings and necklaces of gold, the breastplates of beaten gold, the cloth of her dress, all filled with fire, dazzling and blinding him into awe and silence. He became a statue himself, dazed blind, tongue stuck and a fire in his head. He barely noticed that Gilgamesh was listening and nodding and answering. She talked to the king, who laid the spray of barley on the table, turned and nodded to Barney, who moved as if he knew what to do and put his own bunch with Gilgamesh's, reuniting the divided spray into one, and he realized in that moment that it was a seal on their friendship, that, in fact, it *was* their friendship, the two barley sprays together, now one.

The ritual had meaning to him, a solemn pact made and kept, so although he considered Sumer ancient and barbaric, he also appreciated it for the beauty and strength his own world lacked.

The goddess spoke to him. In English.

"Hello, Barney," she said.

"What?" A hoarse whisper trembled in the thick, brilliant air.

"I said hello."

He tried to meet her gaze, but his eyes responded poorly, darted to the side, down, up to the open squares of the ceiling, the shade and light, everywhere but to her face, which seemed to be hidden in the deepest gloom.

He thought, This is only a statue, but he said, "Who are you?" He knew who she was, of course. The voice was too familiar, too sure, too close, and absolutely real. He didn't expect the voice to be so real.

"You know who I am. Look at me." Fear was an endless reptile uncoiling in his gut, flat evil head and tiny eyes lifting into the clarity of the light, tongue darting, testing the air for his weakness, his death.

He squinted against the intense contrast, the dark of her face hidden in shadow and the terrible brightness of her dress, but he could not see her face; he did not want to see it.

But the voice commanded, was undeniable. "Look at me." He looked.

The face was anger, the wide-spaced oval eyes hard, the mouth a grim line, the lines beside the nose deep and set, the brows drawn together. No, it was not anger, it was more than anger, more than righteous anger. It was divine fury, the rage of heaven, and terror drove Barney back a step, two steps, though his eyes remained fixed on that awful face.

"What have I done?" Punumma's angry words came to him: "I am no mountain girl to be a slave!"

The face did not answer him, but stared him down with its hard, glittering eyes, eyes filled with malice and rage. He knew what he had done.

Nothing.

He had let the clarity of computer circuits feed him, he had worked hard and accepted the esteem of his profession, he had consumed well, and he had assumed that his life was full and real. He had bought a model home in Sunnyvale and thought that the roof that arched over his wife's head was his own protective hand, that the microwave oven he installed in her kitchen was his own warmth. He had put between him and his wife's intangible self all the products that made up the advertiser's litany of necessities and presumed her satisfied. He had *done* nothing.

"Penny," he mumbled through dry lips, "I . . . want another . . ." He licked his lips with a dry tongue. "Another chance."

The face drew tighter, the eyes glowed with malevolence. The lines beside the nose and mouth deepened, gathering his darkness into them, pulling painfully at his guilt. He wanted to fall, to beat his head on the floor, to cry out in his anguish and terror, to cut away from himself all the feelings he had never had until now — remorse, spite, insolence, guilt, envy; they approached him in a gibbering crowd and raked his face with their sharp claws, their slimy hands, and breathed their poisonous breath into his face.

His heart thudded in his chest, a massive clock tolling toward whatever it was he feared most in the world, toward the time when *it* would come and take him. He whimpered, and although his mouth was dry, his face was streaming.

"No," he tried to say. "No . . ." But the hard eyes stared down at him, and the word died in his throat.

He was *frozen* in that terrible light.

"I'm dead," said Penny's voice from the goddess. "I'm dead, Barney. It's too late. And now you too must die."

"No. I . . . didn't know, didn't mean . . ." He looked down, his eyes moved, unstuck at last, and he saw the two sprigs of barley on the table, the grain intermingled, seeds filled with a different kind of future.

When he looked up, the face had changed. She was smiling at him now, filled with love, an unspeakable tenderness. Her lips curved upward, her brows wide and clear, the deep lines beside nose and mouth gone. Relief flooded through him; the hammer of his heart slowed and grew quiet.

Until her words came through: you too must die. He stared at the face, immense above him, at the infinite tenderness in it, and he felt a new fear.

No, he thought. It's the bread, what they put in the bread. I'm hallucinating. This isn't real.

"It is real," the goddess told him. "It is real, and you *will* die, Barney. You must." Her expression held infinite sadness, infinite compassion. That smile held so much love! "But you will be reborn. And you will search, and you may find what you are searching for.

"But it will surprise you, I suspect." Her expression held now a touch of impudence? Mischief? A sly but gentle mocking mingled with the compassion.

"Now go with Gilgamesh, who is your friend and who needs you."

Outside Gilgamesh clapped him on the back. "Aha-ha-ha, that was good, hah? You were speaking to the goddess in the language of the steppe, I think. I never heard words like that."

"What did they put in the bread?" Barney was shaking in the aftermath of shock.

"In the bread? Why, barley, I suppose. Why?"

"Who makes it?"

"Oh, the priests, of course. Holy bread, they call it. But then, priests will say anything, won't they? Why do you ask?"

"It's giving me a terrible trip."

"Trip? Aha-ha-ha, of course. To the Huwawa. Listen, we're going to cover ourselves in glory. People will remember Enkidu and Gilgamesh forever, the two friends who defeated the Huwawa and took away their cedar trees, eh? The trip won't be terrible at all. Dangerous, yes, but not terrible. Glorious!" The king was lost in his vision. "Glorious," he repeated. "The goddess was in a good mood today. She told me. 'Gilgamesh,' she said. 'You must take Enkidu with you, for he is your friend; together you will cut the cedars and be forever glorious.' "

As Gilgamesh and Barney retraced their steps, a small scorpion of absolute zero thrashed at the base of his spine: fear.

At the bottom of the stairway, in the forecourt, ranks of soldiers stood at attention, copper spearheads blazing in the sun, copper helmets shining, every sword hilt at the same angle to the belt. As Gilgamesh and Barney reached the third from the bottom step, a command was shouted and all of them, ten ranks deep by twenty wide, drew their copper swords at once and saluted their king and his friend with a roar. Gilgamesh raised his hands in the air, answering them, smiling; but Barney, standing beside him, heard him sigh, and the sigh echoed in him as they walked along the front rank, inspecting armor, bows, spears and swords.

Close up the soldiers comprised a motley lot: bad teeth, bad skin, bent limbs, broken noses, flat feet, squinty eyes, runny noses, torn ears, plague and sword scars, curved backs; malnutrition, rickets and beriberi had taken their toll. But they looked proud and dedicated and very smart with the polish of copper and bronze, the identical uniforms. These things almost made up for their physical deficiencies.

"Aren't they magnificent?" Gilgamesh asked.

"Mmm." Barney nodded, hearing the sigh.

"Two hundred of them. Forty more with wagons and mules. This is our army."

"Our army. I didn't know we had an army."

"Oh, yes. Of course. We have to have an army."

"And how many Huwawa are there?"

"Many thousands, grains in the desert. But they aren't skilled in fighting."

"Great."

When they arrived at Gilgamesh's office, the king sank wearily onto his bench and closed his eyes. He rubbed the bridge of his nose with his thumb and fingers and sighed again, the same sigh.

"Something wrong?" The scorpion of fear still thrashed, but Barney was worried about his friend.

"Yes," Gilgamesh said. "It won't be enough. It is never enough. Enmerkar built Uruk. Lugulbanda deflowered fifteen virgins. Even if Gilgamesh cuts down all the cedars of the Huwawa, it won't be enough. Even if Gilgamesh builds Sunny Vale, it won't be enough. It will be *done,* finished, over with, and I will still be alive. I won't be able to rest; I'll just have to do something else. Better to go for something great and be killed in the attempt than to have to keep outdoing yourself. Ah, well. I am glad, Enkidu, that you are here. Very glad."

"So am I," Barney said, and he meant it.

12

They couldn't march worth a damn. It took a full day to get
them across the river.

"Who are these people?" Barney asked. He and Punumma watched three soldiers try to climb into a fragile reed
boat at the same time. The last one tipped the boat over.
The three soldiers sank out of sight, weighted down by copper helmets and gear. Two came up sputtering, and the
boatman was fishing for the third when he too came up for
air. The water was only about three feet deep.

"Volunteers. The Sumer summer, as you know by now, is
awful, the crops — what there were this year — are already
in, and there's not much to do but lie around and pant. We
get no shortage of volunteers, especially since there is the
possibility of some good plunder. I suppose most of them
are in it for the money." Gilgamesh was really enjoying himself, for today they were off to the mountains, providing
him with an interruption to his endless round of audiences,
recordkeeping, and orgies.

"I was in an, uh, army once," Barney said. "These are
worse than recruits."

"Well, they're not the best, it's true. But we do have to
leave the best in Uruk in case of Gutians. It is a little late for
Gutians; usually they invade just after harvest. But you
never can be sure. Besides, the Huwawa — "

"I know," Barney interrupted. "Don't know how to fight.
And you have that on the authority of your 'father' Lugulbanda, who has apparently been dead for something like a
hundred and twenty years and who is in any case nothing
but a figment."

"What's a figment?"

"Oh, never mind." Barney was feeling irritable. Punumma had wrung him dry the night before, then revived and revitalized him and wrung him dry again. She softened him up, pounded him firm, threatened and cajoled, stroked and playfully spanked, and this morning he was red-eyed and exhausted, uncertain and once more afraid. On top of it all, it was the middle of July, and the daily temperatures rose well into the hundreds; the sun was a white blast in the cloudless sky. Barney's head felt like a tin drum in an endless paradiddle, a drumroll for an execution.

The three soldiers had finally seated themselves in the boat, which rode low in the water, brown reeds settling into brown water. The boatman dipped his leaf-shaped paddle in the water, straining to move the boat. He paddled more vigorously, then furiously. The boat didn't budge.

"All right," Barney heard him say. "Everybody out." The soldiers, thoroughly soaked, climbed out into the water. The boat did not rise. All four of them heaved on it, but it appeared to be stuck to the bottom. Five soldiers in a wagon with solid wooden wheels pulled by two oxen drove past the boat, hooting with laughter.

"Get an ox!" they shouted. At that moment, the wagon wheels sank into the soft silt of the river bottom and stuck.

"Ha-ha," laughed the soldiers heaving at the reed boat.

"Ha-ha," laughed the others as they climbed out to push the wagon loaded with amphorae of wine and beer and boxes of grain and dried fish.

"Aha-ha-ha." Gilgamesh laughed, pointing and smacking Barney on the back. "You're right, Enkidu, they are terrible. You ever used a sword before?"

"Huh?" Barney didn't follow the change of subject.

"A sword. You ever used a sword before?"

"No, and I don't want to start now. Just think of me as a kind of adviser."

"What's an adviser?"

"Someone who stays away from the fighting and makes suggestions."

"Aha-ha-ha! That's a good one. Makes suggestions, ha-ha." Gilgamesh wiped tears of merriment from his eyes. "It sounds very safe, but alas, Enkidu, it is impossible. The Huwawa will be everywhere, so there won't be any safe place away from the fighting. Oh, oxdung, it's going to be exciting, slash, slash, arms and legs and heads flying, blood and gore everywhere . . ."

"Please," Barney said, holding out his hands.

"Great," Gilgamesh said, mistaking Barney's meaning. "You take this." Unstrapping his sword, he buckled it around Barney's waist. The hilt was decorated with shell and lapis lazuli, the pommel with beaten gold. Gilgamesh pulled the sword from its leather sheath to show off the copper blade, which glowed dully in the sun. "A beauty, isn't it?"

"Listen, I appreciate it, but this is your sword. Really, I couldn't take it."

"Hold it," Gilgamesh commanded, shoving it into Barney's hand. Old Errol Flynn movies unreeled in his head. It *did* have a nice heft. He tried a couple of trial slashes in the air.

"Careful!" Gilgamesh laughed, sidestepping the sailing blade.

"Oh, sorry." Barney slid it into the sheath.

"Tomorrow we'll have some lessons." The king clapped him on the back again. This time Barney braced himself and didn't stagger forward as he usually did.

By sunset the troops were all finally across the Euphrates, the Buranun, or Great Water, as the people of Uruk called it. Everywhere on the broad, flat streets of the new district of Sunny Vale campfires were burning, the army was drinking and screwing and laughing and throwing up, preparing for the long march.

"Well," Barney said, "we made over half a mile today. At

this rate we should get to the mountains in about eighteen months."

They were sitting on the king's pier, which jutted out into the slow, muddy water, watching the activity across the way. Above their heads a reed awning rustled in the slight breeze, and between them a small folding table held beer mugs and dried dates. Punumma stirred at Barney's side.

"Don't worry, Enkidu," she said. "They'll move fast once you leave the city."

"How can they? They're all going to be sick!"

"They'll be sicker staying around here, what with the heat and flies and the swamps. They'll be wanting to get into the mountains as fast as possible." Gilgamesh yawned loudly and belched. "Scribe!" he shouted suddenly.

"Yes, O my Gilgamesh." A robed man with a stylus and a flat board covered with soft clay scurried forward.

"Take a letter."

"Yes, O noble king."

"To the great steward of Enki, king of Shuruppak, the illustrious and noble et cetera, et cetera. I, Gilgamesh, steward of Inanna and Anu, sword of Enlil, son of Lugulbanda, warrior and king of Uruk, builder of walls, et cetera, et cetera, send you greetings, and hope all goes well with you since the locust plague devoured your crops this spring and the plague-ridden refugees from Kish invaded your house, bringing with them the rats and diseases of Enlil, wrath of god, et cetera, et cetera. Know that I, Gilgamesh, steward of et cetera, king of Uruk, am leading an expedition into the mountains of the Huwawa to bring back cedars for my new district of Barbar-buru, the Sunny Vale, and that I would take it as a courtesy for you to keep the aforementioned refugees from Kish inside the walls of your own impoverished and miserable village and to prevent them from proceeding any farther down the river toward mighty Uruk. Should you be able to manage this trifling request, I will send to you, upon my return from the mountains of the fierce and terrible Huwawa, one thousand board-feet of fresh cedar as a token of my gratitude.

"Should, however, you fail in this small matter, I will be up there to wretched Shuruppak in a day to whip your miserable ass and level your pathetic little town. I, Gilgamesh, warrior and lover, decree it. Signed, yours truly et cetera, et cetera. Have someone run that up to Shuruppak tomorrow."

"It shall be done, O my king."

"And get a fresh tablet. I have several more letters to send."

"Well," Barney said, standing and stretching. "I think perhaps we'll go off to bed, if you don't mind. It appears we have a big day tomorrow."

"Sure," said Gilgamesh generously. "You two go on off and give the old god-rod a workout. Knowing you, it will probably be a long period of inactivity ahead. I'll stay here half the night doing the claywork that must be done."

"Well, goodnight, then." Barney and Punumma departed.

"Send me that cute little girl from the kitchen staff," they heard the king order the slave holding the torch.

"Claywork, indeed," Barney huffed. "I think Gilgamesh ought to get married." They were walking through a long colonnade of massive pillars toward their quarters.

"Oh, but he is married."

"He is?"

"Why, of course. He's married to Inanna. You met his wife last week, at her shrine at the top of the ziggurat."

"I'm not sure I understand about that, but I'll take your word for it."

"Of course you will," she said quietly, hugging his arm. "And now I must clean away from you the day you have just had, for you are tired and dirty and unhappy. I will make you happy."

And she did.

He stayed happy during the next day, as the ragged collection of seasoned degenerates staggered and lurched along, singing dirty songs and picking their noses. Most of their jokes involved the events of the previous night, events Barney found so unspeakable that when they marched through the littered foundations of Barbar-buru, he had to avert his eyes and hold his nose. But Punumma had so tenderly washed and loved him and sent him on his way, and Gilgamesh was such a puppy at play, that even Barney's prim midwestern disgust couldn't spoil his own good humor. He even managed to laugh at a couple of the jokes as the day wore on. They made surprisingly good time. The wagons rolled without falling apart, the donkeys and mules jogged without too much coaxing, the land was flat and hard, and for some reason the breeze of their passage made the heat seem less intense and enervating.

Barney began to think everything was going to be all right.

"You know, this just might work out," he said.

"The goddess has promised it, and she doesn't fool around. And Lugulbanda came to me in a dream last night and showed me the cut cedar, stacked and aromatic. There was sweet sawdust everywhere, and on a post was the head of Huwawa, dripping blood. Most auspicious."

Barney grimaced. "I wish you wouldn't talk like that. I get sick at the sight of blood."

"What? You, a wild man from the steppe, who ran with the antelope and drank from the spring with the lion, don't like the sight of blood? You're joking, of course. That's what I like about you, Enkidu. You have a terrific sense of humor. Ha-ha-ha."

They jangled and creaked and rumbled on through the afternoon, and when night came, they camped beside an ancient canal under a row of date palms.

"Tomorrow we will reach Lagash, a moderately attractive city, where the steward is my cousin. We will give him some date wine, and he will give us some grain, and you and I will have a great feast in his hall, and the next day we will push on and cross the Tigris. Lots of swamp there, so we will be slowed down. Then three, maybe four days, and we get to the foothills. We'll be in the mountains! After that, nobody knows how far; we'll have to take some slaves up there to guide us: that's where slaves come from, you know. But we'll find the cedars, and the Huwawa, no doubt."

"What exactly do you know about these Huwawa?" Barney asked.

"They don't know how to fight, ha-ha-ha."

"Besides that. I'm aware that you think they don't know how to fight."

"Well, they are a very unpleasant people. They eat their relatives for dinner. They have lots of diseases, because the gods dislike them; they are the oxdung and offal of the world. They are very fierce but stick-stupid. Very, very stupid. And extremely ugly. Nowhere since the world began have there been people as ugly as the Huwawa. We will be doing the world and the gods a service to get rid of them."

"Nobody could be that bad," Barney said. "They're probably just different from you, so they seem bad."

"No. They are that bad. Now let's go to sleep."

They were that bad. In fact, they were worse.

Barney assumed at first that the degenerate specimen the troops were torturing was a particularly unfortunate example. Probably, he figured, a weakened and unfit member of the tribe. They couldn't possibly all be this bad, with green goop in the nose, dull, sullen eyes, noxious drool on the chin, breath that could kill at a distance, open sores running everywhere on the squat, grotesque body. The prisoner was at the moment engaged in chewing at the Achilles tendon of one of the soldiers who had approached too close to the groveling form. The groveling was a pose, and the soldier screamed in pain as the others laughed.

Gilgamesh was laughing, too. "For God's sake!" Barney cried. "We've got to do something!"

"Sure," Gilgamesh agreed, but before he could act, a soldier clobbered the prisoner with a stick just hard enough to make him drop the ankle he was biting. The gummy eyes glazed over and the green-coated tongue lolled out. Everybody had a good laugh over that.

"Which way to the cedar forest?" a soldier shouted at the writhing form on the ground.

The sun was setting, long slanting rays of golden light falling through the trunks and branches, the needles of the fir and pine. A slight haze hung in the silent forest air, so the light glowed against the trunks, a mazy pattern of light and shade and quiet, an awesome hush. And in the middle of it all the foul-smelling and revolting prisoner tied to a post. At the question, the prisoner quickly thrashed back to life, snapping at his interrogator.

The tranquillity of the huge trunks and rough bark, the rosy light, the drowsy sounds of insect and bird, all contrasted sharply with the thrashing violence of the prisoner. Barney felt the old unreality sliding over him again, a black velvet bag. The interrogator leaped back, laughing, and kicked the prisoner in the face. He was rewarded with a snarl.

"Which way to the cedar forest?" he shouted again.

"May your mother suppurate from the pox she was given by a mule in the outhouse," the prisoner replied. "May your father's prick rot off in the asshole of a camel. May your sister be suffocated by the customers in a brothel for buzzards. May your ancestors . . ." Another kick silenced him for good.

"Let's go that way," the captain of Lion Troop suggested. "That's where he came from."

The ragged troop formed ranks, leaving the inert Huwawa tied to the pole. Two days later they topped a ridge and looked out over endless undulations of virgin cedar, ridge on ridge marching softly to a misty horizon. To their left, the peaks of the Zagros range disappeared into clouds. There had been no sign of people, nothing to break the eternity of this forest, these foothills.

They were now so close to the highest reaches of the range that they marched in shade until noon, but when they broke over the top of the final ridge and observed the cedars before them, the sun too broke free of the peaks and lit the pale, fragrant green with golden light.

"All right, let's get to work," Gilgamesh yelled, and the troops pulled bronze axes and flint saws from the wagons and set to work, hacking and sawing. Sweet-smelling sawdust coated the air, the rhythmic sounds of the saw provided a base for work songs, and the trees began to fall.

Sixty three-man teams were cutting, and soon the din was terrific — sounds of splintering wood, trees toppling into the brush, wrenching branches from their neighbors as they dropped, the layered sounds of chopping, the ripping of the saws, the warm and simple lyrics of the work songs rumbling tunelessly into the scented air:

> Screw, screw — saw this tree,
> Chop it down and make it free,
> It'll make a house where whores will be,
> In Sunny Vale-by-the-sea . . .

"Well, what do you think?" Barney turned and saw Gilgamesh coming up behind him. He'd been seated on a stump, looking out glumly at the leveled hillside littered with cedar trunks, branches and dust.

"What do I think? I think it's a mess. You must have cut down hundreds of trees. It'll take this hill five hundred years to recover. It looks like California, for God's sake. How the hell are you going to haul all this wood to Uruk, anyway?" Barney had never thought much about trees before, but he found himself appalled at the waste and ugliness of this scene.

"We will drag them to the river beyond that ridge and throw them in. Slaves will guide them back to Uruk. Very simple." Gilgamesh grinned.

"I give up."

"Listen," Gilgamesh said suddenly. "I know how you feel. These were pretty trees, they smell very nice. But Inanna has instructed me to bring them to Uruk. We must obey her. Besides, there are more trees in these mountains than there are stars in heaven or grains in the desert. And we will gain much glory for this venture. We will be famous, Gilgamesh and Enkidu, who went to the mountains and brought back the cedars of Huwawa."

"We haven't seen any Huwawa except that one pathetic creature back there."

"So? Who's going to know? I'm certainly not going to say we didn't run into some terrible demon named Huwawa. And you must admit, that fellow didn't know how to fight, eh? No bow and arrows, even."

Just then there was a sinister whistling sound and a long, evilly barbed arrow with blood-red feathers twanged into the stump between Barney's legs. Within seconds the bare hillside echoed with the screams of wounded and dying soldiers and the hideous shrieks of jabbering Huwawa as they fired arrow after arrow into the suddenly grim Uruk army. The natives swarmed out of the trees onto the soldiers, who struggled to close ranks.

Fortunately, there were only twenty or thirty of the Huwawa against the two hundred and forty, so once the copper swords were drawn, the attackers fell like wheat. Soon none was left standing.

"Whew!" Gilgamesh sighed, picking his way through the dead and dying. "That was close, eh, Enkidu?"

There was no reply.

"Enkidu?"

Gilgamesh whirled around, but Enkidu had disappeared. "Where the hell's Enkidu?" he asked the captain of Lion

Troop, who was pinching closed a gaping arrow wound in his thigh with one hand while he chewed on a piece of dried meat in the other.

"Damned if I know. He was hiding behind that log last time I saw him." He spit out a wad of chewed gristle.

Gilgamesh personally examined all the dead soldiers from Uruk and sighed with relief when he found that none of the twelve dead or twenty-six wounded was Enkidu, but he became anxious when he learned that Enkidu was nowhere among the living either.

"You don't suppose they took him prisoner?" he asked the captain.

"Probably," the captain responded, tearing off another hunk of dried meat with his blackened tooth stumps.

"Well, then, we'll have to free him," Gilgamesh said almost gently. The captain understood his tone and limped over to his troops. Gilgamesh watched as he kicked them all to their feet. Soon what was left of the army stood more or less in order, and the king led them off in search of the Huwawa village.

It was half a mile away. "Next time I'll send out scouts," Gilgamesh muttered.

There was a six-foot stockade of fallen cedar branches protecting the twenty rough wooden thatch huts of the village.

"Send out your prisoner or we'll burn this place to the ground," he shouted.

"Your sister picks her nose with the pizzle of a hyena," was the answer. "You lick the asshole of a dog for food. You are . . ."

"Aw, forget it," the king mumbled, as he sat down on a log to think. An arrow whistled past him. "Inanna, what am I going to do?" he asked out loud.

"Wait a while," she said. "You have them surrounded. Enkidu will be out soon."

"You really think so?"

"I'm the goddess, aren't I? Don't worry."

Gilgamesh cheered up. "Maybe we can capture the women as slaves," he said, thinking of the nocturnal tumidities that had been bothering him lately. He was a long way from that cute little girl on the kitchen staff. His kilt rose in response to these musings.

"By the gods," he exclaimed, "we will take some slaves. I'm horny as hell." He stood and paced, waiting, eyeing every so often the gate of the stockade, a rough clump of branches crudely lashed together.

The sun lowered itself toward the treetops downhill, as it did every day. The golden-rosy light returned, slanting through the rough-barked boles and fan-shaped, fringed cedar leaves. The mountain birds sang and darted from branch to branch. Squirrels quarreled and scolded. The soldiers broke out some rations and ate. Several had fallen asleep, overcome by boredom.

Suddenly there was a terrible scream from the village, a tumult and alarum, a roaring of pain and frustration, and Barney came crashing through the wall of the stockade about ten feet to one side of the gate. Branches flew away from his charging body as he demolished the fence, and more of the stockade was crushed by the pack of pursuing Huwawa, easy pickings for the Uruk army.

"The son of a bitch bit me," Barney reported to Gilgamesh after it was all over. "You were right. These people are truly awful. You wouldn't believe the smell. I thought Uruk smelled bad, but at least you have latrines there. These people use the street, if you can call it that. And their breath!"

"How's the hand?" Gilgamesh was distracted because his soldiers were washing the Huwawa women they had captured, and one or two of them were beginning to show some promise, in spite of the dental problems that appeared to be almost universal in Mesopotamia.

"It throbs." Barney cradled it in his uninjured hand, his

left thumb torn, the fleshy pulp shredded by the Huwawa chief's very bad teeth.

"Yeah," Gilgamesh answered. "I got some throbbing myself." His kilt tented in his lap as he watched the soldiers rubbing the naked women. "Excuse me." He started toward the women. "Take care of his hand," he ordered his medical officer on the way.

"Yes, O my Gilgamesh." The doctor had one hand, which he used to pry open the wound while bracing Barney's wrist with the stub of his other arm. "Looks nasty," he commented.

"It is nasty," Barney said. "I'd better wash it."

"Wash it?" the doctor exclaimed. "Whatever for? We'll just smear some beer in it."

"I'm going to wash it," Barney said stubbornly, and walked down to the stream.

"Suit yourself." The doctor shrugged. "Crazy foreigners."

Barney had to avert his eyes from what was happening beside the water. Gilgamesh was riding behind one of the women as she scurried around on hands and knees. His kilt rested on her rump, but Barney noticed before looking away that she was smiling. It reminded him of his last night with Punumma.

"I guess the king deserves a little fun," he told himself as he cleaned the torn flesh of his hand in the stream. It hurt like hell. He wrapped it in a torn piece of his cloak and returned to camp. The Lion Troop captain was bandaging his thigh and cursing.

"You aren't having the doctor take care of that, I notice," Barney said.

"What doctor? Oh, him. He's no doctor. He lost his hand in a fight. He used to be a brickmaker; now he calls himself a doctor. His god told him to because he's missing a hand."

"Oh." Barney strolled on through the camp and began to climb uphill toward the village. His hand throbbed, and he rested it against his chest. It amazed him that the battle —

massacre, he corrected — had lasted so short a time. It was still light out. He walked through the ruined huts, the trampled fence. Shattered fragments of crude Huwawa pottery crunched underfoot. Drying blood was everywhere.

The chief's house, a pathetic one-room affair ten feet square, leaned almost at a 45-degree angle. It was odd that it was still standing. Barney entered and glanced around in the deepening gloom. Everything was still in place; no one had come in during the battle.

He found what he was looking for, the splendid copper sword with the gold pommel, the shell and lapis inlay. He grinned as he remembered the training Gilgamesh had given him in its use. "Hold it in your right hand," the king had instructed. "Swing it as hard as you can at some exposed part of your enemy. Try to hit him with the sharp part of the blade, not the flat part." Some training.

Barney pulled it out of the sheath and attempted a couple of experimental swings. The sword made a satisfying swishing sound in the air, connected accidentally with one of the four posts holding up the roof, and cut it cleanly. The hut started to topple, and Barney had to scurry outside. He watched as the small building sank gently to the ground, then turned and walked downhill in the violet dusk.

Pine needles carpeted the forest floor, deadening the sound of his footsteps. He held the blade loosely in his right hand, occasionally tightening his grip on it and smiling, happy he hadn't had to use it. The Huwawa had been surprisingly easy to escape once the bite had spurred him to it.

He passed a campfire where soldiers were eating and joking about the slaves they had captured.

"The king seems to have found that chief's wife to his taste, ha-ha," one of them was saying. "He's been taking her on like a dog all afternoon."

The birds had fallen silent as the light failed. Barney realized that he was hungry and quickened his step toward the king's tent. There would be fresh-roasted lamb, bread and beer.

He stepped through the flap and saw Gilgamesh, flat on his back, mouth open, snoring. The poor man was exhausted by his afternoon of fighting and screwing.

Crouching beside him, the Huwawa chief's wife held a gilt dagger high in the air, on the verge of plunging it into Gilgamesh's exposed chest.

Barney reacted instantly and swung the blade as hard as he could at the exposed part of the woman, which happened to be her neck.

It occurred in underwater slow motion, the copper blade sliding through the thick air, *thunk*, into the flesh of her neck and through, muscle, cartilage and bone. Once out on the other side, the blade swung free, and time speeded up enormously.

The head flew into the air, trailing a huge amount of blood; at the same time the headless body toppled, spouting from the gory neck, across Gilgamesh's body, plunging the gilt dagger into his blanket. A pool of blood formed there as the body drained.

"Enkidu!" Gilgamesh shouted, shoving the twitching corpse off him. "You saved my life."

Barney collapsed on the floor and started shaking.

13

He shook periodically all the way back to Uruk, but Gilgamesh was so pleased that he had the head impaled on a spear and carried at the back of the troop, a tribute to Enkidu, the mighty warrior.

"Please," Barney begged him, "get rid of that thing. It makes me nervous."

"What's *nervous?*" Gilgamesh asked.

The soldiers were happy, too; the women slaves were properly cowed by the grisly token on the spear, and the wood they had cut was vast and aromatic, enough for the whole district of Sunny Vale, with plenty left over for Shuruppak, should that steward of Enki have done his job and kept the plague-ridden refugees away from Uruk. The entire campaign had been a terrific success.

"We're going to be famous," Gilgamesh said, "just as my dream foretold. The head on the spear, the wood, my friend who saved my life at my side."

"Famous for what?" Barney inquired. "For wiping out a miserable tribe of degenerates whom we outnumbered four to one, who lived in a village you could practically blow over with one breath? For destroying a forest? Or perhaps for crossing the valley between the rivers in summer? For killing a woman? Ha!"

"You sound bitter, Enkidu. For all of those things we will be famous. In time we must die, but our deeds will live on. Already the harpers are composing a song about us, about Gilgamesh and his friend Enkidu who saved his life." Gilgamesh was developing an annoying habit of saying "his friend Enkidu who saved his life" every time he mentioned Barney.

"Well, I wish I could be as happy as you are about it, but I've never killed anyone before, especially not a woman. I don't regret it exactly, or anything like that; I had no choice. But I'm upset about it." He turned in the crude saddle then and mourned, facing into the vast and empty dunes they were crossing. On the horizon to the south he could make out the top of the ziggurat of Larsa, shimmering in the heat waves that danced over the sands, and the desolation out there seemed to be inside him as well.

When they arrived at the city it was well into September, but the heat had not diminished. Nonetheless, Barney felt a lightening of his spirits the closer he came to Punumma, who by now would be heavy with his child, his son, who it was foretold would be a great warrior. At last they approached the outskirts of Kullab and Sunny Vale, and he wondered at how the town had grown in the two months they had been gone. Already homes were built; the central square had taken shape. Dogs scurried through the streets, fighting over scraps of workmen's lunches. A market was flourishing, and people from Uruk and Kullab wandered through it, haggling over bunches of dates, trays of dried vegetables, fresh-baked bread, dried fish, joints of lamb and goat, cloth and leather goods.

The town appeared so prosperous that Barney was shocked when they came to the river, the Great Water, which had been a yard deep. Now it was a mere trickle, meandering through a bog of cracked and glistening mud. People walked carefully across the drier places without getting their feet wet, back and forth to Kullab and Barbarburu. Barney felt a cold undercurrent of unease. Surely the river shouldn't be this low?

"It didn't rain all spring, remember, Enkidu?" Gilgamesh told him. "Inanna is withholding her favor for some reason. There certainly should be water in this river, that's true.

Perhaps, now that we are back with the cedars and many mountain women as slaves, the goddess will smile on us once more, eh? After all" — he poked his forefinger in and out of a circle formed by his thumb and fingers — "I've been doing a lot of fertilizing, eh? Aha-ha-ha."

"Why does everyone look so jovial?"

"Oh, business as usual, eh? We got the wood."

"The wood won't bring water for this year's crops."

"Well, maybe it will rain this year." Gilgamesh refused to get depressed about the drought. He had the wood.

The head priest greeted the king and Barney at the gate to the temple complex, rubbing his hands together and smiling.

"O Gilgamesh," he said, his voice thick with date honey. "We have much news for you: some good news and some bad news."

Gilgamesh frowned and grunted.

The oily voice poured forth, a generous bath of soothing liquid. "Anu is mightily pleased with your venture to the mountains. The cedars you have brought back will cause your new city to prosper. The walls will be firm, the people will multiply, and all your real estate holdings will bring much silver into the temple coffers. Your name will live forever throughout the world and time; you will become a household word; your face will appear on the face of coins. Your people will love you and wish you well. You are a great leaders, a great king, a beloved steward of the gods. Your deeds . . ."

"All right, all right, Enlil! How you do go on! Quit stalling and give me the bad news."

"Well, O mighty Gilgamesh, it's Inanna." The priest shook his forefinger at the top of the ziggurat, towering behind him.

"What about her?"

"She's angry."

"Whatever for? I've been doing lots of fertilizing for her. On this trip alone I have gotten six slave women with child.

She blessed this journey herself before we left. I got the cedars, I got the head of Huwawa. What more could she want?"

The priest looked pleadingly at Barney. "Please, O mighty king, come with me." He glanced at Barney again, wringing his hands.

"What is it? You can talk in fornt of Enkidu. He saved my life."

"O king, the goddess is angered at the slaying of her slave, mate to Huwawa, and wishes, as recompense, that you shall marry Punumma, chief prostitute of her service." The priest's hands slithered rapidly over one another, two oiled mink in a frenzied rut. He no longer looked at Barney.

Who yelled, "No!" as he slid off his mule. Punumma, very large in the belly, walked through the gate toward him, her head lowered, her hands clasped in front of her.

"I am sorry, O my king, but Inanna will not end the drought until you marry Punumma. She spoke it three times at the full moon. She intends to marry you through her priestess."

Barney draped his arm protectively around Punumma, shaking once more, though this time in anger.

"No!" he shouted again.

"I am already married to the goddess," Gilgamesh said. "I marry the goddess every year at the New Year."

"That is, it seems, no longer enough, O king. She wants to, uh, well, she wants to be physical with you, erhmm."

Gilgamesh sat on his mule for a long time, brows knitted in concentration, fingers drumming on the wooden frame of his saddle. The priest's two oiled mink had come to climax, a blur in the harsh light, and were now digging into one another, doing the goddess's work, the only motion in the gateway.

Barney stood still as well, his arm around Punumma's shoulders, while she stared at her folded hands, clasped over the broad shelf of her belly, and refused to look at him.

Heat shimmered over the burnt brick of the open square; it wavered inside the deep shadow of the arched gate; the top of the ziggurat was lost in the translucent curtain of heated rising air. Up there, in the glazed blue shrine, the goddess herself smiled down at the tableau, a deceptive benevolent smile that was heavy with menace, thick with cruelty.

He could not deny the goddess, of course. Even Barney recognized that her presence was so real and powerful that to deny her was unthinkable. Yet Gilgamesh did not acquiesce, but frowned in the uncertain air.

Finally he sighed, and the sigh set the priest's hands to copulating again, oiled sweat glistening as they rutted. "Inanna," Gilgamesh said; then he fell silent again. "Inanna," he went on at last, "has a bad reputation as a wife. I have been thinking about Dumuzi, the last man she married. He was mortal, and he came to a bad end, so you priests say. A bad end! At Inanna's hand. I myself do not want to come to a bad end. And yet, it is dangerous to defy the gods. Well!" He slid off his mule and confronted the priest, whose hands began to whine together.

"I think, however, that I will refuse." He wheeled abruptly, grabbed Barney's elbow, and stalked away. Punumma followed gracefully, an unreadable expression on her face.

"My friend," Gilgamesh said, seated solidly on a stool in his office, elbows on knees, "I could not take your woman away from you. You have saved my life from the Huwawa woman, who was, it seems, Inanna herself, and this is her revenge. The gods, you know, can be very nasty when they want to. And frankly, they want to quite often, as far as I can tell. Dumuzi, for one, did come to a nasty end. So I will take my chances. Punumma is your woman, she will be having your child soon, and I owe you. I owe you both. So I will defy the goddess."

"What will happen?" Barney asked, his voice almost a whisper. His arm was around Punumma again; her eyes betrayed fear and pride at once.

"I don't know." The king sighed. "I'm sure the priests will tell us, though. They always do."

They did.

"Inanna will send the Bull of Heaven," they said, displaying their gift for rhetorical metaphor. "The Bull of Heaven will drink up all the water in the land of the black-haired peoples. The earth itself will crack open, and the young men of the city will fall into the cracks and vanish. The Bull's breath will slay the people of Uruk by the hundreds. The date palm will refuse to give up its dates; sheep and ass will be barren."

"Et cetera, et cetera, et cetera," Gilgamesh said. "I suppose it could be worse."

"They're probably right, you know," Barney told him. "Judging from the condition of the river, it's really not a bad guess that we're in for a drought."

"Hah! But these priests drive me nuts the way they go on, 'the Bull of Heaven,' and all that." Gilgamesh paced up and down the brief space of his office. "Oxdung! There must be something we can do about it. I hate just sitting around drying up like a date and letting Inanna have her way."

"What about the wells the people have been digging?"

"By Anu, you're right. I wonder if the wells have been working. Scribe!"

"Yes, O my Gilgamesh."

"Bring me a report on the wells. Last spring I ordered wells dug. I want to find out what has happened."

"Yes, O mighty king."

The scribe returned in twenty minutes. "The wells were all dry, O magnificent ruler. The priests say they are an abomination before Inanna, O mighty —"

"Stuff that. What do you mean, 'dry'?"

"I regret to report that there was no water in any of the wells the farmers dug."

"You know something, Enkidu. Inanna is being a real prick." Gilgamesh frowned.

"I find it difficult to believe that there was no water," Barney said. "The water table here should be practically at the surface. This whole valley is just silt deposit. It's almost floating on water."

"I don't understand what a table made out of water could be, Enkidu, but if Inanna has dried up the wells, we'll have to think of something else, I guess."

"It might be worth taking a look," Barney suggested.

"That's a thought," Gilgamesh said. They took a chariot, the white horse decorated with purple plumes prancing, the gold and lapis lazuli and copper and shell all dazzling in the brazen sun. The people still smiled their black-toothed smiles as the king and his friend rode by, but Barney could taste the acrid unease in the air, the palpable anxiety nourished by rumors of the king's defiance of the goddess. Somehow it reminded him of that hideous moment in the king's tent when he reacted involuntarily and lopped off the woman's head, and he started shaking again.

He was still shaking when they came to the first well. The farmer stood proudly beside it, beaming, swelling, strutting without moving. Pride was a bag of Christmas toys stuffed full, a pat on the head from the god himself, an ambrosia bonbon. The king himself was inspecting the well.

It was a beautiful well. A lovingly crafted brick wall three feet high enclosed a large square. Above it a pitched roof of woven reed and palm fronds shaded the cool waters below. A long bole pivoted over the wall, with a bucket on the end. It was perfectly balanced for drawing water.

"It is absolutely watertight, O my Gilgamesh," the farmer said proudly. "I filled it myself to test it."

"You filled the well with water?" Barney asked.

"Yes, Lord Enkidu. By hand. Bucket by bucket." The bag

of Christmas toys was splitting open, glimmers of color and shine winking through.

"Let us look at this well," Gilgamesh said, as they climbed down from the chariot.

"It certainly is dry as a bone," Barney said.

"Didn't anyone tell you to *dig?*" The king was incredulous.

"Oh, yes, O my king. And I did dig. It was very difficult, the gound is so hard."

"You did dig? It certainly doesn't show." Barney was inside the well, jumping up and down. The wall came to his waist.

"Perhaps you expected the gods to fill up your well by themselves?" Gilgamesh asked gently.

"Of course, O my king," the farmer answered uncertainly. "The gods will fill up the well."

"The gods will not fill up this stupid well," Gilgamesh thundered, his deep bass booming across the flat land, a bellow to match the Bull of Heaven himself. "The gods will not do a fucking thing with your lousy well. Gods! Are they all like this?" he turned to the scribe standing by.

"Why, certainly, O mighty —"

"Oxdung! Offal! Hyena brain! Oh, Enkidu, you see what we have to deal with here? You have to watch them every minute! First the walls, they drop like flies in autumn, and now we tell them to do a simple thing like dig a hole in the ground, and what do they do? They *build* a hole out of bricks and expect it to fill itself. Aha-ha-ha." There was no mirth in his laugh.

"But the ground is too hard, O king." The farmer's bag of toys had vanished into dust, the pat on the head had turned to a punch, the ambrosia bonbon was dung on the tongue.

"But the ground is too hard, O king." Gilgamesh oozed sarcasm like juice from a punctured fig. "Scribe! I want *holes* in the ground. Holes! Down. Into. The. Ground." His teeth were digging holes in each other, grinding.

The people of Uruk invented the shovel, the pick and the wheelbarrow that day. They dug wells.

"That does not look good." Punumma was unwrapping Barney's injured hand.

"Ouch!" He pulled the linen back and looked. The tooth marks were clearly visible, a double row of ragged tears in the pulpy base of the thumb, giving it a swollen, purple smile. It was true; it did not look good.

"The god Utu is in it," Punumma said. "We must try to coax him out. I will make some offerings at his shrine tonight."

"Never mind that. It probably should be cleaned out. That filthy trip back from the mountains didn't help it much."

"I will make offerings anyway," Punumma said. Her tenderness toward Barney increased as her time drew near. She heaved her awkward bulk to her feet.

"Listen." Barney stopped her. "Don't go out. It's all right. You should rest."

"No," she said. "I will go." She walked through the low doorway without having to bend. Barney always knocked his forehead on the lintel.

Sighing, he lay back on the sheepskins and blankets. In the quiet he could feel the throbbing in his hand, a metronomic pulse beating away the seconds of his life. He remembered the visit to Inanna. There would be danger, there *was* danger. Arrows. Teeth. Falling trees. The pulse in his thumb beat, thum-thump, thum-thump. Seconds, throbbing his life away: danger. He might even die. Much glory, fame, his name, his name — Enkidu, Barney Gamesh. Gilgamesh, friend, king of Uruk. They would dig wells, Inanna would be cheated, the Bull of Heaven. Wells. They would surround the city with wells, cheat the goddess who wanted to take Punumma away from him. His Punumma, his Penny. The oven. Microwaves. Shaking. I've killed someone, someone is dead. Penny. Punumma. No, she is having a child, my son. A son soon.

"Because they have killed the Bull of Heaven." A voice, the voice of Anu, but Anu is pleased. Was pleased. "Because they have killed Huwawa, who guarded the cedar mountain." Anu to Enlil, Lord of Heaven speaking. No, a son, Punumma will have a son. Penny is dead, my thumb is hurt. "One of them must die. Enkidu must die," the voice of Anu went on, speaking to Enlil in heaven. I am dying? I can't die, the Rubber Band Effect. Back to the Accelerator, the CIA. Josh. My son? No, my son isn't born. Soon, soon. Two weeks, it is October, I think. "One must die."

The gods don't care; they change their minds. Pleased one moment, then not. Like people. One must die. Enkidu. Me, scared? No! I don't want to die, to be gone, worms, scared. Yes, scared. I'm. Scared. No, I have a friend now; I've never had a friend before, like this, a friend whose life I saved. I killed for. The head, flying in the lamplight, trailing blood, so much blood! Smoky and red, dusk outside. The mountains, scent of cedar, fire and meat cooking.

One of them must die. Enkidu.

"No!" Barney sat up in the dark, his hand pulsing, the long red tentacles of pain surging up his arm. It's infected. Oh, God, what can I do?

He felt a touch on his face, soft as a mothwing, cool. "Hush," Punumma said out of the darkness. "Hush."

Her touch dabbed slick moisture from his forehead, the fever heat. He began trembling as fear and anger and shock chased each other, three rodents on the cage wheel in his head, around and around. "Punumma, I'm dying."

"No, Enkidu. It is Utu, the sun. He is making you hot. I have made offerings, honey and barley cakes. He will leave you soon. Hush."

Barney slept.

*

By mid-October the people began dying. The Bull of Heaven's breath dried up the land, the winds arrived and piled soft sand against the walls, dune upon dune to the horizon. Cracks opened in the earth; the canals turned first stagnant, then to soft rotten mud, and finally to dry grooves in the land. The smiles in Uruk stopped; unease was dense in the air.

Gilgamesh toured the well project, sometimes in the chariot, often on foot. When he felt strong enough, Barney accompanied him, riding a mule or pulled in a wagon. The hipbones of the oxen pulling his cart jutted, dropping harsh shadows across their flanks.

The head priest frowned most of the time, his oily hands moving ceaselessly in their fruitless rut. "Inanna is very angry," he reported to the king. "She has been rejected, and she does not like that."

"What woman does? Or man either, for that matter."

"She has demanded of Enlil that someone must die for this defiance." The hands slithered, soft, plump, furred.

"What do you mean, 'someone'?"

The hands increased their tempo, intricate and barren interweaving. "Enkidu."

"No." Gilgamesh turned away. "I will not permit it." He left to pick up his friend, to inspect the wells for the thousandth time.

The sun was halfway to the horizon, but there was no lessening of the heat the afternoon the Bull of Heaven stamped the ground, shaking bricks loose from the new walls. In the shrine at the top of the ziggurat, Inanna paced.

"Lord," the priest said, "Inanna has moved in the temple, she has turned her face away from the offerings."

"Lord," said another priest, panting after his run across the river from Sunny Vale, "a house in the new district has fallen on a workman, crushing him. It is the Bull of Heaven."

"Bull," said Gilgamesh. "It's a slight earthquake. Enkidu told me. Nothing to worry about."

"That's right, O my Gilgamesh. A quaking of the earth because the Bull of Heaven is pawing the ground. He is coming closer."

"Three hundred people have died already. Thirst, starvation," the head priest interjected. "We warned you."

"Come on, Enkidu. Let's check the wells again."

Barney was feeling weak, but he was strong enough to follow this project. After all, he thought, I'm an engineer.

The proud farmer was thinner, his beaming smile gone, and he was leaning on his shovel beside a mound of dirt while his two sons worked furiously. Gilgamesh and Barney approached, and one of the sons shouted, "It's dark! The soil is darker. It's wet. There *is* water here!"

The farmer jumped as if stung, joining his shovel in a tangle with the picks and shovels of his sons. Dirt flew, first in dry spatters, then in clumps of thick, wet ground. The tops of their heads sank below the top of the wall.

"Ha-ha," they yelled as Gilgamesh and Barney rushed over. "Ha-ha." They threw handfuls of mud into the air, at each other. Gilgamesh and Barney peered into the well and saw the three dancing madly in ankle-deep water, water that was pouring into the hole.

"We can throw *that* in the face of Inanna's anger," Gilgamesh said. "Aha-ha-ha, water. You did it, Enkidu. You found water for us. We can fill the canals, irrigate the crops. We won't need the river."

Barney smiled at the king's joy. That night his son was born. Gilgamesh declared a double holiday.

"It's a boy? Of course it's a boy. The goddess said it would be a boy." Punumma smiled and smiled at Barney, the infant nursing greedily. "It is the new moon, Enkidu, and we have a son, a mighty warrior."

"Yes," he said, "a beautiful son." He too was beaming, so

broadly his face was hurting with joy. He forgot about his hand, he forgot about his dream. He smiled and smiled, a cramping, face-cracking, tooth-gleaming smile at Punumma. "I want to marry you."

"What?" She was stroking the infant's head, black-haired, wrinkled and red, but hardy and perfect, still oblong from the birth.

"I said I want to marry you. I want you to be my wife."

She smiled up at him, pleased. "Oh, Enkidu. That is nice. No one ever wanted to marry me before. Or at least no one said they did, not since I became a priestess of Inanna when I was thirteen."

"Will you?"

She smiled at her son as he sucked. "Will I what?"

"Marry me." He was still smiling his cheek-cramping smile, but a mouse of exasperation nosed into his voice.

"Why, you mean it, don't you?"

"Of course I mean it."

Her face darkened. "But Enkidu, my lord, my man, you know I cannot marry. I am dedicated to Inanna, goddess of love. This child is her work. She would be terribly angry if I married someone. You understand that."

"She's already angry. Your gods are a confusing bunch, if you ask me. How can she be angry and pleased at the same time?"

Punumma shrugged, a small gentle shrug, not to disturb the nursing child. "Who can explain what the gods do? We are their slaves and can only do what they tell us. No doubt they have their reasons."

"I think it's a lousy system. It's not fair."

"What's that got to do with it? The gods created us to do their work for them, and we must do it. You are from the steppe, so you don't understand. My wild man from the steppe." She smiled.

"Gaah." But he smiled at her too, proud as the farmer whose well struck water in the king's presence, the first in

Uruk to touch the face of Enki, god of water; the god who *was* water and who gave his name to Enkidu, the friend of Gilgamesh. And so it was Enkidu who led the people of Uruk to Enki himself, hiding in the earth.

Sin, the moon, who had gone from the land, showed that night his first new shaving of crescent. A good omen, the head priest said.

"It's a good omen, O my Gilgamesh, this new moon and Enkidu's son. But you have killed the Bull of Heaven with these wells, and the council of the gods *will* find a punishment. Someone will die. It is decreed." The head priest couldn't announce good news without having something very gloomy to go along with it.

"Aha-ha-ha," Gilgamesh boomed, too pleased to be worried by the nattering of priests. He clapped the gloomy man on the back and strode off down the long colonnade, past the massive brick pillars, laughing, "Aha-ha-ha!"

"Come on, Enkidu," he said the next afternoon. "Let's inspect Sunny Vale, eh?"

The cart rattled across the dry riverbed and into the new town. Wood was everywhere, being sawed into planks, framing new houses, doorways, roofs, bracing walls. The streets were straight and wide, the meeting hall and temple complex in the center clean and light of line, the air filled with sawdust, sawdust that seemed to cool the air as it flew.

"Beautiful, isn't it?"

"Yes, Gilgamesh, it's beautiful. And it certainly is sunny." Punumma smiled and squeezed Barney's arm, the child cradled, sleeping, against her breast.

"These are model homes, Enkidu. A new kind of house. These houses are built by the city of Uruk for peasants. Every day more and more people are coming to the city from the countryside, wanting to become artisans or merchants. They move here and get apprenticed to someone, and pretty soon we have a huge population with nowhere to live. Now they will have Sunny Vale, Barbar-buru, on easy terms. Gradually they will repay the city for their homes, and a little something extra goes into the treasury. What do you think, Enkidu? Isn't it a good plan? My father Lugulbanda suggested it."

"It's a very good plan," Barney smiled. But behind the smile, always, he felt the metronome of blood beating in his hand. Red fingers worked their way up the inner arm all the way to the elbow now.

"Furthermore," Gilgamesh gestured broadly, "the fame of Gilgamesh will live on and on for this new invention, a city of wood! Barbar-buru will be my monument. Even Lugulbanda, when he was alive, didn't do this. Even Enmerkar, who first built the walls of Uruk, didn't do it. Sunny Vale will stand forever!"

Barney knew it wasn't true, of course. The wood would disintegrate to dust, while the walls, the burnt brick walls, would make Gilgamesh famous when men dug in the dust of this valley for the bones of the past.

14

As well water flowed into the canals and greened the land around Uruk, Barney deepened into sorrow, his arm swollen and discolored. He tossed fitfully in his bed, and in the next room his son cried. Punumma soothed him, her voice soft and unreal in Barney's fever.

Above the small window the moon fattened toward the end of October.

"Aha-ha-ha." Gilgamesh tried to force more cheer into his laugh as he came through the doorway, ducking as Barney always did. "My friend, you should see the land now. New barley shines green on the ground as far as you can see. The animals are filling out, the farmers all sing your praises: Enkidu, who invented wells, they say. Enkidu, who killed the Bull of Heaven. Everywhere, your name, Enkidu, friend of Gilgamesh." He sat on the edge of the bed.

Barney tossed, his injured hand held close to his chest, the fingers fat and stiff. "I had a dream, Gilgamesh. I dream a lot here. Your gods are killing me, you know."

"No, Enkidu. Punumma has made offerings to Utu. You will be well again. I'm sure of it."

"I'm afraid, Gilgamesh. I'm afraid."

Punumma was singing in the other room: "Lullula lullula, sleep, sleep, my son."

"You cannot die, Enkidu. The land is growing rich and fat; there is water and green; you have a son. So you see, you can't go."

"Dammit, Gilgamesh, I wish . . . Oh, never mind. I've done something wrong. Perhaps I shouldn't have come back here, I should have stayed where I was and mourned. But there were so many signs: the computer, Deathwest. 'Gilgamesh,' it said. And now I'm going to die here, just when I've found things I didn't know existed. Gilgamesh, I curse your gods . . ."

"You're angry, Enkidu. When you get well . . ."

"I know, I know. It's not the gods, I got bit, it's germs, infection, and no antibiotics here. It's going to be close, though, Gilgamesh, very close. I don't know what will happen if I do die here, so far from home, but I feel the pull already, death, the Rubber Band . . ."

"How is he?" Punumma asked from the doorway, their child asleep in her arms.

"Raving. He says he's dying, and a lot of words in the language of the steppe. I'm afraid too, Punumma."

Barney sat up. "No." He looked around the room. "Punumma, I might make it back; I might. They have doctors there. I could get back in time. Nobody can predict what will happen, after all. It's never been done before. *But I don't want to go back!* I don't want to leave you." He fell back and glared at the ceiling.

The ceiling lifted away, and the positrons rained in the sky, a thick swarm, a flock that flowed swiftly and suddenly changed direction, abruptly halted, began flowing again, veiling the brilliant stars that wheeled above him. The constellations of Barney's midwestern childhood were subtly altered, squashed or elongated, glimmering beyond the positron veil. He thought he could see anxious faces, Josh MacIntosh's childish forehead creased in worry, Dr. Milkworth pacing. They were worried about him. But that was impossible, of course. To them he hadn't been gone at all, to him it had been so long. So very long.

"No!" he said aloud again. "No! I'm here. Here, with Punumma, with Gilgamesh, who is my friend. More than friend. Brother. He is more than a brother, he is myself. No." He turned to Gilgamesh.

The ceiling slammed back into place, the room leaped into sharp focus; his head was clear for the first time in days. "I apologize to your gods, Gilgamesh. They're not killing me at all. Time is, simply time. I can't really explain it to you, but I couldn't stay here forever, you know. I've loved you both; and now the child."

The next day he was feeling stronger, so Gilgamesh and Punumma took him outside to enjoy the sunshine.

"This place reminds me of Cal . . . of the place I come from. Brown hills, blue sky. Especially now, as things are turning green. I have a feeling it's going to rain here this winter."

Gilgamesh and Punumma glanced at each other. Enkidu was talking to himself more and more, smiling strangely. As though he really were leaving; and there was nothing in the area that could properly be called a hill.

"Enkidu, let's take another look at Sunny Vale." Gilgamesh was smiling, but his eyes were bleak.

The air shimmered; the veil of positrons reappeared. Barney was finding it more and more difficult to focus on where he was; the reality around him wavered, watery and vague. They rode in the oxcart, which bumped and rumbled through the streets of Uruk, past the market where robed and kilted people haggled, and Barney supposed the RNA injections that had given him much of his knowledge of the language were wearing off, for the speech seemed strange and foreign, the architecture exotic, the qualities of light and air unreal. Even the heat had somehow dimmed, become diluted and thin.

But the bite still throbbed in his hand and arm, and there was a sinister darkness at the edge of his vision.

"Greetings, O my Gilgamesh," Barney heard dimly. He struggled to focus. The great water-knower, the doctor Ur-lugaledinna, who had safely delivered Barney's son, was grinning up at the cart, patting his elegant palms together.

"Welcome, Punumma, priestess of Inanna, and Enkidu, inventor of wells and friend of Gilgamesh. What do you think of it?" He waved at a building going up behind him.

"What is it?" Gilgamesh hopped down off the cart.

"The new medical offices. A special building, just for women. It will centralize this aspect of medicine. And as a side effect, it will remove this practice from the main hospital, where so many of the faculty members are without hands. That was making many of the women patients nervous."

"Could you examine Enkidu's hand?"

"Well, unofficially, I suppose. I can't be held liable, though. I'm not that kind of doctor."

"Enkidu, show him your hand."

Barney shook his head, trying to clear it. His moments of clarity were increasingly infrequent. But he held out his swollen arm.

"Hmmm. Mmmm. Uh-huh. Yes, I see. Mmm." The doctor turned it over and around, prodding the tender swelling with his forefinger. "Very interesting," he muttered. "Hmmm."

"Well?" Gilgamesh asked.

"Not much I could do. You might try packing it with ground tortoiseshell and oil. Use a clean tortoise, though, if you can find one. It probably wouldn't do any good. I wouldn't take on this case if I were the right kind of doctor. Well, if you'll excuse me, O my Gilgamesh, I've got to see about having a sign made for these offices. 'Urlugaledinna, Woman Water-Knower,' eh?"

"Very interesting, I'm sure." Gilgamesh was frowning.

Oddly, Barney laughed after Urlugaledinna had patted his white palms together and departed for the signmaker. "His bedside manner leaves something to be desired, doesn't it?"

"Bedside manner? Oh, I see, yes. The way he talks to a patient. Yes, I guess so. A little abrupt, perhaps?"

"Just protecting himself. After all, he has a reputation to

maintain. Things haven't changed much. I mean, weren't, aren't much different here." Barney laughed again.

They went on.

"Well, what do you think of it, Enkidu? Isn't it splendid? I've got scribes who can draw plans for this town. They laid out the streets, designed the houses, the public buildings, the temples, everything. Perhaps you would like to see one of the completed model homes?"

"Yes." Barney was suddenly in a wonderful mood, his smile back, really there, his eyes, so often fevered and brooding of late, now clear and keen. "By all means, we must see a model home."

The model home was really quite lovely for Sumerian design: a two-story affair built around a central court. It had a private chapel and cemetery, a kitchen with a built-in oven, storerooms and slave quarters. "How much does a place like this go for?" Barney asked.

"Well, of course this is not an example of the low-income housing we are building. This house would be an ideal home for an administrator, a teacher or a doctor. You know, professional people. I'm not sure of the price, though. Scribe!"

"Yes, O my Gilgamesh?" A man holding a rounded pillow of dried clay covered with plans came over.

"How much does this model home sell for?"

"Let me see. This home is offered for about three hundred *gu* of silver, but I'd say that price was soft. I'd say that when the time comes, it will probably go for somewhere in the neighborhood of two hundred and eighty *gu,* or a bit more. This is confidential to you, O king. It's really an excellent buy — good location, near the doctor's offices and the school. Fresh water nearby from a new well, but off the main road. Near the central square. When the landscaping is finished, there will be a lovely garden in back. Cool in summer and warm in winter."

Barney was laughing again. "I'll take it," he said.

"What?"

"I said, 'I'll take it.' I can buy it, can't I?" He asked Gilgamesh.

"Of course." The king was puzzled. "My treasury is yours, you know that. But why?"

"Why not? Do you like it, Punumma?"

"It's beautiful." she answered. She smiled at him, the baby nestled as always in the crook of her arm.

"Then I'll buy it for you. For you and the child. I need a house for my family, and you are my family."

"Aha-ha-ha, that's good, Enkidu. Well done. The house is yours, if you want it."

"But I don't," Punumma said. "The temple takes care of all my needs. I have a place to live, Enkidu." She put her fingers lightly against his jawline, a touch light as a wing brushing air, as light as her silvery laugh.

Barney smiled. "But a place with a good location like this, near the school and the doctor's office, off the main street but near the central square? Garden in back? Cool in summer and warm in winter?" He laughed.

She laughed too, shaking her head. "I really don't need it, Enkidu."

"You could rent it out."

"No."

"Well, OK." He didn't seem unhappy, beaming still at his family. "Let me know if you change your mind. It's a real bargain at two hundred and eighty *gu*." He hugged her with his good arm. "I haven't felt this good in days," he said.

All the way back across the plain, the river, and through the streets of Uruk, past the busy market, the streets of the artisans, metalworkers and potters, cloth-fullers and dyers, brickmakers and builders, furniture makers, seal carvers, engravers and leatherworkers, drug grinders and perfume distillers, Barney watched and remembered, and he talked animatedly about what he was seeing, the smells and sounds of the city. His dream, the ticking beat of pulse in his wrist, all receded momentarily as he drowned himself in sensation.

"This is a wonderful place," he said, acknowledging a greeting to Enkidu, inventor of wells and friend of Gilgamesh. The man who greeted him was happy, and though his teeth were bad, his smile was proud. Barney felt more alive, more proud and clear about his life, than he ever had before.

"Let's eat," Gilgamesh said, clapping his hands for food.

"Good idea," Barney said. "I'm hungry."

The child woke up and started crying, and they all laughed when Punumma began to nurse it and the crying stopped. The boy sucked greedily. "He's hungry, too, it seems," she said.

There was fresh meat, roasted and boiled, swimming in a sweet sauce of dates and honey. There were cakes of honeyed barley, wheat and corn. There were fresh vegetables, some raw with horseradish or goat cream, some simmered in herbs and broth. There was palm wine and beer and water fresh from the well, cold and clean. There was thick meat soup and clear broth. There was fruit, pomegranates and pears, figs and apricots. There were roast chickens stuffed with bread and sausage.

There was far more food than they could eat, so they invited more people in. The head priest arrived, his hands resting at last, moving only enough to carry food to his mouth. Punumma's doctor had returned, and he told them how elegant his sign would be. He chatted amiably about easy deliveries and sturdy children, complimenting Punumma on her natural skill and grace in childbirth. Lugglanu, the handless director of the medical college, arrived, and his slave popped delicacies into his mouth as he laughed heartily at Barney's jokes. Oh, Barney was witty and entertaining that night.

Neither doctor checked his hand, and indeed, he had forgotten about it himself, keeping it tucked under his cloak in a sling. The throbbing was distant and vague, the slightest sliver of darkness at the edge of Barney's otherwise serene and cloudless horizon.

"O my Gilgamesh," the head priest said, "truly today the gods are smiling on Uruk. We have water again, the grain is growing well, the animals have learned to procreate once more. Anu has spoken to me only this morning in the temple, and he is pleased."

"Yes," Gilgamesh agreed. "Today, the gods are smiling."

They were all there when Barney died. Punumma, wrapped in a floor-length black shawl, her round, white shoulders bare, laid the child against Barney's cheek so his breath rasped against the soft skin, and the child made quiet gurgling sounds and did not cry. The priest murmured Enkidu on his way, the doctors soothed him as best they could, Lugglanu waved his handless arms in mystic passes that did no harm; and Gilgamesh sat, his face drawn wire-thin, his cheeks sucked between his teeth, his ripe laugh stilled.

"It's all right," Barney comforted them, seeing in the room the whine of positrons louder than blood, stronger than death or love, clearer than Punumma's hand holding his as the sound increased. "It's all right."

Barney would always remember the anguished "No!" from Gilgamesh, his fingers digging into Barney's shoulders, willing him back, forcing him to live, to stay.

He walked through the front door of the familiar green and yellow building, under the shadow of the huge sign and marquee that read, strangely, WELCOME LEO BLOOM. He was carrying a heavy suitcase of imitation leather, the kind that folded around two suits. He glanced up just before he entered the building, and the sky was low and dark, a dirty gray of dry cloud trailing ragged wisps of virga, a faint rain that evaporated before reaching the ground, which was itself a cracked and dismal landscape of dried weeds and dust. Then he was in the lobby.

No one was there. No night clerk behind the desk, where the rack of keys was empty, the antiquated PBX winking one forlorn light. The Coke machine cast a baleful light, too, the small EMPTY lights shining under every choice. The silence was oppressive. Not even Muzak, he thought, putting down his suitcase. He leaned over the desk. No one there. The soft plush carpeting, worn bare in places, muffled his steps.

Ring for service. He slammed his palm down on the bell and was rewarded by a muted alto note — a clink, not a gong. He hit it a second time and waited. The light on the PBX went out.

He walked over to the glass wall, where the drapes did not quite meet, and gazed out at the central patio. There was a pool, just where it should be, surrounded on three sides by the two-story building, a balcony running along the row of doors on the second floor. There were no lights on in any of the rooms, so it took a while for his eyes to adjust to the gloom outside. When they finally did, he observed that the pool was empty, the cement cracked and rutted with weeds.

"Ah, excuse me." A dry, cracked voice, a voice that joined seamlessly with the desolation of the exterior, spoke behind him.

"Uh!" Barney jumped and pivoted around.

A small, dark-skinned, leathery-looking man in a red fez rubbed his hands together anxiously behind the desk. "Excuse me, sir," he repeated, his hands curiously reminiscent of the head priest's. "Excuse me, but may I ask who you are, sir?"

"What?"

"Who are you, sir? We weren't expecting anyone tonight. I must know who you are."

"Where am I? This looks like a Holiday Inn."

"This is a Holiday Inn, sir. May I know who you are? Please. This is most irregular."

"Irregular? What do you mean, irregular?" Barney found himself growing impatient with this leathery little man.

"I just don't think you should be here, sir, that's all. We weren't expecting . . ."

"I know, I know." Barney chopped the air with his hand and noticed abruptly that it wasn't swollen. He looked curiously at his thumb, and saw only the double-crescent of tooth marks, white against the tanned skin. Now, why should it be swollen? he wondered. Why should my hand be swollen?

Of course, I was bitten. The Huwawa chief, the cedars. But why am I at a Holiday Inn? Where's Penny, Punumma?

"Please, sir . . ."

"What? Oh, yes. My name is Enkidu. Or it was . . . Now I'm not certain . . ."

"Mr. Enkidu? Let me check." The leathery clerk began sorting through a rack of reservation cards. "E . . . Eliot, Everson. Hmmm, that's odd. I'm sorry, sir, but there's no reservation for you here. I don't understand how you got here."

"My name might be Gamesh. Barney Gamesh."

"Oh, well, that's different, isn't it, sir? Perhaps that explains it. An entirely different name, now isn't it? That would be under G and not under E." He riffled through his cards again; they were gray and dog-eared, old. "Let's see, Gallo, Gamble, Gandy. Gamesh, you say? Nothing here for that name either. This is most irregular, by Allah."

"I can't understand this," Barney said. "I should be in Uruk. I remember a room there, the light. A strange light. Something like this ceiling." He glanced up at the spackles, glinting blue in the rough plaster. "Where is this Holiday Inn, anyway? That didn't look like California out there."

"This is the Holiday Inn Deatheast, sir. Uruk would be

right for this inn, but not this time. Let me think, now it seems to me that Uruk would be Thursday. We *are* outside of time here, so it gets confusing *at times,* he-he-he, oh dear, by Allah." He wiped tears of merriment from his seamy eyes. "Allow me to call my supervisor, sir. Please take a seat. I'm sure we can get this confusion straightened out soon. I'd offer you something to eat, but as you can see the restaurant is closed. We weren't expecting anyone."

"Oh, all right. Wait a minute, Deatheast, you said? I was advised a room would be waiting when I arrived. Now where . . ." Barney stared at the empty pool, uncertain. "Aha, the computer! But that said Deathwest, not Death-east."

"Perhaps you came to the wrong inn, sir. I'll just go make that call," he said hopefully. His hands slithered dryly over one another, iguanas trapped in dry heat.

"But that must mean I'm dead!"

"Why, of course, sir. Dead people are the only ones who come here. Now, I must make that call, sir. By Allah, this is most irregular." He dialed.

Barney wandered about the lobby, kicking the Coke machine as he walked past, and was rewarded by the EMPTY lights winking out. He stopped, curious, and they blinked on again. He stood by the drapes for a while, staring at the shattered concrete of the pool, barely aware of the murmur of the clerk's voice on the phone.

He tripped over the suitcase he'd left in the middle of the lobby and stared stupidly at it. At length he said to himself, "Now where did that come from?"

The pliant vinyl felt rich, like good leather. He opened the case. "This isn't mine," he mumbled, pulling out a conservative pinstripe suit.

It was true. It didn't fit him at all: too wide in the shoulders and too short in the arms. He sat down on the sofa, the suitcase at his feet, and rummaged through the clothes, which seemed to belong to a shorter, plumper man.

There was a silver tie with diagonal blue and gray stripes — a bit too garish for his taste, and it didn't go with the suits.

"Excuse me, sir." The man in the red fez wrung his hands.

"Yes?"

"I've spoken with my supervisor, sir. He's confused, too. We were positively *not* expecting anyone tonight at all. He's checking with his superiors, but frankly, this is going to take some time to resolve. My supervisor suggested I give you a room in the meantime."

"OK." Barney pursed his lips, annoyed and confused. "Will the restaurant open?"

"Now I don't know about that, sir. Not ordinarily, if you understand what I mean. Allah is merciful, and he keeps the restaurant open for new arrivals, people who would still be feeling things like hunger. What I'm trying to say, sir, is that, being dead and all, we don't really need to eat. But it takes some people quite a while to realize that they are dead, and Allah provides them with food while they adjust to their new state. I'll see what I can do. In the meantime, if you will come with me . . ."

The room was familiar: green and yellow, the clumsy painting of a harbor above the double bed. An ancient Motorola television sat on the low dresser across from the bed, and an old telephone with a thin neck and round base sat beside it. A typical Holiday Inn room with some anomalies. Barney automatically slapped his pockets for change to tip the man, but they were empty.

"Quite all right, sir," the small man said, rubbing his dry palms together. "No need for tipping here, you know." He failed to smile as he bowed out.

Barney turned on the television; there was a crackling sound and a low but rising whine. From time to time he heard a small pop. At last a brilliant white dot appeared in the center of the screen and expanded rapidly, revealing a snow-ridden, watery and blurred image. The sound came on with the picture, a static blast followed by voices that sounded as though they were underwater. *"This Is Your Death,"* a voice seemed to be saying with a gargle overlay.

Barney sat hunched at the end of his bed for a long time, trying to make out the picture, not paying too much attention to the words, until he heard "guest of honor, the suicide of the year, Penelope Gamesh, of Sunnyvale, California!" The roar of applause stuttered into static, and with a loud crackling the picture died to a sharp, white dot. The sound diminished rapidly to a faint hum.

"Damn," Barney muttered. He slapped the set a couple of times and finally snapped it off. "Damn."

The phone rang. Probably the desk, he thought. It was a hideous jangling ring.

"Hello."

A muted roar of emptiness filled the receiver, a white noise, a hydrogen hiss where galaxies whirled in unimaginable distances: surf, the chaos of the sea, sand sliding over itself, wind in dead pines.

"Hello," he repeated.

"Enkidu?"

"Who is this?"

"Gilgamesh . . . Are dead? . . . grief."

"I can't hear you. Gilgamesh. That's you?"

"Enkidu! Goddess, we are talking! I've petitioned all the gods — Enlil, Anu, and now Ereshkigal of the underworld. You must be down there, in the underworld. What's it like?"

"You wouldn't believe me if I told you. But it's pretty gloomy, I'll tell you."

"That's what they say. The priests. Pretty gloomy. I've had a statue made of you, Enkidu. I've been to Nippur and to Eridu, asking their gods to give you back, but they will not. Or cannot. Ereshkigal is powerful and jealous. The whole city of Uruk grieves for you, my friend, Punumma grieves, and most of all I grieve. But the child is well."

"How can all that have happened? I just got here."

"I don't know, Enkidu. I don't know anything anymore. I held you seven days, but your heart did not beat, you did not breathe. But we gave you a grand funeral. I am leaving Uruk, Enkidu. I cannot be a king and have such sorrow."

"Listen, Gilgamesh, you're talking to me now. Nothing is lost, you know. Patterns of energy, that's all. Everything in the universe. Nothing is lost."

"But you are dead, Enkidu. You are no longer at my side. I have lost you, and my life is dust."

"Gilgamesh, remember the proverb: My knees keep walking, my feet are tireless, yet a man devoid of understanding pursues me with sorrow. Don't pursue me with sorrow, Gilgamesh. Uruk is your city, not mine. Tell Punumma I loved her, love her. And you, my friend. My only friend."

"You are dead, Enkidu. I have lost you."

"I've lost you too, Gilgamesh," Barney said, but the hiss of distances deepened between them, the voice grew faint and vanished. He sat for a long time, the receiver held loosely in his hand, between his knees. "My knees keep walking . . ." He said to himself.

There was a knock at the door, a tentative, questioning, sly, unctuous and queasy knock.

"What is it?"

"It is I, sir. The desk clerk. May I come in?"

"Of course."

The door creaked open; the red fez peeked around it, followed by the thin leather face. "Please, sir," he said, sidling around the half-opened door into the room. "The phone was off the hook, so I couldn't call you."

"Oh." Barney hung up the phone.

"There has been a terrible mistake, sir. We don't understand how it could have happened; it has never happened before. Never, not even in the future. You really were not expected. It seems, sir, that you are not really, uh, shall I say *dead*."

"Oh, come on. This is too much!"

"I knew you would be upset, sir. I told them. I said, 'He is going to be very upset when I tell him.' I told them that."

"And what did they say?" Barney larded his question sandwich with visible sarcasm.

"They said, 'Too bad. Send him back. He doesn't belong here.' That's what they said, sir. 'Send him back.'"

SECOND INTERIM REPORT

*"Buddha, things are getting a bit more urgent on earth.
Sorry to interrupt and all that, but you said . . ."*

"So. What's happening there?"

*Nine types of quark jumped at once, turning into imps
with variable mass and charge and with life spans measured
in billionths of a second. Five high-energy physicists at
CERN in Switzerland frowned as one, puzzled by the ano-
malous photograph from their synchrotron.*

"It's death, Buddha. They've started to work on it."

"Damn," said Buddha. "My foot's still asleep."

PART III

Tomorrow

Cuneiform lesson:

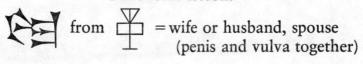 from = wife or husband, spouse
(penis and vulva together)

15

Someone was singing, a drunken, off-key skrawk, a violent lurch in the voice, very far away.

> Well it's just you and me,
> Two bushes and a tree,
> My hand upon your knee,
> My kitty cat's pedigree —
> One big jubilee
> In Sunnyvale-by-the-sea . . .

Barney fell, banging his head against the door. Footsteps thudded toward him, the door flew open, and he tumbled out into the cozy chamber of the Stanford Linear Accelerator target platform straight into the surprised arms of Dr. Desmond Milkworth. The small blue box of Q-tips showered both of them with little cardboard sticks as Barney's naked form bowled them over together.

"Doctor!" Dr. Milkworth shouted from the floor, and the tall, thin form of Dr Schmidlapp, bony wrists furred with black hairs, trotted over with his black medical bag. "Examine this man." Dr. Milkworth climbed to his feet and dusted off his white coat. Then he began meticulously picking up the scattered Q-tips.

Barney, lying on his back, looked up. He saw: Josh MacIntosh's concerned face peering down at him; a large green insect head, extragalactic and warped, a mutant desert locust; Oscar Wilde smiling at his own internal wit; a pirate with eyepatch and stuffed parrot; a man's naked back jutting up from the bottom of an ape suit; and Dr. Schmidlapp's wise face murmuring reassuring nonsense as he probed and thumped Barney's chest, removing EKG sensors.

"Well, Doctor?" Desmond Milkworth probed his ear furiously with a Q-tip. A puzzled frown squeezed the small flesh between his eyes.

"This man has an excellent tan," Dr. Schmidlapp announced.

An amazed buzzing and mumbling went around the solemn group standing over Barney.

"He's crying," observed Oscar Wilde.

"Why are you crying?" the locust asked, bending its bulbous eyes down. "Are you in shock?"

"That's a silly thing to ask him," the pirate said petulantly. "How could he answer if he's in shock?" He scratched his stuffed parrot's head.

"What do you mean, he has an excellent tan?" Dr. Milkworth was asking.

"I mean that the only thing different about him is that he appears to have acquired a very deep, rich tan over most of his body. His heart is fine. His respiration is fine. Very strong," he added, watching Barney's bone-rattling sobs.

"Then why is he crying?"

"Perhaps he's unhappy. Or it could be the effect of the radiation you subjected him to. An emotional effect of some kind." The doctor snapped his bag shut.

"My hand," Barney managed through his strangled sobs.

"His hand," Josh MacIntosh said — his first words. "He wants you to look at his hand."

"Oh, very well." Dr. Schmidlapp turned Barney's hand over. "Hmm, looks like an old bite there. Certainly has healed nicely, though. See, the incisor puncture mark here, bicuspids there. A perfect scar; human, I'd say. Someone must have bitten him a long time ago. Funny I didn't notice it before we put him in that cage."

"Yeah, funny," Josh said.

Gradually Barney stopped sobbing. "Sorry," he managed

through long, racking breaths. "I don't know . . . what came over me. I just felt so . . . sad. So very sad . . ." He sat up. 'How long was I gone?"

"Gone?" Dr. Milkworth looked surprised. "You weren't gone at all. We gave you the positron shower for .73254 seconds, as scheduled. Then you fell against the door and I opened it. You fell out. You haven't been gone at all."

"The Rubber Band Effect," Josh murmured.

"Mmm. Possible, I suppose. Theoretically. But I doubt it. I don't believe in your Rubber Band Effect. Anyway, how would we know?"

"He does have a tan. A tan that could be from the sun. The well-known, extremely *hot* sun of ancient Mesopotamia. Now couldn't it?" Josh was becoming decidedly sarcastic. Barney found himself approving. The effects of SUM?

"Probably not." Dr. Milkworth was unruffled. "More likely a side effect of the positrons. The pion branch effects could have induced ultraviolet fluorescing inside the booth there. Or prompted melanin production in the skin. How about it, Doctor?"

Dr. Schmidlapp was pulling a large pipe from his white lab coat. "Eh? Oh, well, I suppose so. Something like that. Though it would be unusual for the effects to be visible this quickly. But we really don't have any data on this sort of thing. I'd like to get him over to the McWhirter Clinic for a complete physical. Blood tests, skin biopsy — things like that could give us a hint about this positron effect. I must say, it is surprising. A good tan. Do you think there could be a market for this sort of thing? No, I suppose not. Too expensive, I imagine. Oh, well." He sighed, tamping aromatic tobacco into the huge bowl of his pipe.

"I've been away almost a year," Barney said.

"Hah!" Dr. Milkworth snorted. The pirate and Oscar both smiled. Sure, fella.

"I had a son," Barney said, and he started sobbing again.

"It is funny I didn't notice that bite scar before," the doctor was telling the half-ape, half-man. "It's quite prominent once you notice it."

"I got it from the Huwawa," Barney explained through his racking sobs.

"Hmmm." The doctor nodded and turned back to the ape. "The human bite is really quite dangerous," he went on. "Outside of a positively venomous bite, the most dangerous bite in the world is the human bite. You wouldn't believe the numbers of infectious bacteria present."

"I've lost them all," Barney told Josh. "I found Penny there, and I had a friend. A real friend. I've lost them all."

"Come on, Mr. Gamesh. Let's go on over to the Mc-Whirter Clinic so Dr. Schmidlapp can examine you." Dr. Milkworth helped Barney to his feet and draped him in a terrycloth robe. Barney felt like a boxer who had fairly lost the fight and was being accused of throwing it.

It was dark outside; a chill wind rose and fell, a wind from the northeast. Thin razors of cloud sliced across the full fat moon, trailing silver-edged shadows down the length of the accelerator to the highway, under which it disappeared. The small group hurried through skidding leaves to the car — Josh, Barney, Dr. Milkwoth and Dr. Schmidlapp. They drove through the dark to the McWhirter Clinic on Sand Hill Road, in the foothills of Menlo Park. On the way, Barney began to laugh suddenly, a low, private chuckle, a rising giggle, a blurted laugh, a guffaw that roared and roared and collapsed into renewed sobs. "I don't know what's happening to me," he said. "I keep getting these waves of feelings, sadness, pleasure."

"Interesting." Dr. Schmidlapp nodded at the wheel of the car, steering up the hill to the clinic. "Well, here we are." Clouds were piling up to the east, across the bay.

"No residual radiation," he said later. "You should be pleased with Project April Showers. Mr. Gamesh has survived in fine shape. Not just fine shape, better shape than before. Muscle tone has greatly improved. Another odd effect, I suppose. Totally unexpected. Looks like he's been doing a lot of work in the sun lately. This could be used as a new program for executives, perhaps, people with desk jobs, eh? Seven tenths of a second of positron radiation and they're fit as a violin. Mmmm. I'll suggest it."

"You don't seem to believe me," Barney said. "I've been working in the sun. I've been gone almost a year. Ten or eleven months, anyway, I was in Uruk, with Gilgamesh. I had a child."

"Yes, Well, history is not really my field. You might want to talk to someone else about that. Meanwhile, all I can say is that you are in excellent health, far better than you were before. The one thing I don't quite understand is that scar."

"It was horribly infected yesterday," Barney told him.

"No. There was no infection yesterday. I'm quite positive of that."

"Not yesterday *here*. The yesterday *then*. *My* yesterday." He saw the disinterest on the doctor's face. "Oh, never mind."

There was a brief, businesslike knock on the door, and Junior Arkwright sauntered in. "I guess I missed all the fun, huh?" he said. His knobbed and bony nose appeared to be stuffed up, a fall cold. He was wearing his red plaid suit. "I went over to the accelerator, but they told me you'd already left, so I came on over. How did it go?"

The scientists stared at him so intently that he began to jiggle in his shoes again, doing a tap dance without taps, a soft-shoe shuffle on the Congoleum. "Eh?" he queried.

"It went fine," Barney said. "Just fine. The project was a big success."

Junior sighed dramatically. "Well," he said, the dance subsiding. "I'm glad of that. You certainly do look fit. Must have been hot there, eh?"

"Hot where?" Dr. Milkworth asked, fingering a Q-tip from his pocket.

"Why, wherever he went. You *were* going somewhere, weren't you?"

"Yes," Barney said.

"Oh," Dr. Milkworth said. "Sumer. Mesopotamia. Well, I don't think he went anywhere."

"The computer might show something," Josh said.

"Hmm."

"Well," Junior went on, his marbled eyes glowing in triumph, undiminished by Dr. Milkworth's skepticism, "I only ask because the computer gave me a printout on the total cost of equipment and freight for this project, and I was a bit worried if it didn't go well. The institute doesn't like it when we overspend on unsuccessful projects, and the projected figures were a bit above the initial estimates we made last week."

"How much over?" Barney wanted to know.

"Seventy-six thousand dollars." With his lavender hand-kerchief, Junior mopped his sweaty brow and running nose.

"That is a bit over." Barney winked at Josh.

"More than double." The lavender slithered into his pocket.

"Well, rest assured, the project was successful in spite of what Dr. Milkworth here says."

"I'm glad of that. Well, I'd better be getting on. I have a late date tonight."

"A date?" Barney was feeling calmer, for some reason, now that Junior had appeared.

"Oh, yes." Junior was very pleased with himself. "You remember Miss MacHunt? Pete Boggs' secretary?"

"I don't think I ever met her."

"Well, I think I'm in love. She has the most beautiful feet I've ever held."

Junior sauntered out, leaving an aromatic trail of Sauvage cologne in the air.

"Sometimes I wonder about the quality of the people the institute hires these days," Dr. Schmidlapp said mildly.

"What institute?" Dr. Milkworth burrowed in his ear.

"The one at MIT that designed this project," Barney said.

"Oh."

"What was that about feet?" Dr. Schmidlapp wanted to know.

"His father collects string," Josh was telling Barney. "Prue told me Pete Boggs told her."

"String?"

"In a nursing home. He used to collect it at home."

"Feet he ever held," Dr. Schmidlapp was saying to Dr. Milkworth.

"I couldn't help overhearing," Barney said. "He used to be a podiatrist."

"Ah."

"Shall we go home?" Barney said to Josh.

"I'll come around tomorrow afternoon," Josh told Dr. Milkworth, "to see the computer analysis of the shower."

"The photos will be ready then too," Desmond told him, crumpling a Q-tip and throwing it away. "But they won't show anything."

"I've called a taxi for you," Dr. Schmidlapp told Barney.

The clouds had piled high in the east by the time they emerged from the McWhirter Clinic, and the wind had picked up, sending small whirlwinds of yellow leaves twirling around their ankles. The shredded cloud was racing so fast that the moon was racing too, a fat white wheel in the silvered sky.

"Were you really gone ten months?" Josh asked once they were settled in the back of the taxi.

"Josh, you wouldn't believe it. I can hardly believe it myself, now that I'm here again. It was so strange. I even killed someone."

"Wow! Killed someone! What was it like?"

"Awful."

The taxi driver, a graduate of Josh and Barney's SUM class, one of the blinding bulbs lit by SUMUS, the Rumanian named Tiglash Apsu, haunter of funerals, twitched his ears when he heard the words about killing. Tiglash was a firm believer in the old Rumanian proverb, one his mother often mumbled to him when he was a child: Always kiss the hand you cannot bite. Since SUMmation, Tiglash had been kissing imaginary hands.

"How did you do it?"

"With a sword. It was Gilgamesh's own sword with lapis lazuli and gold on the hilt, a copper sword. I saved his life with it."

Saved someone's life, thought Tiglash Apsu, steering the taxi through the windswept streets of Menlo Park toward Sunnyvale. Killed to save a life. Always kiss the hand you cannot bite.

It reminded him of funerals. Ever since SUMmation, when he had wandered out into the streets and failed to return to his Las Vegas employers, Tiglash had begun to hang around funerals, triggered by the billboard outside the Milpitas Holiday Inn: WE TAKE THE STING OUT OF DEATH. The image of the Boston cream pie lady's inert cadaverous form snoring on the floor beside him tormented him; visions of all the hands he had kissed and all the hands he had bitten. And now he knew death was a rip-off. He loved it.

He had stopped killing people himself, though. He didn't get so involved anymore. He let other people, other things, do the killing for him. He just attended the funerals.

"Why was it awful?" Josh asked.

"Well, for one thing, it was a woman I killed."

That was almost too much for Tiglash Apsu. He began to squirm in his seat, a vague sexual excitement rising from the warm, slick seat under him. The taxi swished on through Palo Alto, past more motels than there were in the entire state of Nebraska, past more car dealers than there were in all of Albuquerque, New Mexico, past more drive-in restaurants than there were people in Nevada. And all the while, Tiglash squirmed.

"Wow," Josh said. "A woman! That must have been really strange. And with a sword. Yuk."

"I didn't like it at all. But good things happened too. Wonderful things."

"You had a son, huh?"

"Yeah. I thought of you."

"Really?" Josh was pleased.

Tiglash was annoyed. He didn't understand the strange excitement that was moving in on him, but it seemed to have something to do with women lying still and limp on stainless steel. He'd never killed a woman and wasn't likely to, not anymore. He wasn't going to get involved. So what was this squirming?

They passed a billboard at the Mountain View–Sunnyvale border: WE TAKE THE STING OUT OF DEATH.

"That's Pete Boggs' new slogan. Prue's very interested in Pete Boggs these days." Josh watched the sign go by.

"Lovely," Barney said. "I know what it's really like, though. Death."

"Oh? What?"

"It's a Holiday Inn."

"Oh, come on."

"I'm not joshing you. It really is."

Tiglash Apsu had been to the Holiday Inn. Next to a fat lady who played with Boston cream pie. It wasn't the pie that had gotten to Tiglash; it was the way she lay on the floor, mountainous, inert. Unconsciously, Tiglash pressed harder on the accelerator and the taxi picked up speed. A few fat drops of rain flattened against the windshield, though the moon still raced westward over the clouds, clouds that by now crashed into one another in the east, covering half the sky.

"That's a terrible joke," Josh said. "And I've heard it before."

Barney was smiling. "I didn't mean it as a joke. Really."

"Hmmm."

The taxi climbed up Puerco de Esmeralda Lane and ground to a clashing halt in front of Barney's model home.

"Come on in," he said. "I'll run you back to Prue's later."

"OK."

Barney paid the taxi driver, and they went on into the house. Tiglash stood beside his door for a moment, dully watching them close the front door behind them. Then he gripped the frame of his door and rammed his huge bald head through the closed glass window, right up to the first layer of fat wrinkles at his neck. He pulled his head out, got in, and drove slowly back to his apartment in Redwood City, a tiny red light winking on and off inside his eyes.

"How about a beer?" Barney asked.

"Prue won't let me."

"Hey, why don't you move in with me? There's plenty of room."

"I'd like that, but Prue won this big single-parent custody case with me, and I don't think she'd like to give me up. A matter of principle with her, you see. She doesn't really like me all that much."

"But what about your parents? I mean, were you an orphan or something?"

"Well, my father was a hunter. A real fanatic. He had killed almost everything that moved in the world; even when it was something that didn't move, like a tree or something, well, half the time he shot that too. The only thing he hadn't killed was a tiger. He really wanted a tiger bad, but tigers were protected. The only time anyone could kill a tiger was when there was a man-eater loose in India somewhere, and even then the tiger had to have eaten at least thirty people or something before it could be shot. My father had his application in for years, waiting for a tiger to eat thirty people.

"Finally he got a telegram. I was about nine then, and a bit distracted because that was when I was into being a phone freak, so I hardly noticed when they went off to India, he and my mother. They went for the tiger, and they never came back."

"Never came back? You mean the tiger got them?"

"No, no. The tiger was dead by the time they arrived, shot by the local district commissioner. They'd had a terrible journey up there, days on an Indian train and all that, and the disappointment was too much. They both got a terrible dysentery, dried up like prunes. When their train got back to Calcutta they were found in their seats, mummies. That's when I got interested in high-energy physics."

"I'm not sure I see the connection." Barney had a puzzled frown, a blinking question mark between his eyes.

"Me either," Josh grinned. "But that's when Prue, who was a cousin of my mother's, saw an opportunity to take on a controversial single-parent case for herself. She won."

"Well, she doesn't own you, and you're old enough to make up your own mind, I'd say. Remember what A. Spencer Sparling would say: You want to go on being the silly out-of-control asshole you are?" He was smiling again.

"You're right. I'll have a beer."

They sat in easy chairs in the living room, the computer console between them, and sipped at their beers. Barney sighed and wiped foam from his lips. "I haven't had a cold beer, a cold anything, in a long time," he said. "Now listen, I have to ask something fairly serious. You realize we have committed a fairly elaborate crime, don't you? We've manipulated the government's supposedly secure computer network to the tune of something like a hundred and thirty thousand dollars in time and equipment. We do have a follow-up program to eliminate any evidence of tampering, but at the very least we have committed fraud, grand larceny or a breach of official secrets. If we get caught we're going to be in trouble."

"We won't get caught," Josh said confidently. "That was a good program we wrote."

"I was hoping you'd say that. Because I have a proposal for you."

"Yes?"

"You'd better be sure about this. It's a lot bigger than a mere hundred and thirty thousand dollars."

"How much?" Josh finished his beer.

"I figure somewhere around one point three billion dollars."

Josh spit his final mouthful of beer back into his glass. "Did you say billion?"

"Mmm-hmm."

"Dollars?"

"Roughly. It's a little hard to be precise in places."

"You want to *steal* that much?"

"Good grief no. Not steal. No, I don't think we would ever see any actual money. I'm thinking more in terms of computer time, research assistance, hardware modification and development and programming talent."

"That's a lot of money, even for something as expensive as computer talent."

"This is a big project I have in mind."

"OK. What is it?"

"You're sure?"

"I'm sure. Come on, you're killing me."

"Death." Barney sat back in his chair.

"Death?"

"Death."

"I don't get it. What about death?"

"Look. I went to Uruk for ten months. I was sent to a Holiday Inn. I got in touch with a Holiday Inn called Deathwest on this computer here. You designed the physics that got me to Uruk and back. I guess what I mean is that there seems to be more to death than just dying."

"Go on."

"We're going to write the final program on death. Everything that anyone has ever said or written or experienced on the subject. There has already been a lot of research on it — DNA, cell death, psychiatric investigations of the death experience. I read somewhere that there's no reason we can't live forever. And then the mystics have studied it. We will program everything — physiology, psychology, religion, the physics and chemistry of it, the sociology and anthropology of funeral rites, politics, everything, and run all the correlations we can think of, or that anyone we hire can think of. We will solve death, find out what it is.!

"You see, I want Penny back, now more than ever. I was with her back there, even if she didn't know it; she had my child. I certainly can't go back there again: I died there; and besides, the Rubber Band Effect would keep bringing me back here. I couldn't stand that."

"You are thinking big, aren't you?"

"I've been SUMmated, haven't I? It's time to take charge of things. I've been pushed around long enough."

"Yeah, but . . ."

There was a tremendous crash outside, a long, rolling, descending gut-rumble of thunder — *thunder* — and a sudden flurry of rain, a quick patter of drops against the picture window, and a shattering fork of lightning speared the radio tower of the Sunnyvale Police Department dispatcher downtown, knocking out police communications for two hours and sixteen minutes, long enough for twelve armed robberies, twenty-nine burglaries, twelve breaking and enterings, sixteen assaults with a deadly weapon and a homicide.

"What was that?" Josh put down his second beer and joined Barney at the window.

"It's raining!" Barney exclaimed. He recalled water flowing from the wells into the irrigation canals of Sumer. "Wasn't there a drought here when I left?"

The fat drops streaked the window, sluicing down to the cracked ground and brown grass of Barney's yard.

"That was yesterday," Josh told him. "You haven't been gone, remember?" Smiling.

"Yes, I have . . . Oh." Barney saw the look and smiled too. "Anyway, thunder in California, that's a treat."

"Didn't it rain in Sumer?"

"Not while I was there. I haven't seen rain in years." Barney noticed, among the rivers of rain flowing down his window, that bubbles of soap were forming, loops and squiggles and streaks of soapy writing turning now to suds. "I forgot! It's Halloween! All those guys in costume at the accelerator."

"Not Halloween anymore. It's the first of November, now." Josh looked at his watch. "One forty-three in the morning."

"Hah!"

The moon finally sank into a sea of thick black cloud, and the light went out. They could see nothing outside, only their two faces staring back at them from the rippling sheet of water against the glass. The thunder had rolled away to the east, leaving only the wet sounds of rain falling through the gutters and drains, washing the hard-baked ground, greasing it with a thin layer of oily mud.

Tiglash Apsu, back in his one-room apartment at the Killborne Hotel in Redwood City, stared redly at the ceiling as the green neon of the hotel sign lit the walls with the first four letters of the hotel name, on and off, a green ghost quoting an old detective movie. The thunder jolted Tiglash to his shoes, which he had worn to bed. It was an omen, loping through the Rumanian forests of his brain. "Many dogs will eat a lone wolf," he said to the ceiling. "Kill, Kill, Kill," the walls signaled back, the "borne" of the hotel name out of sight one floor down. Tiglash didn't notice the message on the wall; he was concerned with the vague excitement, now somehow augmented by the thunder, an excitement he still had not recognized, though the solemnity of funeral parlors had something to do with it.

Prue Nisenvy was squirming atop Pete Boggs' "tort" when the thunder struck and startled her into such a shuddering orgasm that she collapsed around his quivering "stiff" like a hot water bottle breaking on a lit cheroot, quenching them both.

"Hot damn," Pete said, "it's raining."

"I'll say," Prue said, not understanding him.

"No, I mean outside."

Sergeant Masterbrook had been chasing Halloween prank calls all night, so when the lightning cut him off from the police dispatcher, he felt released. Switching on his red light and siren, he raced through the drenched residential streets of Sunnyvale, whooping and laughing and shaking the sleeping citizens into wakeful recognition of the rain.

Junior Arkwright was holding Miss MacHunt's slender left foot in his trembling hands, caressing the sole tenderly with his fingertips and murmuring words he had never spoken before to anyone but his mommy. Miss MacHunt did not find the words displeasing, and wriggled her toes in a way that sent shivers of ecstasy down Junior's bony back to the tumescent lusts at bottom, swirling all into confusion. Sweet confusion.

The thunder sent his nose between the big and second toes, a sliding skid that sent shivers *up* her delicately curved spine.

"Oh, Junior," she breathed. "I can't describe how that feels."

"Doh Deed," he replied, his nose pinched between her toes. "I dow. Woderfuh." He wiggled his nose, and the ginglymoid joints responded with orgasmic flexion, curling tightly around his greater and lesser alar cartilages, sending emergency messages in two directions: one to his throbbing hammer, which exploded on its own, and another to his CO_2 sensors, triggering the "incipient suffocation" signal.

He popped free, and they both gasped in the afterglow.

Barney turned away from the bubbly lather on his window. "How about another beer? To celebrate."

"OK with me." Josh was grinning such a mouth-breaking, tooth-exposing grin that Barney was alarmed for his face.

They toasted the rain. They toasted Sumer. They toasted Gilgamesh, whose fame had lasted through the centuries, a hero of epic proportions whose grief was great. They toasted Punumma, and Barney collapsed into sobs again and called her Penny.

They got very drunk together, and Barney wanted to adopt Josh on the spot.

"Prue wouldn't like it." Josh sighed. "She's a lawyer too. A good lawyer."

"We'll get another good lawyer," Barney said. "We can afford it. A small slice of our budget."

They emptied the refrigerator of beer. They sang a couple of songs, but neither one of them knew a song all the way through. A police car roared past the house, siren wailing, red light flashing.

The only song they could finish was "Sunnyvale-by-the-sea":

> It's just you and me,
> The computer fac-to-ry
> In Sunnyvale-by-the-sea . . .

The night grew darker and wetter, and in the dim gray morning, the sky was filled with dismal glorious sebaceous cumulonimbus that dumped inches of welcome rain on the entire West.

"When do we go to work?" Josh asked, holding his aching head over the bathroom sink, a sickly grin on his face.

"How about today?" Barney asked, mixing them both an Alka-Seltzer.

16

Pete Boggs was happy. Very happy. He stood at his office window, staring out at the rain-flooded streets, and smiled. In the reception room, his secretary Miss MacHunt hummed a pleasant tune. She was also happy.

The indirect source of all this happiness was on the El Camino Real, the road of kings. It was the rain, of course. Out there was a monumental traffic jam, for people had quite forgotten how to drive in the rain. The traffic jam was sending tempers, and after tempers, blood pressures, soaring. And the rain would bring a terrific upsurge in respiratory ailments. Flu season was on the way. All this meant that business was picking up. Pete whistled "The Sound of Music" under his breath. The hills are alive, he was thinking, with people dying.

A new shipment of coffins was due in from Hong Kong, and Pete really needed those coffins. Already this week he'd had seven funerals; he'd had to direct three in one day, Tuesday. That was good, especially the second one, but they were all good. Very, very good. And it was going to get better.

Pete loved directing funerals: the long lines of limousines pulling out of the parking lot one after another, just so, headlights on, purple flags snapping; the flowers arriving right on time, exquisitely arranged by Pete's *ikebana* master; the condolence cards; the tasteful candles, the incense. Lighting, drapery, everything, just so — a production. Pete considered himself an artist, a great director who put on a different show every time, who faced a new challenge with every stiff, and all on a very limited budget.

Hence the coffins from Hong Kong.

The phone rang. Miss MacHunt's musical voice answered. Pete had not been missing Caroline's attentions these days. Too busy. He chuckled, thinking how busy he was these days, business, pleasure, a rosy blur. Prue had even figured out a way to deduct Pete's new CIA income. Business. Pleasure.

"It's for you, Mr. Boggs. Mr. Gamesh."

"Put him on."

Pete fingered his gold chains and smiled into the phone. His voice smiled too. "Barney, old friend, how the hell are you?"

"Pretty good, Pete. Surprisingly good, in fact. How are you?"

"Brisk, my friend. Brisk is the word. Couldn't be better. What can I do for you?"

"I wondered if we could get together. I have a couple of things I'd like to discuss."

"Such as the disposition of the sti — uh, your wife?"

"Actually, I wasn't thinking about that just now. In fact, I'd like you to sort of hang on to her for a while longer if you could. Something's come up."

"OK, sure. By the way, I wanted to talk to you too. A little dream of mine for some time now — I want to computerize the crematorium. Business is good, and I think I could afford it now."

There was a long pause. "Really?" Barney asked at last, his voice thoughtful.

"Yeah. Don't you think it could be done?"

"Oh, certainly it could be done. It's a wonderful idea, Pete. Let me give it some thought. Yup, I think it's a wonderful idea. I'm sure I could help you out with that."

"Great, Barn. Where shall we meet?" For Pete, everything was pushing up daisies.

"Ceramic Lobster?"

"Swell, Barn. Just swell."

"He says swell. Just swell," Barney told Josh after hanging up.

"Great." Josh put a check mark beside Pete Boggs' name on the list in his hand. "Who's next?"

"We need a lawyer. Let's see who the computer can dig up for us."

"We could use Prue, I suppose," Josh suggested doubtfully.

"Mmm. Do you think so?" Numbers flowed across the screen.

"She *is* going to be a little pissed off when I leave. She may not exactly volunteer."

"True, Josh. Too true. We'll just have to find another way, another way." Humming. "What does Prue like most of all?"

"She sure likes to humiliate people. That's one thing she likes for sure. And I don't think I care for it much anymore."

"Can't say I blame you there, Josh. Well, we'll have to use that to our advantage. How about this dummy corporation we're setting up? We could hire someone to front for us and let her humiliate him. Or her. That might help out. She need never know she works for us."

"That's great. Me employing Prue. Ha."

"So much for that. Now for the details. For example, what shall we call our company?"

Josh said, "Something anonymous, that won't give a clue to what it does."

"Right," Barney said. "Some kind of research group. A name that sounds dull. Society for the Investigation of Corpses?"

"SIC? I dunno. Too specific, perhaps. Besides, every death nut in California will be coming around."

"I guess you're right, it's not so good. How about Shadow Research, Inc.?"

"That sounds OK."

238

"Good. Now, here's what we need. First, set up the dummy corporation. For that we'll need a lawyer. Prue. But before that, I guess we need a figurehead president, someone Prue either knows or who we can introduce her to . . ."

"Pete Boggs."

"Mmmm. That just might work. Make a note of that for my lunch with him."

"Check."

"Then we'll need to arrange offices for the company. We'll have to divert several phone lines to forward calls here; untraceable diversion."

"That's easy. I can make a couple of calls about that. The phone company's network is so complex, now, only their computer can trace it all. There shouldn't be anything to tapping into the data links and establishing a subsystem. What's next?"

"We'll have to register the corporation with the state; that means tapping into the state computer and sticking the articles of incorporation into it so that anyone checking will find everything in order and won't be able to trace the principals. Because the principals will all be dead."

"The principals will be dead? I don't get it."

"We're going to use what are called dead souls to run the company — except Pete Boggs, of course. We raid an insurance company for a roster of deceased policyholders, and we revive them."

"Next."

"Next we need operating funds for Shadow Research payroll. We're going to hire a lot of expensive talent."

"How do we work that? I don't have any money to speak of?"

"Three ways. First, we do the deposit slip scam, an almost foolproof idea. If you're careful. We open an account at a bank. We have deposit slips printed with that dummy account number. Then we put them back on the counter at the bank. All deposit slips go into the computer, where every deposit made using our slips goes into our account. Only good for a month, of course, because once the statements are mailed out and people haven't been credited it all hits the fan. We'll be gone by then, of course. If we do it at enough banks it should give us a stake. Be a bit of work, of course."

"What isn't? And second?"

"We use the interbank clearing procedure to get dummy checks caught between two cities — probably New York and Los Angeles. We print one bank's checks with another bank's code number. Then when it goes for clearance, the computer bounces it back because there's a different code on it. It could get stuck there until a bank official gets into the act. Meantime, we get to use the money. And third, we use the old salami slice technique. We reprogram the bank computer to divert fractions of pennies in interest into our accounts. There's no way to get caught with this one, so it's good indefinitely. Takes only fractions from thousands of accounts, so the money is never missed. We make the system work for us."

"Sounds a bit illegal."

"Actually, some of it is and some of it isn't, but it's very difficult to get caught, and more difficult to be convicted even if caught. This type of crime is pretty new."

Josh was delighted with the whole thing, despite the dubious morality of it. It was all a game.

"Then, of course." Barney continued, "we need some time and information sharing from some of the larger computer systems around — the government, NORAD, in fact all federal security computers, and Intergalactic Orgones, which has one of the largest available memory storage facilities in the world at this time. They're using some top-secret very large scale integration circuits, and VLSI is where it's at, computer-wise." Barney laughed.

Josh was laughing too. "Right," he said.

"And then, I think, we could put our employees to work

writing grant proposals. That should be pretty easy, and the money is legal. Lots of people make their living doing that, getting government grant money."

"And after that?"

"After that we're ready to get to work. Now let's call Prue and tell her you're going to move."

"Goddammit, Pete," Prue was shrieking over the phone at him. "The sunuvabitch is going to move out on me. After I won that *extremely difficult* custody case, too. The ungrateful little bastard is moving out. He's moving in with that Barney Gamesh, a goddam *client* of yours, for God's sake. A client! I've never been so furious in my life. To think —"

"Now, Prue, don't you —"

"Don't interrupt me, you blinking sot. Keep your goddam mouth shut! When I get my hands on that little twerp I'm going to make him suffer, I'll tell you. Little Josh MacIntosh, the poor orphan waif I took into my own home, took to my bosom, fed like my own child, treated with love and tenderness —"

"Now, Prue, I heard —"

"You've heard nothing, you sleazy lounge lizard, you Mantanned California gigolo, you bloodsucking, belly-stabbing, frivolous, overdressed pimp. You've heard not one bleeding goddam of a thing! Nothing. When I get through with those two, there will be nothing left but hair and bone, if that. Then I'm going to stuff their reputations into your goddam furnace for good luck. That's what I intend to do." She hung up before Pete could protest that it was a crematorium, not really a furnace.

He found himself cowed in spite of SUM. Such magnificent anger! He was really impressed. Such passion. She may be wrinkled, but she certainly knew how to hurt someone. He fingered his golden ankh where it winked among the chest hairs and leaned back in his office chair.

He discovered he was shaking. Time for SUM exercise

number three. He closed his eyes and sank into the chair. Think of the most humiliating thing that ever happened. He searched through the attic of his memory. He prowled through rusty implements, dusty compulsions, minute failures, tricks played on him at morticians' school, tricks he had played on others, hasty words, impotence, shame.

Soon he was blushing furiously under his perfect health spa tan. He squirmed in his seat. Oh, awful! Spanked! Awful, awful. He was enjoying it. Worse and worse. He leaped suddenly to his feet, ready to shout "Bullshit!" in accordance with the dictates of SUM exercise number three.

But, alas, he caught his thighs, just above the knee, sharply, under the edge of his desk, so that it came out "Bullsh —" followed by a terrific crash as he went over sideways, taking with him in his desperate grasp for something solid everything on his desk — desk pad, pen and pencil set, a heavy silver statuette of an erotically entwined couple in a coffin, the sketch he'd been doing for his current funeral — and his chair.

He was squirming on the floor holding his thighs and squeezing back tears when Miss MacHunt came in to remind him it was time for his lunch at the Ceramic Lobster with Barney Gamesh.

The Hispano-Suiza purred through the downpour, engine throbbing in time to the throbbing in his thighs, the pulse of life and power and pain. Pete's tan lips were thinned in concentration, the great "Bullshit" pulse beating in his brain. Parking beside a hydrant, he ran through the rain to the restaurant.

Mel Mellows' mellifluous melodies wafted through the vast room:

> My neighbor down the block
> Has a brand-new garbage pail
> In which he puts great stock —
> And a copper rooster crows in Sunnyvale . . .

Mel was singing. Mel's new hit. Bullshit, bullshit, bullshit, throbbed in Pete's injured thighs.

Barney was already there, studying the huge menu, seated under the rehung mermaid figurehead that had almost fallen on Prue a few weeks before, the evening of the quake.

> He got it down at Sears
> Because it was on sale
> When he went to buy some shears —
> And a copper rooster crows in Sunnyvale . . .

Nina Choklat was hanging over a table next to the piano in her pilgrim outfit, buckle shoes crossed, a welcome she did not feel on her face as revolutionary rhetoric unreeled in her brain. She smiled a smile that masked distaste as she eyed the customer's Scottish three-piece wool suit that still exhaled damply the smells of rain and wool. Fascist pig-fucker, she was thinking, almost loud enough for Pete to have heard it had he not been so absorbed in his own thigh pain.

"Hiya, Barn," Pete said with false cheer, grimacing over the throbbing. "How's tricks?"

"What's that?" Barney looked up in alarm, tricks flashing. "Tricks? Oh, hi, Pete. Sit down." He went back to the menu.

Mel Mellows' marshmallow voice launched itself spiritedly into the next verse:

> And now he's working hard
> Each weekend without fail
> Out there in his yard —
> And a copper rooster crows in Sunnyvale . . .

The bland chords flowed from his piano, Mel's style of tapioca music somehow in conflict with the decor of harpoons and whale bones.

"Whatchya gonna have?" Pete wanted to know, studying the menu.

"Thought I'd have the Pilgrim's Progress," Barney said.

The Pilgrim's Progress was a low-calorie, low-fat, guaranteed sinless, organic sandwich of watercress, sprouts, sliced eggplant and goat cheese on twelve-grain, stone-ground, unleavened Puritan bread. Pete always thought eating it was a bit like wearing a hair shirt; Pete never wore hair shirts.

He preened his own pure silk, puff-sleeved, open-neck shirt, the one with the Mondrian prints on it, and waved his brown hand at the menu. "I guess I'll have the Sybarite Special myself." The Sybarite Special was a high-calorie, high-fat casserole of pastry stuffed with game bird, filet and pâté. In no way did it approximate wearing a hair shirt.

> He's glad to have his bin,
> His bright green garbage pail,
> To put his clippings in —
> And a copper rooster crows in Sunnyvale . . .

Mel flowed to a flourishing finish and presented his faultless teeth to a smattering of applause from the bar. "Mom is especially proud of that song," Mel told his audience after blowing into the mike to make sure it was working. Then he left the room.

Nina Choklat took Pete and Barney's orders and left, her lovely behind swaying sensually within the prison of her Puritan dress. In her head she was building bombs to blow the class-ridden oppressors into oblivion right along with their goddam computer society. The Pacific Gas and Electric Company had turned off her power that morning for her failure to pay her bill. She had paid the bill, of course.

"So you want to computerize your crematorium?"

"Right, Barn. I figure we might be able to lay off some of the extraneous employees that way, especially the ones who demand extra pay for night work and weekends. The gas company said I'd save money if I could maximize production, keep the burners going all the time somehow. It would eliminate the daily fire-up, which is when most of the gas is consumed."

"Hmm, I'll tell you what we can do. I've been ap-

proached by some people, people I don't know, I must con-
fess, to find someone to act as a kind of consultant for them;
it's some type of death research center."

"Death research center?"

"That's what they said. You'd be an officer of the company with a fairly hefty retainer."

Pete whistled. "What kind of retainer?"

"Well, they spoke somewhere in the neighborhood of a
thousand a week."

Pete whistled again. "I'd just be a consultant?"

"Right. Probably only take an hour a week or so, on the
average. Some weeks there probably wouldn't be anything
to do at all, but the retainer would continue. Now, I think I
could persuade this outfit to help finance computerizing
your crematorium as part of the package."

"That's a sweet proposal, Barn. A very sweet proposal. It
would be very hard to turn it down. I mean, what have I
got to lose?"

"I figured you might say that, Pete." Barney smiled. The
mermaid over his head also smiled, arms outstretched,
breasts hard and round and perfect. "The only thing you'd
have to do initially is a sort of favor for me."

"What's that?" Pete was gazing thoughtfully at the mermaid, recalling the evening he'd been there with Prue when
the quake struck.

"Contact Prue Nisenvy for them."

Pete jumped. Barney read his mind. "Huh?"

"A lawyer is needed for drawing up incorporation papers.
A lawyer with discretion. They don't have to be filed, just
drawn up."

"And you want Prue to do it?" Pete rubbed his palms
over his aching thighs. They left damp streaks.

"I don't know any other lawyers, Pete. And this group
left it all to me. They have their own legal talent, of course,
but they wanted a local lawyer to handle this part. Now, I'd

talk to Prue myself, you understand. But she's just a tiny bit annoyed with me right now." Still smiling.

Pete's palms sweated into the pale beige flannel of his trousers, awakening the pain in his thighs. "Annoyed isn't really the word for it, Barn. She called me this morning. Sort of let off steam."

"Ah." Barney was still smiling, a warm, clean, fun-loving, buddy smile.

Pete basked in it uneasily for a while. The mermaid smiled on as well, and slowly the painful throbbing subsided. "All right," he said, "I'll talk to Prue. What's the name of this company?"

"Shadow Research, Incorporated. Tell her to draw up the papers in that name and send you the bill. You can give it to me and I'll take care of it. My name mustn't be mentioned, you understand? I'll send you the names of the principals as soon as I get them — in a day or two, I expect."

"What's your part in all this?" It was beginning to sound a little too good to Pete.

"Oh, I'm just a temporary consultant. I'm working on a little invention of my own and am going to be awful busy soon. I'm helping out with a couple of computer problems they had. Just to get them started."

"And they wanted me? I don't quite understand . . ."

"Well, they wanted someone with an intimate knowledge of death and the funeral business. Naturally you seemed a perfect choice."

"Naturally. OK, I'm your man. I'll give Prue a call."

"This afternoon, please, Pete. They're in something of a hurry."

Pete was remembering the necessity for SUM exercise number three. "OK," he said at last. "I'll call her this afternoon."

"I'll come out tomorrow to look over your furnace."

*

Mel was in the back of the restaurant, trying to get the furnace started; the rains had brought declining temperatures, and the old furnace hadn't been fired up in a long time, not since the beginning of the drought and its unusual warm weather.

He kicked the furnace. Nothing happened. He took the plate off the burner at the bottom and peered inside. Nina Choklat came in then, just in time to see Mel's round behind sticking into the air as he bent to the bottom of the furnace.

"Oh," she said, "excuse me." *Voice Bank* drifted through her head.

Mel was startled. He jerked his head up, knocking it against the metal hood on the furnace. "Ouch!"

"Oh!" Nina dropped to her knees beside him. "I'm so sorry," she said, all her maternal functioning at the commune rushing back to her, augmented by what she gave her kids. She cradled Mel's injured head in her hands.

Mel liked her hands there. Only his mom had held his head like that. He'd never really noticed Nina before, but she had soft hands. Maternal hands.

He's such a big baby, Nina thought. He can't do anything right. Oh, he sings OK, and he does pay his employees well, and takes care of them. And the food isn't really *too* bad. Not great, but not too bad. Especially the Pilgrim's Progress; now that is good organic food. Her hands stroked his hair, his balding crown, his soft round cheek.

She looks good in that hat, Mel thought. She looks good in buckle shoes. Black suits her. And she does have nice hands. She's a good waitress, too, always cheerful with the customers, always pleasant to have around. Mom likes her.

He slumped a little into her welcoming palms.

Barney clapped his palms together. "You should have seen it, Josh. It was wonderful. Good old Pete Boggs is going to be a consultant. He's as happy as one of those spring birds that's always singing and flying."

"A lark?"

"Yeah."

"I bet. And I've got some news too."

They were sipping beer, the remains of take-out pizza scattered on the coffee table. The computer hummed softly to itself in the background.

"Shoot," Barney said, stuffing the last bit of sausage and mushroom into his mouth.

"Well, we got the printouts and photos from the positron shower, and they confirm all my predictions. The photos show you *were* gone, for well over twelve nanoseconds, though that nitwit Milkworth maintains you weren't gone at all and it's a flaw in the negatives. And I've been dipping into the Bunker Hill Insurance Company."

"Mmm-hmm," Barney drank deeply from his beer.

"It's full of dead souls."

"What do you mean?"

"I mean that the Bunker Hill Insurance Company has been stuffing its life insurance rolls with dead people. Around a hundred and twenty thousand of them, all very dead or imaginary. Whenever they're audited, they invent biographies for these bogus people to show the auditors. They've been doing everything you suggested — taking out loans to pay back old loans, putting the policies up as collateral, and investing in highly speculative ventures. Fact is, they've been cleaning up and no one suspects. No one but us."

Barney whistled. "Can we raid their computer for some appropriate people?"

"Whoo, not only that. We can have Bunker Hill Insurance back Shadow Research. We won't have to do any of the scams you were talking about. Made me nervous anyway, taking money from ordinary people. But Bunker Hill has done everything for us."

"Mmm. Banks are insured, so the investors wouldn't lose in the long run, but you're right. This is far better, and it won't even inconvenience anyone but Bunker Hill. The officers of that company will be protecting us as diligently as they can — they won't want anyone looking too closely at their insurance rolls. And the people we select will already have some kind of existence. It's too lovely." Barney was almost hopping up and down in his chair. "Now, I'll have to get to work on the search program. What's the number."

Josh gave it to him, and Barney went to work. Data flowed across the screen; it queried him, and he started writing the search program. He entered biographical parameters for the directors of Shadow Research: age, work experience, medical record, psychological profile, marital status, number of children, average income, driver's license, police record, life insurance, blood type, childhood diseases, everything. Once the program was complete, all he had to do was enter the position he wanted to fill, and the computer would search the insurance company's tapes for the appropriate dead person with the requirements. Then the name would be entered as an officer of Shadow Research, Inc. Pete Boggs was the only "real" person on the payroll. He would never know that, of course, since all his communications with other staff would come through computer-written memos.

"I'm going to need a total business program," Barney said as he typed in "President."

"I don't know anything about that."

"I think we can use Intergalactic Orgone computers. They manage a lot of wholly owned subsidiaries. We'll install a central processor in the office in Milpitas and use other companies' memory and subsystems to store and process. All our central processor will do is assign the jobs. Shadow Research will be impossible to trace because it will really be a shadow — parts all over the place. Day-to-day business — entirely spurious, of course — will be handled by Intergalactic through a new subsidiary of theirs we'll invent. They'll write and send all the memos. All we have to do is hire some programmers and put them to work."

The screen winked and beeped and spit up a name: "Luther Hadley McWhirter." The biographical data looked fine, so Barney signaled the "accept" code, thinking dimly that the name was familiar.

"Same name as the clinic," Josh commented.

"Oh." Barney dismissed it, the Luther Hadley McWhirter Memorial Generator at the Stanford Linear Accelerator, and the Luther Hadley McWhirter Memorial Life Insurance Bonus — all almost a year in the past for him, buried in memory. Barney would regret forgetting.

He proceeded with the selection until he had the entire board of directors. Then he phoned the names to Pete for forwarding to Prue.

By Monday, Shadow Research, Incorporated, was a fully functioning company, doing seventeen million dollars' worth of completely fictional business a year.

It was still raining.

17

Hadley Grimm draped his short, plump arm around Barney's shoulders. Barney could see highlights gleam off his elegantly manicured nails where the hand rested beside his ear. Hadley was an instant intimate.

"Mr. Gamesh," Hadley was saying, "you are welcome to my humble home. Most welcome." He urged Barney across the marble foyer toward the sun room. A marble staircase spiraled up, aided in its lift by a long series of original artworks — Keanes, Mexican señoritas on black velvet, expensive landscapes by retired naval officers.

"Thank you, Mr. Grimm," Barney said, lost for a moment in the huge, exophthalmic eyes of a Keane halfway up the stairs. Somehow it reminded him of Penny, that wide gaze.

Barney regarded the home as anything but humble. Narrow Gothic windows rose two stories beneath the stairs, the small leaded panes running with rain. Marble spread before him, a black and white checkerboard meadow. Every inch of wall space was covered with the tacky but expensive paintings. They looked just fine to Barney, though.

And Hadley Grimm was the best. "I checked you out, my boy. I checked you out even before you called me. It's very important to be thorough in these matters. It helps with the contact, you know. Yes, Yes." He prodded Barney through the enormous double doors into the sun room.

Hadley was a medium; his clientele was the most discriminating in the world, and Hadley had a solid reputation. He really could talk to the dead.

"What did your check reveal, Mr. Grimm?"

"Why, you are bereaved; you are a scientist. And I welcome scientific investigation, Mr. Gamesh, believe me. You have, or had, some vague connections with the government. Not too surprising in light of your profession . . ." Hadley waved his small hand, dismissing Barney's government ties. "What is of interest to me is your bereavement, your loss. People come to me in such times of loss. I hope I am not being presumptuous in assuming that that is your reason for coming to me?"

"As a matter of fact —"

"Ah! You're going to dissemble. Quite all right. But I have an instinct for things like this, my boy. Quite an instinct." His voice reeked of duplicity.

"As a matter of fact," Barney went on, "that was part of the reason."

Hadley Grimm smiled encouragingly, his hand now resting gently on Barney's arm. They were standing in the center of the sun room surrounded on three sides by floor-to-ceiling windows, windows that only a few days before had looked out on a sparkling sweep of lawn, garden, Japanese maples, oleander and rhododendron hedges but that today was displaying only a blur of rain-smear.

"Only part, you say? Well, well. And what may the other part be?" Hadley beamed.

"I do want you to get in touch with my wife; but you were recommended by a company called Shadow Research. I wondered if you had heard from them?"

Hadley Grimm pursed his small mouth into a bow. "What makes you suspect I might have heard from them?"

"They investigate death, I understand."

"As a matter of fact, I did receive a communication from them." Hadley visibly relaxed, taking Barney into his confidence. "This communication told me to expect you. I must say, my curiosity was piqued. Mmm, piqued. So I checked you out, as I said, before you called me. And what is it exactly you'd like me to do?"

"I was hoping you could tell me what you can do. This is, you must understand, a bit new to me — this spiritual stuff."

"Of course. You are a scientist, Mr. Gamesh. Interested in hard fact, not the vague arena of the spirit world. Quite. It is indeed possible for me to help you if you want to get in touch with your late wife. It was your wife, wasn't it? I thought so. I have been of service in this area in the past; it is in the nature of my business to provide this service. I can do it. Sometimes. But it is unusual for an agency, a company at that, to recommend me. Usually I am recommended by former clients. I am discriminating in whom I serve. I have expenses, Mr. Gamesh. My clients — and I do hate to be crass, but these are, I'm afraid, the necessities of life — my clients must pay for my services. What I do is very difficult. Few people can do it. It is very much in demand. I am not in the charity business, Mr. Gamesh. No. It is, as they say, a seller's market. I am, in a word, expensive. I am expensive because I am the best. My profession requires a great deal of, shall I say, ectoplasmic *enthusiasm*. It is very draining."

"Please, Mr. Grimm," Barney put out his hand to fend off a speech. "No need for jargon. I am, as you said, a scientist. And I know you are the best. Shadow Research said so. But I don't exactly want to get in *touch* with my wife; not to just talk to, that is. No, I don't want to merely talk to her at all."

"What exactly is it you want, then, Mr. Gamesh?" None of Hadley's urbane manner faltered, but there was a noticeable coolness, a vagrant breeze imparting the slightest hint of distance to his tone.

"I want her back. Shadow Research told me there were several avenues of approach open to me. You are one of them. Shadow Research, I understand, is a nonprofit tax-deductible research organization investigating death. You were recommended by them as an expert in death. Or after-death. So here I am."

"Ah! Well, that explains it, then." Hadley was warm again, and from the warmth his voice emerged, concerned, paternal, reassuring and soothing.

"Let me show you around, Barney," he said, sliding his plump arm around Barney's shoulders again. "This house was built almost a hundred years ago. It has ten-foot ceilings and thirty-seven rooms. Eight bedrooms. Six baths. A gatehouse, gardener's cottage. Stables, unused now, alas." He gently urged Barney from room to room, dining room, bar, sunken living room fifty feet long, greenhouse, and back, at last, to the sun room. "You must understand," he went on, after they settled into a purple wicker settee, "that it costs a great deal to maintain a place like this. A great deal. The heating costs alone, you wouldn't believe. So you see, I cannot afford to give my services away. Not like the nonprofit, tax-deductible research outfit you mentioned. As I said, I am exclusive. I do not maintain my standard of living — and this counts as overhead, you understand, since my clients come here — by giving anything away." He beamed at Barney, radiating good fellowship, camaraderie, sincerity.

Hadley was just one of the stones Barney was not leaving unturned, but at the moment he thought he had found something unpleasant under it: Hadley Grimm seemed like a grub, a complete phony. But he said, "Shadow Research, in the interests of their investigation, has told me that they will support me in this. You are to send them the bill. Surely they mentioned that?"

"Ah, yes. They did. But who are they? I ran a credit check on them, naturally —"

"Naturally," Barney murmured.

"— and could find nothing on them. They are too new to have paid any bills yet, although they do seem to have assets. They *seem* quite respectable and aboveboard, but until they have established a line of credit there is no way to know if they will pay or not."

Details, Barney thought. I should have anticipated credit. "How can I reassure you, Mr. Grimm?"

"Perhaps" — Hadley tented his pudgy fingers, a fence made of breadsticks — "perhaps you could give me some assurance, based on your personal assets —"

"I understand," Barney said. "You have my word your bill will be paid."

"Wonderful!" Mr. Grimm leaped to his feet. "Well, then, shall we get started? We can at least begin to try to contact your wife. About getting her back, well, I don't know . . ."

He led Barney to a room he had not seen before, a room filled with Victorian apparatus of the "spiritual sciences," as Hadley referred to his profession.

The spiritual sciences seemed to consist of just as much movie hokum as Barney expected them to be: dim lighting, candles, mist in the air. Hadley sank down in his chair, his eyelids fluttering, and went into a trance. In a hollow voice he requested the presence of Penny's spirit.

She did not, however, respond to Mr. Grimm's ectoplasmic enthusiasm. No trumpets, no tables knocking, no visible manifestations of the Beyond, no strange winds. Nothing. The ether remained stubbornly silent.

"You must understand," he told Barney after they left the room, "these techniques are the most elementary, the most commonplace and ordinary. In view of your rather extraordinary goal, we really cannot expect them to work immediately. I shall have to meditate on this problem. Please come back tomorrow, say, at three?"

"I wonder if you would mind if I brought along some equipment? And a technician?"

"Why, not at all, my boy, not at all. You are thinking I am a charlatan, a phony. You are thinking I have gotten rich off the credulity of others, of those in a bereaved and vulnerable position. You are thinking, because nothing happened in there, that I am a con artist. No, no, quite all right." Hadley held up his hand to stop Barney's protest, his confidence unshaken. "I assure you nothing could be farther from the truth. I have a real talent, but it cannot be forced. You will simply have to see for yourself, won't you. Good day, my boy. Until tomorrow."

Barney found two letters waiting in his mailbox. The first was from Shadow Research. He opened it just inside the door.

Outside, the rain was falling in gentle loops and swayings, a soft, misty curtain blocking the street. Barney's refurbished Silver Sword stood at the curb, carefully braked, wheels turned in, to prevent another runaway into Mrs. Bunyon's picture window, still boarded over with a plywood sheet.

"Dear Dr. Gamesh," the letter read. "I know what you are up to. You can't get away with it. Yours sincerely, Luther Hadley McWhirter."

"Josh," Barney shouted. "Come here a minute, will you."

Josh emerged from the bedroom trailing the smell of hot solder; he carried a fistful of alligator clips and a pair of needlenose pliers. "What is it?"

"Take a look at this letter, will you?"

While he waited for Josh to read it, he opened the other one. It was a check for $500. The note read: "Here is your Luther Hadley McWhirter Memorial Life Insurance Bonus. Hope you enjoy spending it. Your agent, Willy Apple."

"My God," Barney breathed.

Josh said, "Luther Hadley McWhirter. He's the president of Shadow, isn't he? Of course. And remember, he's the guy Dr. Schmidlapp tried to do the head transplant on."

"I don't remember that, but the name was familiar."

"Well, that's right. It's been over a year for you. What are we going to do?"

Worry lines had formed between Barney's eyebrows. "I don't know. The computer threw up his name and we punched him in as president. Didn't seem anything wrong with that. But where's this letter coming from?"

"I don't know. I sure didn't send it. Nothing in the program should be sending letters like this. This thing's only been going two weeks."

The phone rang. "Yeah?" Barney answered.

"Hiya, Barn, Pete Boggs here. Listen, I need to ask you something. I received a couple of memos from Shadow Research, and I'm a bit puzzled."

"What's the matter, Pete?" An acid uh-oh sank in Barney's stomach.

"Well, one of them is from a Wilbur Scaggs, the comptroller. He accuses me of padding my expense account. Now Barn, I swear I didn't pad my expense account. Oh, I rounded it off, you know, to make it easier. But that's not really padding, you know." Pete's tan voice sounded pale, as if it had spent a month in the basement. "It was only a couple of lunches anyway."

"I'll look into it, Pete. What else?"

"This memo. I'll read it to you: 'In order to maximize our potential and define optimum parameters of operation it will be necessary to develop a flow-through information integration for goal-oriented synthesization. This should improve the overall production picture and finalize henceforward developmental plans with an eye toward general favorable annual economic implementation. In other words, Boggs, let's get in there and land the Big One.' It's signed by Luther Hadley McWhirter. Now I went to morticians' school on a McWhirter scholarship, and he always used to talk about landing the Big One, and I guess it makes sense that he would be involved with a research company that investigates death, but I thought he was dead. I went to school on a McWhirter *Memorial* scholarship."

"Uh-oh," Barney said aloud.

"What's that, Barn?"

"Nothing, Pete. McWhirter can't be dead if he's president of the company, now can he?"

"I guess not, Barney. I guess not."

"We got a problem," Barney warned Josh after he hung up.

"I had a thought," Josh said. "We've routed a number of fairly elaborate computer circuits together through our central processor. I mean, the phone company, three banks, a huge insurance company, four major computer companies themselves, NORAD and CIA and other government agencies, all tied together; even the Intergalactic Very Large Scale Integration banks. That's an enormously complex structure."

"I think I see what you're driving at. This could be a computer simulation; our business programs could just be inventing business. But why is this letter to me threatening? That's the question. Look: 'I know what you're up to. You can't get away with it.' What does that mean?"

Josh was stumped for an answer.

Tiglash Apsu drove his taxi through the gentle misty rain taking a fare to Cupertino, but the passenger, a neat, elderly man with smooth pudgy hands, was annoyed because the rain kept blowing in on him through the broken window of the driver's door. Mopping a round pink face with a scented handkerchief, he thought: This would be the day the Rolls breaks down.

Tiglash drove through a rain of his very own, a sad, dismal, funereal rain that fell straight from a featureless sky into the oblong hole in the ground at his feet. Tiglash could smell the thick, viscous mud at the bottom of the hole. It gave him immeasurable pleasure.

He was in love. It was a vague, unsatisfactory kind of love, a subliminal yearning, an erotic itch somewhere between the slick seat of his taxi and the hard plastic of the steering wheel. But he knew it was love. When he lay down on his bed at the Killborne Hotel and watched the green neon light his walls and ceiling, he knew it was love. When he drove his bright yellow taxi through the light rain, he knew it was love. When he ate his gray, unappetizing, cafeteria meals he knew it was love.

He was in love with the woman his fare the other week had killed with a sword. Whoever she was. Love at first hearing, that was. Tiglash Apsu knew. He was looking for her. He was going to find her.

His erotic itch had almost been satisfied, once. When he put his bald bullet head through his taxi window. Almost.

His fare was talking. "Huh?" he asked.

"I said, 'Either close that window or let me out.' It's very damp back here and I'm catching a cold."

"Window don't close. Broke."

"Then hurry or get me another cab. Use your radio or something."

"Don't got radio."

They drove on through the rain, the fare fretting, past the Sunnyvale Police Department, where Sergeant Masterbrook sorted through his papers, trying to find all the tickets he had written over the past two months. The copies were on his desk, but the computer had no record. Sergeant Masterbrook scratched his head.

In Cupertino, Tiglash dropped his fare in front of a large Victorian house in the oldest part of town.

The neat, pudgy man scurried through the rain to the front door, which gave before his touch, opening into a foyer with an umbrella stand.

"Hello," he called.

"Ah, Mr. Grimm, come in. I've been expecting you," a voice responded from the sitting room to the left, an oily, smooth, lubricious voice.

Hadley Grimm sniffed. The air positively reeked of ectoplasmic enthusiasms: the house was full of ghosts.

The sitting room was a back-lot version of Victoriana: overstuffed horsehair chairs, a love seat, a hissing gas fire, a welter and confusion of bric-a-brac and knickknacks, memorabilia, marble statuettes, heavily framed photographs of starched women and bearded men, tassels, fringes, lace doilies and antimacassars, Tiffany lamps, heavy drapes, and an acrid haze of fusty dust everywhere.

Except for the furniture, though, the room was empty. "Come in, Mr. Grimm," the fat voice said.

"To whom am I speaking?"

"Ah, Hadley, you don't recognize my voice? I'm your cousin Luther, of course."

"Cousin Luther? Don't be silly . . ."

"There, there, Hadley. It is I, Luther Hadley McWhirter. Your cousin."

"Nonsense. Luther's been dead for six years. Since the unsuccessful head transplant."

"Well, that could be why you can't see me, Hadley. But what you say is interesting. Most interesting indeed. The head transplant — so I tried that, did I?"

Hadley was peering around the room. After all, he was an expert in this sort of thing. Where were the hidden speakers, the machinery to move the tables, to make the air fill with mist and light?

Ah, over there, behind the photograph of, yes, Grandfather Hadley in a wing collar and a righteous frown. Yes.

"You are looking for the hidden speakers, aren't you, Hadley? You will find the speaker ov ‑ behind the photograph of Grandfather Hadley. But this is no trick, Hadley. It is really I, Luther. I've summoned you here because I have a small problem." The violet-scented voice chuckled urbanely. "A small problem."

Hadley checked behind the photograph and glared at the speaker. A quite ordinary affair, not at all concealed. Housed in a carved wooden box, possibly Indian.

"Where are you, really?" Hadley followed the speaker

wire down to the baseboard, where it connected to an ordinary if somewhat old-fashioned telephone jack.

"Ah, a number of places at once, Hadley. All over the place in fact. I have access to machines, telephones, hardcopy printers, vocal reconstruction devices. A quite remarkable sensation, I don't mind telling you. Not at all." A thin layer of phlegm formed over the voice as it chuckled once more.

The air was crackling with etheric emanations. "Luther, you're dead. How did you get access to all this stuff?"

The chuckle stopped. "I don't feel dead," the voice said petulantly. "Really I don't."

"I planted you myself, Luther. Six years ago. Your body gave out on all fronts at once, as it were: heart, arteries, liver, lungs. Dr. Schmidlapp made medical history trying to put your head on another body."

"Or another body under my head, eh, Hadley? Hee-hee."

"Mmm." Hadley couldn't find any more evidence of trickery, so he sat on the love seat and folded his neat hands in his lap, waiting.

"Enough of this chitchat, Hadley," the voice said sternly. "Let us get down to business, eh? I am apparently president of a company called Shadow Research. I have a staff of twenty-five life programmers in Milpitas, people with bodies. The board of the company is made up of people like myself: dead people. Wilbur Scaggs, for example, of Los Angeles. Been dead for fourteen years. Boating accident. Public relations man named Haig Despot, a former CB radio salesman, electrocuted."

"I've been contacted by Shadow Research, too. This morning."

"I know, Hadley. I contacted you."

"Not just that. A man was sent to me by the name of Gamesh. He wants his wife back."

"Ah." There was a long, thoughtful silence from the

speaker, a quiet electronic hum that sounded exactly like pursed lips. "Some things are becoming a bit more clear, Hadley. A bit more clear." The voice was smiling an oily smile.

"For instance?"

"For instance, I have no memory of dying. For a time it felt like a hospital — I couldn't see, couldn't hear, couldn't feel a thing. Then I started getting orders."

"Orders? That's very interesting, Luther." Hadley took a small leatherbound notebook from his jacket pocket and jotted notes with a gold pencil. "What kind of orders?"

"Send a memo here, write a letter there. Have money transferred from this place to that and back again. Things like that. I found I could do all those things, and more. It was a remarkable sensation, very odd. I believe I am inside some kind of computer, Hadley."

"What?"

"I said, 'I seem to be inside some kind of . . .'"

"OK, Luther, or whoever you are, this has gone far enough. Who is this?"

"Oh, this is Luther, Hadley, you may rest assured of that." The chuckle rollicked from the speaker, a cascade of phlegm. "The interesting thing is that the orders come from a Barney Gamesh."

"Ah!"

"It seems, Hadley, that you have been on the wrong track all these years. People don't die, they go into some kind of computer. Get it?"

"Frankly, no." Hadley jotted a few more notes before putting his book away. "But perhaps this Gamesh situation could be lucrative, if what you say is true. She is quite dead, I understand. She isn't in there with you, is she? No, I thought not. But if we can re-create her, get her back the way you are, this could be quite profitable for me, us."

"Money doesn't mean much to me in here, Hadley. I have

access to millions, billions, even. I think, Hadley, that this time I have really landed the Big One. And it is giving me ideas."

"Oh?"

"Oh, yes, wonderful ideas." The chuckle dribbled to itself as Hadley let himself out.

"We could make millions." A. Spencer Sparling was lounging in his penthouse living room atop Russian Hill in San Francisco. "What do you think about that, Snow, baby? We could make millions. You want to make millions, don't you?"

"Sure, Spence, if you do." Snow was in the middle of her Tibetan Rhamba-Bhuku meditation exercises in front of the glass wall. Crippled firefly traffic crawled through the streets below, forming a carpet of lights to the bay. The rain had let up for a time, leaving ravaged tatters of cloud hanging just in front of the penthouse windows.

Snow's small round breasts bobbed forward as she bent to clasp her toes, legs straight. They wobbled as she straightened again. Her tight, boyish bottom clenched as she stretched. She preferred to do her Rhamba-Bhuku meditation naked.

"*Dharma-Dhātu,*" she grunted, straightening. Then slowly, and to A. Spencer Sparling, lasciviously, she did the splits, all the way down to the shag carpet. Tightening her thighs and without touching the floor with her hands, she rose to a standing position again. She pivoted and started down again. "Rhamba-Bhuku," she breathed, in through the nose, out through the mouth, uncoiling the cobra of her spine.

"I probably could do it now," Spencer said, watching the slow agonizing progress of his assistant, her round heels dragging through the shag carpet away from her body.

Snow's pale blond shag rug dropped slowly downward,

approaching the golden-white shag on the floor. As the space between them diminished, Spencer squirmed on the couch. "Yup, I think I could even do it now."

Snow's blond-white hair fell forward, hiding her face. She watched, fascinated herself, Rhamba-Bhuku forgotten for the moment, as the two rugs, small and large, moved toward juncture, her gorgeous pubis inching closer. Spencer found himself falling backward off the couch, his head near the floor, trying to watch the progress, his groin twitching. He thought of grazing animals, soft lips moving toward the wheat-colored rug, a fertile field of floor.

As the space narrowed, A. Spencer Sparling's leather-clad body slithered off the vinyl couch and inched, supine, backward toward the narrowing gap. His breath quickened into short, spasmodic rasps, his eyes rolled violently up. He wanted to intercede, to interpose himself between the small blond triangle and the floor. "I. Think. I could do. It. Now." The words ground from his throat like walnuts from a crusher.

"Do what, Spence?" Snow's golden voice was cool, smooth and distracted. Fascinated by her control, she continued to watch the descent of her venereal mountain toward the carpet.

"Have, you know, *more than one!*" Only a foot to go. Spence would have to hurry; he was still four feet away from that closing gap.

"More than one what, Spence?" Another inch vanished, devoured by those soft nibbles at the air.

Spencer's heels scrabbled at the floor, pushing him toward the gap. "Orgasms," he ground out. "We can make. Millions. If. I. Can do it. Aaargh." He made a final, desperate lunge toward the opening, but was a fraction of a second too late for complete success. The bridge of his nose collided with her pubic bone, and she toppled forward onto his leather shirt, her pert round breasts flattened on either side of the line of buttons. Her cheek splashed against the throbbing bulge in his leather pants. "My goodness," she said.

"That was a nasty crack," Spencer said, rubbing the bridge of his nose.

"Oh, Spencer. You have such a mind." She gently unzipped his fly, easing her long, delicate fingers inside, and he flew out, cocked and ready to fire, the fountain of youth, and somewhere down in the basement of his pumphouse the caretaker turned on the spectacular formal fountains of Versailles.

"Wow!" Snow said. "Do you really think you can?" She twirled around, rolling over, and flipped Spencer's still-spouting hose into her firehouse, and with a powerful flick of her Rhamba-Bhuku conditioned hips she crossed her ankles between his shoulder blades, forcing his nose down into the yellow and white shag carpet, where his squinted eyes could discern every fiber. His own hips kept right on twitching, a one-lunger engine generating enough power to send him airborne.

"Uh," he grunted, "huh." Shag rug filled his eyes, his nose, his mouth. "Uh. Huh. Uh-huh. Uh-huh uh-huhuhuhuhuh." And he did. And so did she. Twice.

"We can make millions," he said into the delicate pale whorls of her ear, his curled toes twitching against her lean calves, his short body dry-docked on her long blond grace. "I could package this. Think of it! Multiple Orgasms for Men! Millions!"

"Whatever you say, Spence," Snow responded, uncorking him.

18

Haig Despot waved his fork, drawing ideographs in the air with the small, curled, pink, sauce-drenched shrimp speared on the end of it. "I'm getting ideas about this place," he said.

Penny stared down at her cocktail and didn't answer. She was feeling a multitude of confusions, not the least of which was what, exactly, she was doing here.

Haig popped the shrimp into his mouth and chewed solemnly for a moment. "Ideas," he said again.

"Uh, what kind of ideas?" Penny sighed, picking up her own fork. Might as well eat. Seems a little pointless, though.

"Well," Haig went on between bites. "You know we're dead?"

"Of course I know we're dead!" Penny wondered why Haig seemed to be enjoying his meal so much. "I mean, this Holiday Inn is nothing if not dead!"

"Well then," he said, as if that proved something. "Why do we eat?" He waited for a response, looking at her. When she said nothing, he added, "Why do we sleep?"

Penny made a fretful gesture. "Cripes, I don't know. I wish I did."

"I've been having dreams," he said, and he fell to his shrimp cocktail, finishing it with relish and gusto. Penny felt queasy.

"Breaker, breaker," Penny said softly to herself, thinking, Now I wonder where that comes from?

Haig heard. "Like that, for instance. That 'Breaker, breaker.' I have a memory, or a dream, that I used to say that. Something to do with CB radios. But I keep forgetting things."

"I don't remember. You used to say it? Breaker. I keep forgetting, too." Penny put her fork down. She wasn't hungry.

"How long have we been here?" Haig asked suddenly.

"Been here?" Penny felt vague, stretched across an endless time, suspended in a vat of lemon Jell-O. "I don't know."

"You see!" Haig shouted triumphantly, almost jumping to his feet.

"No," Penny said, "I don't see. What are you talking about?"

He collapsed back in his seat and sniffed, his eyes leaking sudden tears. "Neither do I," he said dolefully. Penny couldn't adjust to these sudden changes.

"Oh, I didn't mean . . ."

"It's all right," he said, holding his hand in front of his mouth in the old microphone gesture. It seemed vaguely familiar to her. "It's all right," he repeated, sobbing violently now. "It's just that I have these dreams, dreams that I'm alive, but dead. That I have a new job, nothing to do with radios, but computers. What do I know about computers? I work for a research company. It's so vivid, so real, in the dreams. More real than this restaurant, that woman." He waved toward the angular yellow woman from the DMV at the entrance to the dining room frowning at the reservations book. Someone was late.

"She doesn't seem very real, does she?" Penny mused, her mind wandering away from her confusion.

Haig brightened, his mouth smiling despite the glistening tear on his sagging cheek. "No, she doesn't. Now why does that make me feel better? Anyway, I bring all this up because it seems to have something to do with you."

"With me? What do you mean?" A thin red edge of alarm sliced through her fog.

"I'm not sure. It's just a feeling. I write press releases for this Shadow Research company. But the dreams, well, they're *fuzzy*. I can't follow them very well. But your name keeps coming through, in and out, like one of those blinking signs. Should I discuss this with someone?"

"Who can you talk to around here?" Penny unfolded her napkin and covered her shrimp cocktail with it. It was less offensive to her that way.

"You're not allowed to do that." A voice grated at her shoulder. The woman from the DMV glared at her. Uh-oh.

"I'm not hungry."

"Doesn't matter. The rules are, you eat. We've had enough trouble around here today. First, McWhirter doesn't show up on time — not at all, in fact — and now this. I won't have it." The bony finger extended toward the white mound of napkin. "Take that off."

"I'll throw up. I don't feel well."

"You can't throw up. You're dead."

"So are you, bitch," Penny shouted, jabbing her fork violently into the white tablecloth.

"Well!" the lady from the DMV sniffed. "I'll speak to the manager about this. I've never seen anything like it. First McWhirter and now —"

"You do that, bitch!" On the last word, Penny stabbed the table again, bending the tines of the fork. DMV left.

"What can they do?" she asked. "They can't make us eat. We're dead."

Haig Despot was smiling, his mouth stretched tight smiling a cheek-splitting smile. His nose was pinched with smile. His eyes were squinted and leaking genuine laughter. Haig Despot guffawed. He tittered and roared. He chuckled and giggled. He dabbed at his teary eyes with the back of his hand and started laughing again, his laugh ascending the scale of pleasure to belly-shaking, knee-clacking, toe-curling helplessness.

"Oh, breaker, breaker," he gasped through his laughter, "That was wonderful!"

Penny found herself smiling too. Then giggling. Then laughing as helplessly as he. She whipped her napkin away from her shrimp cocktail and scooped out a handful of sticky red saucy shrimp. She threw it at Haig.

He grabbed his water glass. "No!" Penny shrieked, strangled with laughs, but he hurled it straight into the air, dousing the Frenchman at the next table, who turned with a laugh and overturned his salad — crisp lettuce, cucumber and sliced green pepper spattering over the tough carpet. He grabbed a double handful of the salad and poured it over his own head, laughing.

The dining room of the Holiday Inn Deathwest collapsed into pandemonium. Steaks sailed serenely through the green and yellow air to splat against the windows overlooking the pool. Custards and ice creams flew to the ceiling and hung there momentarily, dripping. Soup sloshed across the pristine tablecloths and drowned laps. Someone started a song. The Frenchman marched around the room, a baked potato skewered on his knife held aloft, singing *La Marseillaise*. Other national anthems joined in, conflicted, fought, dissolved in laughter.

Standing on her table. Penny shouted, "It's not real. Not real!" She tossed hard-crusted rolls and pats of butter at the milling crowd, into the glorious confusion. "It's not real. We're all dead!"

She performed a short tap dance on the table, then began to sing.

> We're sure you all agree,
> It's a Gilgamesh jubilee
> That our kingly king did decree,
> Our Sunny Vale-by-the-sea.

She kicked and jigged in the muffin litter, laughing, and did not wonder until later where she'd learned that song.

Everyone had a wonderful time. The lady from the DMV did not return. What could she do? They were dead.

"A. Spencer Sparling says death is a rip-off, but of course he's full of it," Barney told Josh. "Death is a lot more complicated than that."

They were in Milpitas, walking between the two rows of programmers' desks toward the central processing room. The office was effectively modern, air-conditioned, decorated in pleasing pastel graphics, filled with indoor plants. Small areas of couches and chairs allowed the employees to socialize and discuss their work. Barney was pleased with the setup.

"Since that letter from McWhirter I believe you're right. It is a bit complicated. After all, he's dead."

"Nothing final about that," Barney said.

"Yes. And he also is inside the computer network."

"It must be something like that — he's in both." Barney pinched his lips together, a fish-mouth gesture. "He's certainly in the computer, but he's also probably at a Holiday Inn somewhere. Or reborn as someone else, if we can believe *The Tibetan Book of the Dead*." He stopped at a desk. "How's it going?" he asked the programmer seated at a terminal.

"Pretty well. We had some difficulty translating the more mystical passages into an appropriate code, but I think we've got that licked now."

"You're doing the Tibetan thing?"

"Egyptian. Thoth is saying, 'The heart of Osiris hath in very truth been weighed, and his soul hath stood witness for him; it hath been found true by trial in the Great Balance.' We're working out the parameters for the Great Balance. It eats up memory like crazy."

"Are you running out?"

"Oh, no. It seems to be unlimited." The programmer turned back to the book and started typing.

"How come we can ask questions like this?" Josh inquired after they moved on. "We're not on the board; don't even work here."

"Oh," Barney explained, "we're clients. Have the run of the place." He pushed open the door to the central processor room. "Let's check up on McWhirter."

The room was spare, the processor rather small, about the size of a suitcase. But a thick cable ran from its back into the floor, a cable that in one way or another connected to the information network in North America and via satellite to private and public computers all over the world. It would take at least ten years to straighten out the mess once Shadow Research pulled out, so deep was this clandestine penetration, so intertwined its program subroutines.

Barney had his private code for access to everything the machine knew. The console at home was too weak and small to handle the complexity of this job.

"Budget?" he asked first.

"677 million dollars," the screen informed him in luminous green characters.

"McWhirter?" Barney typed, and information filled the screen. Biographical data — "See," Barney said. "He was president of something called Thoth Communications. Curiouser and curiouser" — and a minute-by-minute log of his actions since installation as president of Shadow Research.

"I'm sure glad I had this watchdog program built in. Now look at that. Very odd," Barney murmured, pointing to a period late in the previous day. "He ordered a speaker installed in a house in Cupertino. Why?" Barney typed some more, and the display answered. "My God, look at that! He bought the house. He's certainly become independent. I wish we could get the tone of voice . . . unless his conversation was recorded. It *was* recorded, and then erased . . . strange. But we do have a transcription." Barney and Josh read through McWhirter and Grimm's conversation. "Well, it seems Grimm is interested in money. The question is, do we try to fox him or let him continue." He glanced at Josh.

Josh had a wolf-grin. "Let him continue," he said.

"Mmm. I see what you mean. We might have a fall guy here, just in case. Interesting. And McWhirter still seems a bit confused, though it probably won't last long — he's talking about ideas. 'Wonderful ideas,' he says. I wish I knew what ideas he has in mind. The personality profile is identical with that of his material existence. I think he's really alive in there somewhere." He leaned back in the chair, tugging at his lip.

He leaned forward. "I want to clear this up before we start working on Penny directly. Let's put a protect around our own communications with the computer so McWhirter can't get at us again." He went to work.

"There's one thing I don't quite understand," Josh said while they were driving to Hadley Grimm's. The back seat was filled with recording equipment, and a large cloud was heavy and gray above them, though it was not raining. Josh had been humming, "Prue Nisenvy, Prue Nisenvy," under his breath to the tune of the Hallelujah Chorus from Handel's *Messiah*. He broke off to ask his question.

"What's that?"

"Why do you want your wife back? I mean, it sounds as though you didn't really get along very well when she was alive."

"You know, before I went to Sumer I thought I wanted her back because I wanted to apologize, though I wasn't sure quite what for. I guess I felt guilty, responsible. But since I've been in Uruk, well, I want her back because I love her, I guess."

"Oh."

They drove across the bridge, low on the gray bay water, beneath the low gray sky, caught in a sandwich of gray wetness, suspended in a gray view, concealing the urban sprawl. There was nothing in their world but the road, the car, and themselves. Josh hummed his Hallelujah Chorus for a while and stopped again. "This is what I always imagined death was like," he said, pressing his forehead against the wind-shield, staring out at the empty gray.

"It's a Holiday Inn."

"That's what I mean. What time is Grimm expecting us?"

"Three o'clock. We'll make it. Might be a good idea not to mention anything about the link between him and Mc-Whirter. Imagine, they were cousins. There certainly have been a lot of coincidences in my life since Penny died."

"I read somewhere that there is no such thing as coinci-dence," Josh said. "Besides, physics proves there isn't. Ev-erything is connected."

A police car roared past them going the other way. Inside, Sergeant Masterbrook gripped the wheel tightly, his mouth grim. He turned on the siren and flashing light. He was on his way to his cousin in San Leandro, a dentist, who would help relieve this toothache. He didn't notice Barney at the wheel of the Silver Sword.

Barney didn't see him, either. Just another coincidence that failed to connect. The siren sound died away behind them as they rolled down off the bridge into the city. Josh started singing again, the same tune. "Pe-ter Bo-oggs, Peter Bo-oggs, Peter Bo-oggs," he sang. "Pete 'n Prudence, Pete 'n Prudence, Pete 'n Prudence." He waved his hands in the air, conducting an invisible chorus as the Silver Sword swept through the damp streets to Hadley Grimm's house, and Barney smiled at the wheel, liking Josh.

On the Bayshore Freeway they passed a panel truck. On the side, in gilt letters, was printed: SUM — SPARLING UNI-FIED MEDITATION. Underneath that, three capital letters: MOM.

"What do you suppose MOM is?" Barney wondered, glancing over at the driver of the SUM truck.

"Dunno," Josh sang. "Don't know-ow, don't kno-ow . . ." fitting it into the chorus.

"Look." Barney pointed.

WE TAKE THE STING OUT OF DEATH on a huge billboard.

"Pete sure is advertising a lot," Josh observed, pausing in his song. "Seems a little morbid, but I suppose they could say the same thing about what we're doing."

"We take the sting out of death. What do you suppose he means by that?"

Josh grinned his skinny-kid grin, pushing the freckles together on the bridge of his nose. "He means, probably, that he charges so much that the sting of your bill will be bigger than the sting of your grief, and you forget it."

"You could have a point there," Barney laughed.

They swept up Hadley Grimm's spiral drive and stopped under the porte-cochère. The front door swung open as they climbed out of the car, and Hadley Grimm, smiling broadly, his plump hands extended in welcome, met them. "Welcome, welcome," he said. "And this would be your assistant, I trust. A bit young for this kind of thing, don't you think? But never mind, never mind. Today I believe we might be able to do something. Really I do. There's a tang in the ether. Come in, come in."

"Certainly is a genial man, isn't he?" Barney mumbled to Josh as they struggled their equipment from the back of the car.

"Well, well, well, my boy. You've brought a great deal of complex equipment, didn't you? Well. I thought perhaps today we would try a simple trance. Sometimes that works best, especially when some of the more, uh, superficial but shall we say showy techniques haven't worked. You must understand that the expectations of the client have a lot to do with how well they work."

"Right," Barney said briskly to conceal his skepticism. "Ectoplasmic enthusiasm and all that."

"Quite, my boy. Quite." Hadley led them to the sun room and sat tranquilly in a vast wicker chair while they set up their instruments. "What does all this stuff do, I wonder?" he asked guilelessly.

"Most of it is designed to record and detect small variations in a number of radiation spectra," Barney told him, connecting cables to metered boxes. "This device here will telemeter all the data to a computer for analysis, though we may be able to form some preliminary judgments on the spot. Since we're not quite sure what we're looking for, we have detectors to monitor everything we could think of. Most will indicate nothing, of course, but we hope one or two things — EEG, electrical potential, things like that — will show something."

"I see," said Hadley, closing his small, good-humored eyes. "Shall we get started, then?"

"OK." Barney and Josh turned everything on, started the recorders, and waited.

Hadley sank back so the high wings of the wicker chair concealed his face. His back was to the windows, so the damp garden and gray sky surrounded him on three sides. No dim lights, no table-tapping, no ghostly manifestations, no scented candles. Just the three of them, Hadley apparently asleep, Barney and Josh watching meters and dials. Silence filled the room, first merely the absence of sound, then a palpable presence, a tension, a carrier wave of silence. Barney could hear his own breathing, Josh's breathing. He felt he could almost hear his own heart beating time, a beat that pulsed in the old bite scar at the base of his thumb. He remembered the bite, the fever, the metronomic throb, the pulse of his life beating away, lessening, fainter and fainter. He was growing drowsy, but it didn't seem to matter. The computers were listening.

Penny was in the shower at the Holiday Inn Deathwest, washing the ghostly effects of the Great Dining Room Rebellion off her face and hands, out of her hair, enjoying the soap and hot water, the steamy air. She was singing in the shower: "I'm dead, I'm dead, It's off to death I go," she sang. She also sang:

> Oh, it's just you and me
> And the computer fac-to-ry,
> A Gilgamesh jubilee
> Mmm-mmm, Sunnyvale-by-the sea.

"Now I wonder what that song is," she murmured, soaping and lathering her body. At that moment she was feeling beautiful. She did not miss the starched, uncomfortable prison of her life in Sunnyvale.

"Hello," said a voice through the misty shower. "Hello, Penelope Gamesh." The voice came through the hiss of falling water, a voice of soap and lather. "Hello. Hello."

"What?" Penny stopped her singing. She stopped soaping; her hands fell to her sides. She looked around. She opened the shower door and peered out. No one there.

"Hello. Hello. Can you hear me?" A cultivated male voice, nobody she recognized. But warm, grandfatherly, sincere and friendly.

"What? Yes, I can hear. Who is this?" The bathroom, the familiar green and yellow tile, the white towels stacked in chrome-plated clips against the wall. The green writing on the towels, HOLIDAY INN, the glass in its waxy paper bag beside the sink, the paper band over the toilet seat. Everything gleamed. The voice seemed to be behind her, in the shower with her, speaking conversationally in her ear.

"You don't know me," the voice began, then faltered a moment, as if talking to someone with a hand over the telephone mouthpiece. The the voice returned. "You don't know me," he repeated, "but I'm a friend of your husband."

"My husband? What are you talking about? Whew, this place is weird." Penny recalled a husband. A nice college boy, wasn't he?

"Your husband, Barney Gamesh."

"Oh, him. Listen, mister" — Penny put her hands on the

soapy swell of her hips — "I don't know who you are, but you better tell me what this is all about. For instance, where the hell are you?"

"I'm in my sun room. Oh, I see what you mean. I'm on what we call the other side."

"Other side? You mean, not dead? *Alive?*" She rubbed her soapy palms together, suddenly hesitant. She remembered Barney, his open face, his distracted eyes, his casual gestures of affection. She remembered touching him along the line of his jaw. The memory was filled with pain, and she didn't know why. It made her mad.

"That's right, Mrs. Gamesh. Alive. Do you remember being alive."

"That's the dumbest question I've ever heard. Of course I remember being alive! I . . ." Penny's eyes unfocused on the rippled glass of the shower door as a sudden memory surrounded her with tastes and smells, sounds and sights, a memory that had nothing of Sunnyvale in it; instead, it was a tiered, four-story building and blinding sun. She held a child cradled in her arms and nursed it. At her side stood two men, one of them . . . Barney? Her husband, the nice college boy. I've lived before, two lives overlapping. The memory was more vivid suddenly than her life in Sunnyvale, more vivid and more . . . more something she couldn't quite place. More confident?

"Yes, Mrs. Gamesh. I didn't quite catch . . ."

The memory vanished, washed away with the falling water, the warm lather, the sudden tears she felt. "Yes, yes. I was married to Barney," she said, a catch in her throat. "But it seems so long ago. So long . . ."

This is silly, she thought. A hallucination, I'm imagining this, the white light of the *devas,* the dull white light . . .

"This isn't your imagination, Mrs. Gamesh," the voice said. It was clear, this voice. Too clear. And it was reading her mind.

"All right," she said. "What do you want?"

"Not me, Mrs. Gamesh. I don't want anything. It's your husband. *He* wants you." There was a pause, another whispered conversation with the hand over the mouthpiece. The voice returned. "He says he wants you back."

"He *what?*" Penny's neat fists smacked square on the smooth swell of her hips.

"He says he wants you back."

"Well, I . . . I can't quite understand that." She reached out to touch the line of jaw, wavering in her memory there in the mist, and the pain frightened her. She lashed back. "Did he say *why* he wanted me back? Huh? Did he say why?"

The falling water hissed against the white dazzle of the ceramic tub. It swirled cleanly to the chromium drain and circled there. Water beaded on the rippled glass door, on the white tile walls. It pooled in the soap dish, milling whitely with the scented bar of soap. Wreathes of ghostly steam twisted slowly near the ceiling light, dipped toward the mirror over the sink, and adhered. Tiny droplets of water condensed against the cool glass, fogging her image as Penny stepped out of the shower, forgetting to turn it off for the moment. She stood, dripping, on the white Holiday Inn bathmat, staring at the dim outline of her body in the misted mirror, and started in disbelief at the letters spelled out there, as though drawn with a finger, the flesh of her body clear in the glass inside the letters, in the H and the E, the two L's and the round rudimentary face of the O.

"She said, 'Did he say why he wanted me back?' She sounded genuinely puzzled. Angry, even."

"I think I can understand that, Mr. Grimm. I think I can, now. Well, Josh?" Barney shook his head, trying to clear the peculiar fog that had filled his mind, a coastal updraft dense with vapor. He had fallen asleep. For a moment there he could almost hear Penny's voice. "Did we get anything? I seem to have dozed."

Josh was surprised. "Dozed? You answered all Mr. Grimm's questions. Are you OK?"

"I feel . . . No, I'm all right. Did anything happen?"

"All kinds of things were happening. We'll have to see what the computers come up with, but needles were dancing all over the dial."

"You know, Mr. Gamesh." Hadley was pensive. "I had the feeling it was raining there. I've never had that feeling before. Why would it be raining on the other side? Why would they need rain?"

"Look outside," Josh suggested, pointing to the garden through the windows.

It was pouring, a deluge, a torrent, a roar of rain, beating the brilliant green grass, the oleander and philodendron, the maples, the beautiful Japanese maples, whose leaves, turned now in autumn, flashed scarlet and orange in the gray fall of rain.

Hadley clapped his pudgy soft hands together. "It's raining again," he laughed. "Wonderful, isn't it? After all this drought, three weeks of rain. Something to be thankful for, eh, this Thanksgiving week?"

Barney couldn't help smiling too. "Yes," he said, "something to be thankful for."

Hadley turned serious again. "I'm sorry the connection was broken off just then. But now that we've made contact we can probably do it again. And we shall, eh, my boy? We shall."

Barney and Josh drove back through the rain, both silent as the Silver Sword hissed through the rain-slick streets. The hills, brown and bare for so long, were green now, visible through the gaps in the low clouds hanging down across them like a paternal arm, hugging them to life. Emerald green.

"It's so different from the Midwest," Barney mused, glancing at the hills. "In the Midwest the autumn is the time when everything turns brown after the summer green. It's the opposite here: Everything gets green and lush in November. There's something backward about California, Josh."

"You can say that again," Josh responded, grinning.

"OK," A. Spencer Sparling said. "Let's do it again." The technician readjusted his connections, flicked on his electromyograph and EEG, and ran a test.

"Everything's working fine now, Mr. Sparling," he reported. "We're ready to go again."

"Let me hear the tone once more."

The technician adjusted a rheostat and a pure middle C 128-cycle tone pulsed through the room.

"Right," Spence said. "OK, Snow, baby, let's get it on."

Snow, lying naked on the bed, reading a back issue of *Psychology Today,* glanced over at Spencer, also naked, trailing wires from forehead, navel, buttocks and the base of his tumescent member. She yawned and closed the magazine. "All in the interest of science, eh, Spence?" she said, giving her fine pale hair a shake that sent it cascading around her face, a swift wind across late wheat.

"And in the interest of money, Snow, baby. Science and money. That's where it's at." He bobbed toward her, swinging his small but shapely erection from side to side, trailing wires. Snow's hand reached out to stop the swinging, closed warmly around the length and tugged gently, easing Spencer's short, neat form on top of her languid and graceful form.

The technician started his EMG and EEG machines and the paper rolled smoothly beneath the pens, tracing the graph of Spencer's excitement. Paper poured from the end and piled on the floor, twelve wriggly lines on each inked darkly along the paper. The needles jumped sharply as Snow eased Spencer into her and he began a steady thrusting, looking the while over her shoulder at his watch, set now on stopwatch mode, electronically ticking off one-tenth-second intervals.

She mused about the article in *Psychology Today:* "The Masochist's Way to Mental Health." Dimly she was aware of Spencer's steady ins and outs, his panting breath at her ear, his glinting eyes. The dimness throbbed, in and out of clarity, an answering warmth in her groin, a rash on the insides of her long pale thighs as she began to work back and forth in response.

She forgot about *Psychology Today.* For the moment. A balloon full of warm milk broke in her lower abdomen and Spence's breath rasped in her ear.

"That's one!" he shouted, increasing the tempo of his movements. The middle C was beeping endlessly in the background, *beep, beep, beep* . . . Thump, thump, thump, his pelvis bammed against hers, and another balloon broke. Waves of warmth coruscated up and down her delicately boned spine. "My. Goodness," she gasped demurely, eyes closed.

"Two!" Spencer suddenly shouted, with no break in either rhythm or the beeping of middle C. "Three! . . . Four! . . . Five!"

He jumped to his feet, dripping and dropping at once, and jogged back to the console where the technician was pulling the heaps of paper from the floor, tracing the peaks of the graph.

"Seven minutes and twenty seconds," he said, pointing to his watch. "And three tenths. Five orgasms! Five *male* orgasms, do you hear?" He was almost shouting in the technician's ear. "Multiple Orgasms for Men is a reality! MOM is real!"

"Spence," Snow called plaintively, "I'm not finished yet!"

19

Irving Gowanda, owner of Del's Quarter-Hour Cinderella Car Wash, a completely automated, computerized 200 yards of brushes and rollers, sudsers and buffers, scrubbers, waxers, blowers and sensors, was eating a Delmonico steak sandwich from the Louis Quatorze Hamburger Castle down the block when Barney and Josh drove in for a wash.

It was mid-December, and it had been raining off and on since the beginning of November. The drought was officially over; greater than average rainfall had soaked the West, a mixed blessing as flooding had drowned much of Washington, Oregon, the central valley of California, parts of Colorado, Idaho and Utah. Only Nevada remained relatively dry, though flash floods had carried away a famous brothel near Reno, taking with it all the women, twelve customers and the piano player. The trailers that had housed the establishment were located four days later about 120 miles south, rocking to the most exuberant party the converted mobile homes had ever seen. The sheriff was later quoted as saying that it was "hell on wheels."

"But why are we having the car washed now?" Josh wanted to know as Barney steered the Silver Sword up to the lead-free pump.

"Tell you later," Barney said. Irving Gowanda scarcely looked up from his steak sandwich. Except for the pumps, the fifteen-minute car wash was entirely self-governed. There was never any trouble. Once the front tires had been grabbed by the pullers there was nothing for a human to do until a sparkling automobile rolled out the other end.

Once gassed, Barney settled back in his seat, prepared to enjoy the ride. It was not raining at the moment, although large round biscuits of cumulus floated through a crisp winter-blue gravy of sky. The car moved toward the yawning tunnel of the building, and large black and white roller brushes opened wide to receive it. Josh shuddered, thinking, oddly, of Prue Nisenvy, still hounding them both. The Silver Sword glided in and the brushes closed around it, top and bottom, munching.

"Why are we washing the car?" Josh asked again as soapy film fell like a curtain down the windshield.

"We're being followed," Barney said, frowning. "Two cars behind us. Junior Arkwright's car, that lavender sedan. He's got someone with him. This is the only place I could think of where we couldn't be eavesdropped on. In case I'm being bugged." He was right. The noise was deafening.

"Are you sure he's following us?" Josh had never been able to take Junior seriously.

"No. But there are things we've got to talk about anyway. For instance, I received a call from Prue. It seems McWhirter is attempting to blackmail us, and Prue has sensed something is up, though I don't think she has any clear idea yet."

"McWhirter! I thought he was taken care of. And he's dead, after all."

"Yeah, he's dead all right. But that hasn't stopped him. I tried building a trap for him in the program, a place where he'd fall through and disappear. I even had a fictitious death worked out for him. But he spotted it and stayed away; he's damn smart. Now he's threatening to send a letter to the newspapers."

"But what could he want? I mean, there can't be much we can give him. He doesn't exist." Josh worried at his front teeth with his fingernail. Outside, the huge brushes swept their way down the back of the car. Ahead, two more, side brushes, began to whir.

"That's precisely the problem. He seems to have developed something of a grudge. Apparently, he intends to be mean."

"A grudge about what?"

"Well, for one thing, we're alive and he's not."

"So?"

"Anybody willing to attempt a head transplant in order to stay alive has got to have a strong will to live."

"I guess. That was Dr. Schmidlapp, wasn't it? Some people! But can't we program him out somehow? After all, we control the computer, don't we?"

"Not exactly, anymore. It's begun to self-program. I discovered this morning that it has tapped, by itself, into three major medical center computers. McWhirter has developed an interest in the medical aspects of death. Prue told me, and I don't blame her for sounding puzzled, that McWhirter is searching for a body. He plans to come back, with a body."

"Whew!" Josh breathed.

Two cars behind, just entering the building, Junior Arkwright's lavender sedan was bitten by the two upper and lower brushes. As darkness descended on the car, he and Miss MacHunt clambered into the back seat, where, by the dome light, she provocatively removed her shoes. Junior was panting loudly, loud enough to be heard over the din of the car wash, through his lumpy nose, and when the toes of her right foot sprang free of the shoe, he plunged that organ between them, inhaling deeply. "Whew!" he exclaimed, tongue nudging out to caress her sole.

Irving Gowanda finished his Delmonico steak sandwich and crumbled the remains in the Louis Quatorze Hamburger Castle wrapper. He threw the wadded paper and plastic into his trashcan and went outside to watch the stream of cars in his car wash. He knew that no one entering his building was really coming to get his car washed. Not on a day like this, with more rain threatening. No one would be here at all if his car wash didn't last fifteen minutes. Long enough, he was thinking, for a couple to enjoy themselves if they hurried. He felt that the gods had given him this idea, for the car wash was replacing the drive-in movie in the busy culture of California — it took less time, was completely private, and folks could go during the day. Lunch, say. Irving Gowanda smiled. He often smiled these days. He would soon stop smiling.

"It's funny," Barney was saying. "I asked the computer outright how much memory it could access now. It said, 'None of your business.' I had to sneak the request in through another subroutine. Frankly, I'm growing nervous."

"How much memory does it have?"

"Twenty-seven times ten to the fifteenth power bytes. That's twenty-seven mega-giga bytes. Several thousand orders of magnitude greater than anything ever assembled before. It's no wonder it's getting out of control. I don't have any idea anymore how many computers McWhirter has gotten into. Why, he could even have control of this car wash, for all I know."

"Ha-ha," Josh laughed.

Irving Gowanda heard the first premonitory rasp as he turned toward his office. A few fat drops of rain had begun to spatter the blacktop among the pumps. A drop trembled at that moment from his upper lip, and his hand rose halfway to his mouth to wipe it away. Distracted in this way, he was scarcely aware of the sound, a faint, unpleasant grating sound inside his building. Shrugging uneasily, he wiped the drop from his lip and went inside.

Junior, in the back of the sedan, didn't notice a thing. Not at first. He was curled awkwardly under Miss MacHunt, her delicate metatarsal arches cupped around his cheeks. She was leaning back, presenting his feebly stabbing member with her glistening mound all asmile. Junior heard nothing but the roar of blood in his ears as he successfully navigated into Miss MacHunt's drowsy harbor. Her feet writhed on his cheeks and she cried out.

Barney heard the ominous rasp, however; it was the sound of his right front fender being forcibly peeled away from the Silver Sword's body as a rubber roller moved fractionally out of position. The fender wound around the roller like a window shade, so as the car moved on past the defective roller, a long strip of Detroit steel peeled away.

"What the hell . . ." Barney exclaimed.

He barely got the words out of his mouth before the left front fender began to wrap around the roller on that side, metal rent away from his Silver Sword, rivets popping, bolts shearing with tiny pinging sounds as the small metal parts flew into the bowels of the vast machine.

"You don't suppose McWhirter *is* into this computer, do you?" Josh asked, ducking as the side mirror was snapped off by a waxing brush. Barney's reply was swallowed by the sounds of the front bumper being devoured by the brushes in front. The chrome pulled loose, and was unreeled over the hood of the car, dragging the grille along with it. The scarping din of metal dragging over the hood and up the windshield was awful, a high-pitched fingernail-on-blackboard screech. The sheared bolts from the front bumper etched deep lines vertically up the windshield. Then the bumper rattled away over the top.

"Something's gone wrong!" Irving Gowanda shouted at the sullen teen-ager manning the pumps. "Do something, for the sweet Reverend Moon's sake!"

"Huh?" said the teen-ager. "Do what? I don't know nothing about that thing." He pointed a stubby, well-chewed finger at the vast building, from the aluminum vents of which small tendrils of smoke were beginning to emerge.

"Turn it off!" Irving shouted.

"Oh," the boy answered. He trotted into the glass shack and flipped a switch.

Nothing happened.

Then a terrific screeching sound came from the building, muffled by brushes and distance.

"Turn it off again!" Irving shouted, dancing back and forth in the gradually increasing rainfall.

The boy flicked the switch two or three times, but nothing stopped the awful sounds from the car wash as it munched its way through the seven automobiles inside.

Junior Arkwright and Miss MacHunt united in an extravagant mutual orgasm of sudsy water and dripping wax-rinse as the roof of the lavender sedan was ripped suddenly away. By the time the car rolled out of the wash their clothes were soggy and they were laughing hysterically.

"I haven't had anything like that in my whole life, ever," she gasped, clutching at his dripping red-checked lapels, collapsing with the laughter of relief and satiation.

Barney and Josh walked around the remains of the Silver Sword. Three of the tires were chewed to ribbons, a black plasma goo running from the shreds. Three of the doors were wrinkled, as if not simply metal fatigue but perhaps some kind of metal *senility* had set in. The fourth door was completely gone, as was the roof, trunk lid, hood and hubcaps, chewed to filings by the rapacious machine. The distributor had been ripped out, dragging the air filter with it. Both parts had landed in the back seat trailing wires.

The radiator was bent into a V, and hot coolant sizzled out of the crease in spurts. Oil pooled under the corpse of the Silver Sword.

"This car is ruined," Josh said, a strange smile twitching at the corners of his mouth. The rain was falling on his head, plastering his hair around his ears and eyes, giving him a curiously elfin look.

Barney kicked one of the doors, and it fell off so suddenly he had to dance backward to get out of the way. "I think you're right. We'd better call a cab."

Irving Gowanda was pulling hard at a clump of his hair. "I'll get sued to oblivion for this," he wailed. The Delmonico steak sandwich was turning rancid in his stomach.

Fire trucks arrived, ready to add more water to the now crackling car wash, and somewhere in the acres of silicon chips around the world Luther Hadley McWhirter was silently laughing. Haig Despot, composing press releases for Shadow Research, a shadowy figment himself, might have considered that laugh a bit nasty, but he said nothing to Luther Hadley McWhirter. McWhirter was in a position to pull the plug, and, vague as his existence was, Haig did not want to have his plug pulled.

Barney and Josh watched the firemen pump steady volumes of water on the blaze until their taxi arrived. Tiglash Apsu was seated stolidly at the wheel, his window fixed. But his head was more awry than ever.

He'd taken to skulking around the Boggs and Boggs facilities. We take the sting out of death. Little bees buzzing. Bzzz, bzzz. Wheee.

Pete Boggs was growing a little desperate. Prue was slipping away from him, and although business was going especially well this year — the flu season having been the most promising since 1917–18, his crematorium being fully automated and computerized, providing a broader profit margin, reduced labor costs and full-time production — still, he was troubled by Prue's gradual cooling.

So he had enrolled in A. Spencer Sparling's new, also computerized, biofeedback MOM training. He had his own body hooked up to wires and electronically monitored — the starfish pulsing of his anus, the twitchings of eschio and bulbo-cavernosus muscles, the crackle of dendrites whispering electrochemical messages from brain to spine to penis and back.

Prue found the whole thing delightful and wonderful for a time. It was totally humiliating to Pete, who for once, reaching for the thin gold chains around his neck, found no comfort there.

"Ha-ha," she laughed, multiple wrinkles radiating away from her grating rasp. "Ha-ha." She would point, and Pete would wilt, and they'd have to start again.

"I'm doing this for you," he complained as she worked him up again between her leathery palms. She laughed. "Ha-ha."

It was a long, hot weekend, but finally Pete achieved four better-than-average orgasms inside the arbitrary seven-minute limit.

"See," he said, touching the inky peaks on the rolls of EMG and EEG printout paper. "Four."

"So?"

"So, that's better than one, isn't it?"

"Mmm. I wouldn't know, actually," said Prue. "I'm not you. Let's take another look at that tort."

All this electronic monitoring flashed through the wires and radio relays to silicon chips resting in medical center memory banks, and Luther Hadley McWhirter, president of Shadow Research, former head of Thoth Communications, philanthropist and benefactor of humankind, chuckled to himself. "Landed the Big One, eh, Haig?" He flashed electrons through flipflop gates to his PR man. It was a rancid chuckle that bothered Haig a lot. "Yes, sir," Haig replied.

But Haig sent Barney a letter, printed out on his CRT screen at home. It was there when Tiglash Apsu dropped the two off at 34½ Puerco de Esmeralda Lane.

"Look here," Barney said after they shed their umbrellas and raincoats at the front door.

"Mr. Gamesh," it said. "I feel compelled to warn you. McWhirter is becoming a bit mad. Fragments of program come through my circuits from time to time. He laughs all the time and plots awful things. I'm worried."

"That's not really news, is it?" Josh asked. "I mean, he's almost certainly responsible for the car wash incident, isn't he?"

"Mmm," Barney replied, reading: "He's withholding information from you. Certain connections are being made, certain results coming up. Things I don't understand; only fragments come through my sector. They have a lot to do with sex. A. Spencer Sparling's name keeps popping up. He used to be my partner in the CB radio business. And Hadley Grimm. I don't know him. I have a very bad feeling. Haig Despot."

"Who's Haig Despot?" Josh asked.

"Let's see, he's our PR man, as I recall." Barney frowned. "That's not what concerns me. We've now got two live ones inside the computer . . ." Just then the message on the screen vanished, to be replaced by another.

"Not anymore," it said. "I pulled the plug on Despot. McWhirter."

"We're in trouble, Josh. The whole program is nearing completion; we're going to be finished if McWhirter gets completely out of control before we finish this operation. Damn, and we're so close to solving death."

"Let's continue awhile longer. We must figure a way of getting the results out without alerting McWhirter, that's all. Shouldn't be too hard." Josh had great confidence in Barney.

Barney wasn't so sure. He suggested they visit Hadley Grimm.

"Well, well, my boy," Hadley greeted, ushering them into the sun room.

He beamed, he wreathed, he radiated; his sneer almost showed. He tipped onto his pointed shoe-toes and dipped back onto his heels, his soft white hands clasped before him, his lips constantly in motion, stretching and pursing, twisting and thinning, teeth glinting in the darkness of his mouth. "Well, well," he repeated.

"Any news?" Barney asked, pretending not to notice. This pigeon, he thought, is going to be plucked. Barney had a printout at home of the total funds McWhirter had diverted into Hadley's account.

"News, my boy? I have been in contact with your wife, and that's a fact. Again. Well, I fear for you, my boy. Really I do." Solemnity chased bubbles across his bland face, immediately replaced by those pleased twitchings.

"Fear what?"

Barney stared at Hadley's pudgy rocking form. He was a walking definition of self-satisfaction, was Hadley Grimm. Or rather, a rocking definition.

"Well, your wife says that she still doesn't understand why you want her back. I must say, she seemed quite ambivalent about you. Kept forgetting and calling you Enkidu. Something like that. But the gist was that she didn't think you liked her very much, and she doesn't understand why you want her back. Anyway, she says she's dead. She says she doesn't want to be afraid of the glorious blue light of the Wisdom of *Dharma-Dhātu*. That's from *The Tibetan Book of the* . . ."

"I know." Barney sat there for a long time, looking up at Hadley Grimm.

Josh stared out the window at the wet lawn, the soggy oleander. He was thinking that oleander was pretty but very poisonous. The rain fell. He was thinking that it was appropriate that rain was falling.

Abruptly, the rain stopped; the clouds began to break up, becoming once more fat, juicy cumulus drifting to the southeast, across the bay. A shaft of sunlight lit up the oleander.

"She says she's dead?" Barney asked.

"Yes."

"Mmmm."

The taxi was idling when they left Grimm's house. Tiglash Apsu smiled his vast, gap-toothed grin and drove them away.

"What are you going to do?" Josh asked him.

"I'm thinking about it."

"Do you think he's for real? You believe him?"

"You know, I do. Penny, Punumma, could be very determined when she wanted something. And she apparently wants the blue light of *Dharma-Dhātu*. Can't say I blame her . . . Anyway, there were so many kinds of energy activities when he contacted her before, there must be some truth in it; he probably did talk to her. Josh, we are so close to solving this riddle; we are going to understand death. I think I went through it just before the Rubber Band Effect brought me back here — a Holiday Inn. I suppose that's some kind of hallucination, some construct of the mind to deal with an unfamiliar experience. Anyway, I'm not giving up. I want Penny back, and I intend to keep trying." He lapsed into silence, staring out at the wet, shining streets. The clouds were almost gone; a crisp chill was in the air, an aching blue in the sky.

"I'm thinking of a Feynman diagram," Josh said suddenly.

"Huh?"

"I'm thinking of a Feynman diagram. Look, a lot of people have been working on a unified field theory, a general theory of relativity, things like that. Something that would explain everything, all phenomena, one big metatheory. But nobody has thought of including life and death in such a theory."

"Go on."

But Josh was glaring at the back of Tiglash Apsu's neck. "We seem to spend an awful lot of time riding around in this particular taxi. I wonder . . ." He trailed off.

"What?"

"Never mind. Anyway, it seems to me that no theory would be complete without including the phenomena of life and death. After all, they are both energy states. We've managed to move around in time, within limits, so that dimension is now open to us. And apparently we can move around in life and death too."

"So . . . ?"

"So death is another state of life, like ice and water. We

can't perceive it very well since we are limited to our six senses and whatever instruments we can invent, and *they* are limited by our six senses too. I'd swear that driver looks familiar. I've seen him before."

"We rode with him before. Never mind him. Go on."

"Energy moves around us, right? But energy is not the same as life, right? So life is something else, a form of energy we haven't been able to measure yet; something on the subatomic level, perhaps. It could be a form of quark. We have up quarks and down quarks, strange quarks and charmed quarks, top and bottom quarks, truth and beauty quarks. Quarks also have what is called color. And all quarks have antiquarks. These are all forms of energy, but energy is nothing but a pattern, like a whirlpool or a knot. It doesn't matter what matter is going through the pattern. Buckminster Fuller used to hold an imaginary rope and tie a knot in it; everyone could see the knot, it existed as a pattern. So it's not merely the raw energy that is life, but a specific *pattern,* and it's a truism that on the subatomic level there are *always* patterns present. Even in a state of total entropy when there is no visible structure. Matter itself is made up of these patterns of energy, moving so fast that matter seems solid. You see? Patterns."

"I think so," Barney said. "And friendship is a pattern, and love is a pattern, and kinship — social patterns. So death could be a variant of the life pattern. Funny, you know, we've been working with them all our lives, patterns, without really noticing them, the small, invisible ones, the conceptual ones, like love. But they have been everywhere, always, as long as there have been people." He stared out the window for a while, musing, and as he stared, electrons flowed in computer circuits all over the world or flashed as microwaves through satellite relays; and they danced a complex pattern, solving problems.

One of the problems they were solving was the problem of Pete Boggs' coffins.

"Someone on the phone for you, Mr. Boggs. Won't give his name." Miss MacHunt was crisp and efficient this morning.

"Oh, all right," Pete sighed, picking up the receiver. He had finished his MOM training the night before and still ached.

"Who is this?" he asked.

A horrible rasping voice said, "Boggs, we're on to you."

"What? Who is this?"

"We're on to you, Boggs. We know all about your little coffin scam, Boggs. We know. Ha-ha-ha-ha-hah." The rasp degenerated into a stagy fanatic laugh, a hacking Dracula guffaw. In spite of the stagy manner, Pete felt a chill. It wasn't that there was anything really *illegal* about his Hong Kong coffins, but if it got out it could be bad for business.

And business had been so good lately. There was a waiting list for Pete's new cryogenic freezers in the basement. Plots were selling like hotcakes, four deep and glad of it. Real estate in the Whispering Cypresses Memorial Park, where Pete had most of his holdings, was at such a premium that Pete had started to hold auctions for it. The computerized crematorium was cooking day and night, and Boggs and Boggs had installed a splendid new line of burial urns.

So the rasping chuckle unnerved Pete Boggs. "What about my coffins?" he asked, deciding, I'll tough it out. I'll stonewall.

"Ha-ha-ha, eh?" The voice caught up short in midlaugh. "What do you mean, Boggs? Come on now, Petie, ha-ha-ha, don't fool around with me. I'm everywhere. I know everything. You can consider me a deity, ha-ha."

"Ha-ha," Pete replied sarcastically. "OK, deity, what about my coffins?"

"Stonewalling, eh? Well, it won't work, Boggs. Never does. Not with old deity around, eh? Everywhere, ha-ha. Let's just say, since you don't believe me, that your coffins are a tiny bit, shall we say, used? Secondhand, eh, Boggs? Ha-ha-ha."

A finger with a long pointed nail trickled up Pete's suddenly calcified spine, laying open flesh and bone to pluck at his nerve cord itself, flayed and open to the conditioned air, a high-pitched twang miles above the middle C of MOM.

"They are not," he tried.

"Now, now, Boggs. It's no use. I *know*. I know everything. Everything. Everywhere, ha-ha-ha . . ." the laugh itself degenerated into a mumble, a buzz, a carrier wave, and then abruptly someone was singing, "I'll be down to get you in a taxi, honey," in a ghastly electronic larynx-voice. Pete hung up.

"I wonder what he's going to do about it," he said aloud.

Miss MacHunt spoke up from the reception room. "Did you call me?"

"No. It's nothing." He wished he could believe it. But his coffins were secondhand and very cheap, shipped over from Hong Kong, where their original contents had been dumped after the mourners had left so they could be used again. Hong Kong was short of burial space, and the funeral home Pete bought the coffins from had a French-intensive garden in back where high-quality marijuana was grown for export. The marijuana was shipped out in the lining of the coffins, but Pete was unaware of this sideline since the shipper removed the grass at the warehouse, before delivering the coffins. Nothing was wasted. Everyone was happy.

Until this minute. The phone call was upsetting. Upsetting enough to make Pete forget about MOM for a while.

He phoned Prue. "I'm in trouble, I think. Someone has found out about the coffins. I don't know who, he didn't say. He just said he was everywhere, knew everything. I should think of him as deity . . . crazy . . . No, he didn't say what he would do. He had a horrible rasping voice, like a rusty can opened with a screwdriver. You heard from him too? Why didn't you say . . . You do? You did? Oh, my

God." Pete sat down on the word "God," and as he did the rasping voice interrupted.

"You rang?" the voice inquired, starting its maniacal laugh all over again, then treated Pete to "I'll be down to get you in a taxi, honey." Then silence.

"Prue, are you there?"

Prue was not there.

However, the taxi was. Now equipped with a two-way radio, Tiglash Apsu answered calls. Tiglash was not sure where they came from, but somehow they always sent him where he was needed. Since he was not a very reflective man, he didn't pause to question those calls. He simply obeyed them.

Sitting in his cab in front of Boggs and Boggs Funeral Home he picked his teeth, probing with his flat fingertips at the gap between them.

The phone call, that ghastly laugh tinkling down the scales, made Pete frantic. He stumbled down his stairs to the parking lot, climbed into his 1910 Hispano-Suiza, and discovered that the battery was dead.

"Goddam!" he shouted, and kicked the tire furiously, knowing even as he did it that A. Spencer Sparling would call him an asshole for losing control of his life. He pretended the tire was A. Spencer Sparling and kicked it again. "Goddam!"

Then he noticed the taxi idling at the curb, the flat-faced, fat-necked driver picking his teeth.

"Taxi!" Pete climbed in.

Tiglash Apsu didn't budge, his finger still hanging from his mouth, his eyes as empty as Sunday afternoon in Sunnyvale.

"Take me to the Ceramic Lobster," Pete said. "I need a drink. God knows, I need a drink."

20

It was dim, cosy, and warm in the Ceramic Lobster. The harpoons gleamed over the door; the hardwood figurehead, arms back, breasts bare, gazed out over the corner table and across the room, sighting just over the horizon a destination, a newfound land, a vast and fertile America of the mind. Outside, the sky was clear and vivid blue, devoid of clouds, empty of the usual brown residue of life, pure and washed clean; it throbbed with the dance of orgones and energy; it whizzed with health and negentropic structures.

Nina Choklat loitered beside the swinging doors to the kitchen and gazed at the engagement ring on her hand. It was a simple star sapphire, a blue as rich as the sky outside, winking with perfect rays from its inner star. She gazed from the ring to her lovely Mel, seated at the piano bar, his broad bottom spread comfortably on the wooden stool, his plump fingers restlessly caressing the keys, soft arpeggios tinkling up and down the whites and blacks, mingling in subtle modulations. "Mmmm-mmm," he hummed, picking at a tune, aimless and free, a sunny afternoon, his only worry his sainted mom, to whom he had yet to relay the joyous news; tomorrow, perhaps, he would share with her his bride-to-be. For now, a quiet melody wafted through his mind, soft as panther's paws, as serpent's tongue. "Mmm-mmm," he hummed, "mm-mm, Sunnyvale-by-the-sea," almost to himself.

Nina smiled at him as she hugged herself, so good, so soft, so childlike, she thought. Like one of her kids, a big baby boy, with a great talent and always a song. Her only worry was meeting his mom, a minor terror. Tomorrow, perhaps. Always time, tomorrow. Meanwhile, she had the cold blue fire of the ring and a warm fire in her belly. A small, bourgeois smile twitched her lips. Fascist pig, she prodded herself, smiling secretly.

When the bell rang, she entered the kitchen to get the order it announced. Cape Cod salad with yogurt and sprouts and a Whaleburger Deluxe for the boy.

"Does she seem different to you?" Josh asked, watching Nina's Pilgrim-dressed body sway away from their table.

"Mph. How do you mean?" Barney picked at the chunks of yogurt-smothered cod in his salad.

"I'm not sure. More alive, happier."

"I didn't notice," Barney confessed. "Listen, Josh, about this idea of yours, you know, patterns. Is there anything we can do? Penny apparently doesn't think she *can* come back. I'm not even sure she would want to. She seems to have only a fuzzy memory of Sumer, when she loved me . . ."

"You're positive that was Penny? It could have been someone else, someone who looked like her."

"No, it was Penny. I could tell; there was a way she touched my chin . . . Anyway, we had a son there, we loved each other. And I've been different since I came back."

"True," Josh said, splattering his whaleburger with catsup. "You took me in, for one thing. We can talk about things besides physics and computers. You're more fun. Hrmph." Josh cleared his throat and grinned at Barney. Barney returned his grin.

"The thing is, Josh, is there anything we can do?"

Nina appeared at their table. "Phone for you, Mr. Gamesh."

"OK." Barney went to the phone.

"We're engaged," Nina told Josh. "Mel and I. See my ring?"

"Nice," Josh answered. "A pure blue form of corundum, isn't it? With an asterism?"

"It's a star sapphire," Nina said.

"It's beautiful." Crystal lattice structures formed in Josh's mind, the rigid elegance of pure math.

"Hmm," Nina said, and wandered away, staring into her star.

Barney sat down heavily. "McWhirter," he said. "He wants a body. He was very insistent. That man is out of his mind."

"Wants a body? You mean he's subverted the whole program just to get himself into a body?"

"We're so close. So very close. But I'm afraid we'd better pull the plug. McWhirter is completely out of control. He's tapped into the phone company — not just the computer, but the phones: he's the ultimate phone freak. He's *inside*. Frankly, I'm very nervous, Josh. Very nervous."

"Hiya, Barney old pal, sweetheart, how the hell are you?" Pete Boggs stood over the table, martini clutched in his tan hands. He was chewing vigorously on the olive, the plastic skewer bobbing in the corner of his mouth.

"Hi, Pete. Fine."

"Hey, I hear ya, Barn. I hear ya. Listen, I have to talk to you. I've been receiving these weird phone calls . . ."

"You too, huh? OK, sit down, Pete. Are they from McWhirter?"

"I don't know. I've never heard his voice. But you'd expect he would approve of me. After all, I've landed the Big One, eh? He claims he's everywhere. Like he's some kind of deity, you know, God. Of all things." Pete slumped glumly in the third chair and stared into his round martini glass, reading his invisible future in the bottom.

"That's McWhirter, all right. He wants a body, Pete. You don't have a body handy, do you? One he could take?"

Pete's head jerked up. "Are you kidding?" The wire in his

spine tightened, hingeing his head up and around. "Oh, I see you are." The head flopped down again.

"You do recognize that McWhirter is not real, don't you, Pete?" Barney stared at the hip mortician curiously.

"What do you mean, not real? Of course he's real. He keeps calling me up, threatening me, trying to blackmail me or something. Why, just this morning he called about my coff . . . Well, he seems to know things. Things he shouldn't know. I can't figure it out." The future, there in the bottom of his martini glass, was bleak. It was empty.

"So think I'm kidding," Barney said. "But I'm not. McWhirter really does want a body, and he's attempting to maneuver us, you and me, into locating one. I have no idea how he plans to get into it, but he has access to an incredible amount of computer power, and he may well have found a way. We must stop him."

"I don't understand." Pete's face, tan and thin-lipped, sagged into a vertical stack of inverted V's, mouth down, lines beside his nose, eyebrows down, a portrait of depression. "I'm ruined," he whispered. "I've had it."

He didn't know the half of it. At that moment, Prue Nisenvy, a walking tribute to the concept of wrinkle, entered the Ceramic Lobster trailed by a short leather popinjay named A. Spencer Sparling. She didn't notice the threesome near the piano bar, where Mel continued to trill the keys absently, but swept on to the corner table and seated herself once more under the flying mermaid, her hands clasped before her on the creamy white tablecloth, high priestess to Spencer's leather suppliant. She was hearing his confession.

"It's the most incredible thing that's ever happened to me," he was confessing. "MOM is sweeping the country faster than instant fried chicken. I can't keep up. *Cosmopolitan* is running an interview. *Newsweek* and *Time* call every day. *Ladies' Home Journal, Reader's Digest, Playboy* interviews! I can't keep up. What should I do?"

"How about some kind of franchise arrangement," Prue suggested in a voice like nerve gas percolating through stale beer.

"What do you mean?" Spencer's eyes acquired hope.

"License the operations out. MOM is a boon to mankind. But there should be a way for you to reap the profits without taking any legal risks. It was your idea, after all."

"Reap the profits," Spencer breathed. "Yes, well, I promoted it, actually. A couple of researchers in Milpitas dreamed it up. I just sort of got wind of it and acted as an entrepreneur for the idea. But it's fantastic! You should see it in action."

"I have," Prue responded, the percolator of her voice cooked dry.

"Oh, you have, huh? Oh. Well, dammit, the money is rolling in faster than I can keep track of it. It's all getting away from me. What if there are bugs in the system somewhere, someone has a heart attack and sues? What then?"

"Oh, we can fix that," Prue said. "Dummy corporations, false fronts; liability laws have loopholes in them we can use to protect you. After all, you have a product. The world wants it. The world should get it, and you certainly shouldn't have to suffer for giving the world what it wants. Simple."

"I marvel," Spencer said, "at the clarity of your mind."

"Mmm," Prue said. "This is going to be fun."

"My God." Pete stared over Barney's shoulder at the corner table. "That's Prue. And she's with A. Spencer Sparling."

"He's probably a client," Barney said.

"I don't think Prue has clients anymore," Pete moaned. "All her clients are like me: men. She eats men up. I even went through MOM for her."

"MOM?" Josh said. "We saw a truck with that on it. What's MOM?"

Pete was surprised. "You haven't heard about it? It's been written up in *Newsweek* and everything."

"Don't read *Newsweek*. No time."

"It's Multiple Orgasms for Men. It's all done with biofeedback. You train with a partner, get hooked up to a machine, and get trained to have more than one. Several. It's amazing."

"I'm amazed," Barney said. "How does it feel?"

"Wonderful. I think. You forget everything. But it is a bit exhausting."

"Sounds to me like it isn't for everyone," Barney commented, smiling.

"Free drinks for everyone," Mel told Nina. "I'm announcing our engagement."

"OK," she said, and the bartender went to work.

"Nina and I are going to be married," Mel murmured into his microphone, backing himself with cheerful chords. "We got engaged yesterday. Everyone is invited. New Year's Day. Three-thirty, right here, mmm-mmm, Sunnyvale-by-the-sea, mmm, mmm."

Loud applause filled the room, applause that grew louder when Mel announced the free drinks.

"Thank God for this," Pete said, lifting his new martini in a toast to the room, to Barney and Josh, to Mel and Nina. He gulped it down and sank instantly once more into his morass of gloom. "I've had it," he mumbled. "Had it."

"How much do you charge?" Spencer inquired.

"I'll have to think about it," Prue answered, slipping off her shoes. "It all depends."

Alarm flashed through A. Spencer Sparling. A muted bell in the abdomen. "Depends on what?"

Prue's leather feet slithered across the carpet under the table. "You have deep eyes," she said, "very deep eyes. I find myself strangely attracted to your eyes."

"You do?"

"I'd like to plumb the depths of those eyes," she continued, her toes wriggling under Spencer's leather cuffs. "I'd like to sink down into those depths. I'd like to drown in . . ."

The alarms were ringing loudly. Spencer retreated, jerking his pointed platform shoes out of reach of her prehensile toes. She sank farther into her chair, hands clasped serenely on the tablecloth, face composed and professional. Settling brought her feet into range.

"I don't think . . ." Spencer began uncertainly. He needed a lawyer, it was true, and she was the best.

"You leave the thinking to me," Prue said. "Would you care to plumb the depths of my soul?" Her crackling toes climbed his calf to the tops of his socks and made electrical contact with skin. "I certainly would like to plumb the depths of *your* soul," she continued, hot blue cyanide gas bubbling merrily through the vat of flat warm beer. A sharp stab of fear plumbed the depths of Spencer's soul.

"I've often wondered about the soul," he began. "How exactly do you define the soul?"

"Ah," Prue said, settling lower. "Ah."

"I'm going to sit at the bar," Pete said. "I can't stand to watch this. I don't know how anyone could stand to watch."

"Our backs are to it," Josh reminded him. Pete wobbled away.

"Ah," Prue said, her long wrinkled toes scaling the heights to Spencer's knee.

"You're wrinkling my pants," he said. "This leather can't stand much wrinkling."

"Isn't that suit awfully hot?" Prue asked, her fingers hooked over the edge of the table. "Wouldn't you like to take that suit off?"

"It does seem a little warm in here." Spencer's eyes were dancing around like two gobs of spit on a hot griddle.

Nina Choklat brought their lunch. "Boy, are those two

weird," she informed Mel. "That woman's always doing something with her feet. Weird."

Mel beamed at her, his chubby fingers lingering on the piano keys, a syncopated wedding march, jazzy.

The phones rang, the phone in the kitchen, the pay phone by the entrance, and the phone behind the bar. Next door, at the Naked Van (recreational vehicle accessories), the phone rang. At the smoke-blackened ruins of Irving Gowanda's car wash the phone rang, all alone in the shattered wreckage of his glass office.

Every telephone in Sunnyvale rang, all at the same time. The clamor was terrific.

The cook in the kitchen of the Ceramic Lobster answered his phone; the bartender answered the bar phone. Nina Choklat answered the phone beside the entrance.

"Hello?" Sunnyvale residents said into their receivers. Irving Gowanda, his shoes crunching shattered glass on his office floor, said it. Mrs. Lotte Bunyon, holding an armload of Rice-O-Roni she had just purchased at the Los Cojones de Santa Teresa Thriftee-Shoppee, said it. In all, 47,317 people said "Hello?" at the same time. Sergeant Masterbrook, at the station, said it.

"Ha-ha," the telephones answered. "Ha-ha-ha-ha, heh-heh-heh, he-he-he-he, ahh ha-hah-hah," the telephones cackled. Forty-seven thousand three hundred and seventeen people stood or sat or lay down listening in disbelief as their telephones poured obscene, cackling, demented laughter into their ears, laughter that trickled down the scale to the subsonic; laughter that rose up the scale to the limits of human hearing; laughter that made every one of the 47,317 standing, sitting, or lying down extremely uneasy. "Hoo-hoo-hoo," the telephones laughed. "Kak-kak-kak."

"Who is this?" Nina Choklat asked.

"Eh heh-heh-heh," the phone answered. "Aw haw-haw-haw."

She hung up. "That was very weird," she told Mel, who

didn't hear because the chef had hurried from the kitchen to tell him the same thing.

"It was very weird," the chef said. "Laughter. Insane laughter."

"It was awful," the bartender added. "Like a crazy person."

"Wait a minute," Mel said, hands extended. "You mean the same caller was on all three phones?"

They looked at one another and shrugged. "How do I know?" Nina asked. "But there was laughter. Horrible laughter. Really grotesque."

"I'm going to call the police," Mel announced. "Sounds like a crank to me."

He used the phone behind the bar. He carefully dialed the Sunnyvale Police Department.

"Hello," Sergeant Masterbrook said. "Sunnyvale Police."

"We just got a call from a nut," Mel said.

"What's that you say?" Mrs. Lotte Bunyon said. "Who is this, anyway?"

"Isn't this the police?" Mel asked.

"Of course this isn't the police. You have a wrong number. Who is this?"

"Sorry," Mel said. "I guess it is a wrong number."

"I'll say," said a different voice, a very nasty voice that sounded like a shovelful of rusted thumbscrews tossed into an iron maiden. Then the voice began to laugh.

Mel hung up. "Something's wrong with the phones," he told Nina. "I got two different people and then some guy who started laughing. Wires crossed or something."

"What's going on?" Barney asked Nina as she whisked past. "The phones keep ringing."

"I don't know. Seems to be something wrong with the system." She was carrying a double Scotch to A. Spencer Sparling.

"I've got a bad feeling about this," Barney told Josh.

"Me too."

"Phone for you again, Mr. Gamesh," Mel said. "Something is wrong with the phone systems, so be prepared. Weird things are happening."

"Mr. Gamesh? Hadley Grimm. Could I see you?"

"What is it? I'm a little rushed right now."

"McWhirter just called me. My cousin. He's dead, you know, but he's been getting in touch with me. I think he's been setting me up. Several government people were just here, asking questions; I think they were from the IRS. Luther says he's inside a computer of some kind. I thought maybe you would know about that — that's your field, isn't it? And I did get in touch with your wife for you, didn't I? I'm worried, Mr. Gamesh. You've got to help me."

Hadley sounded worried. His words spurted forth with a fluctuating pressure, rushing and falling back, then dribbling away at the end into hard breathing. Worried.

"Something is going on, Mr. Grimm. I'm sure of that. I'll try to look into it for you. Maybe I can get in touch with McWhirter, find out what's happening."

"Oh, thank you, Mr. Gamesh. Thank you. I'd appreciate that. Really I would."

"I'll do what I can." Barney returned to the table. "We've got to do something," he told Josh. "Soon. McWhirter is crazy. We must stop him. We can't let him go on like this."

"How?"

"What do you mean, how?"

"How? We can't pull the plug anymore. Which plug do we pull, anyway? He's into so many computers by now. Which ones do we turn off to get rid of him? He's a program, isn't he? And he can relocate himself anywhere in the system. If we turn off the entire phone company, he moves to an insurance company, and if we turn that off, he moves somewhere else."

"We'll have to send a program after him," Barney said, tugging at his earlobe; Josh's gesture. "We'll have to trap him somewhere and turn him off."

"He'll probably have a duplicate waiting somewhere. That's what I'd do."

"I didn't think of that. You're right, of course. Someone will have to go in after him somehow, track him down. A hunter. What would happen if he got a body *and* had all that computer power?"

"What about Penny? That's why we started all this."

"I know, I know. I haven't forgotten. I just haven't been sure what to do about her. Until now." Barney sank into silence, inward as a shell curled tight around his pain.

Phones rang sporadically all over Sunnyvale, rippled up and down the peninsula, jangled in San Francisco, in Washington, D.C., in Pretoria and Minsk, in Chicago and Ulan Bator; there might be chuckles, then silence, or silence, then chuckles. At the Sunnyvale Police Department Sergeant Masterbrook put his head in his hands for a moment, then went out to his squad car.

"That's what started all this." Barney repeated Josh's words to himself, his elbows on the table, chin cupped in his palms. "If McWhirter figures . . . Oh, my God!"

"What is it?" Josh asked, alarmed.

"Penny. Penny's body is frozen in the basement of Boggs and Boggs. This is getting awful. Josh, I've been a fool. Penny can't come back; we've got to bury her, and now. McWhirter is fooling around with death, with life and death. What if he wants Penny's body?"

"We've been fooling around with life and death too, Barney."

"That's what I mean. Perhaps we shouldn't have. I only hope it's not too late."

"Too late for what?"

"Too late to give Penny a funeral, before McWhirter gets ideas. Let's get Pete."

"What are you doing?" Pete asked as they hauled him away from his fourth martini. "Where are we going?"

Barney dragged him toward the front door, where they collided with Hadley Grimm.

"Well!" huffed Hadley, brushing his suit. "Oh, it's you. Where are you off to? I must talk to you."

"Boggs and Boggs," Barney gasped. "It's urgent. Where the hell's that taxi?"

He looked up and down the street. It was an ordinary street, though curiously empty of traffic for the time of day. The sun banged down on it like a child with a tin drum. There was no taxi in sight.

"That damn taxi is always around when I need it," Barney muttered. "And now it's not. Oh, I have a very bad feeling about this."

"We can take my Rolls," Hadley offered, gesturing at the great Silver Cloud at the curb. His chauffeur lounged at the front door, smoking a cigarette. He straightened when Hadley spoke and opened the back door, throwing away his smoke.

"OK," Barney said. They climbed in.

Pete stood on the curb, dazed, his martini still in his hand.

"There's room for one more inside, sir," the chauffeur said, bowing Pete into the back.

"Huh? Oh." Pete got in.

The Rolls swished through the clean December streets, and the only sound they heard was the dashboard clock. And breathing, especially Barney's, loud in the conditioned air.

Hadley started to speak, saw Barney's face, and lapsed into silence again.

"How did you know I was at the Ceramic Lobster?" Barney asked at last.

"McWhirter."

"Oh."

There was a muted buzzing from the front.

"The phone," Hadley said.

"Oh. I've got a bad feeling about this."

"For Mr. Gamesh," the chauffeur said through the intercom.

"A very bad feeling."

"It's for you," Hadley said, indicating the phone in back.

Barney picked it up.

"I know what you're up to, Gamesh. It won't work. I'm way ahead of you."

Barney placed his hand over the mouthpiece. "McWhirter," he said.

Hadley groaned. Josh tugged his ear. Pete frowned into his martini glass.

"I don't know what you're talking about," Barney bluffed.

"Ha-ha," McWhirter laughed. "You think you're going to beat me to Boggs and Boggs. You forget, I'm already there. Very foolish of you to help old Pete computerize his crematorium. Very foolish, Things are already under way there. Already under way. This is the Big One, Gamesh, ha-ha-ha."

"You can't do anything," Barney said, the elevator falling abruptly to his basement, yanking his stomach with it.

"Can't I though? Well, I have help. Very qualified help. Ha-ha-ha."

"Oh, for God's sake, stop laughing like that. It's too corny. What kind of help?"

The laughter veered out of control, but Barney caught the words "taxi driver."

"Uh-oh," he said, hanging up. "McWhirter's already into the crematorium computer. He intends to snatch a body. Please tell the driver to hurry."

The Rolls sped up, racing through the almost deserted streets. The sun shone merrily, a happy gold, an Indian summer gold on the emerald hills, shining in a clean sapphire sky, as though earth and heaven were engaged.

Sergeant Masterbrook might have arrested the speeding

Rolls, but his police radio was giving him conflicting orders: robberies here, homicides there, domestic arguments in vacant lots, brawls in churches. Zooming from one nonexistent crime to another, he grew increasingly confused and frustrated. He passed the Rolls going the other way, his siren wailing, off to a holdup in progress at a gas station that had been recently closed.

The Rolls rolled on. As they swung into the parking lot at Boggs and Boggs, throwing the passengers to one side in a heap, Josh had a thought.

"Barney, you said someone would have to go into the computer after McWhirter, a hunter. You didn't mention whom you had in mind."

"Oh," Barney said as they piled out of the still-swaying auto, jouncing on its elegant shocks. "I expect it'll have to be me."

"Buddha!"

"What is it this time?"

"They're using computers on earth."

"Oh. My foot's asleep. Damn, this left foot is really giving me problems."

"Right," said the voice. "Your left foot is death. Wake it up. It's connected."

"Tell me something new," Buddha mumbled, blowing out a dozen Main Sequence stars in the neighborhood. "All right, all right."

He stretched out his foot, and hadrons danced, exchanged, and danced again, changing states like hats, structures flowing, degenerating and reforming, energies blazing and moving, slowing and increasing, endlessly shifting, popping, zapping, slinking, splitting and combining, fluid as thought. It was Judgment Day in another universe; dragons hissed and slithered, two clouds of hydrogen kissed and fell in love, bodies rose from their graves and linked hands, fingerbones falling through fingerbones, skulls clacking, teeth still heavy with dental work and inlays where the precious metals glinted by the light of dying stars.

He wiggled his toes, and sparks danced through the ecstatic visions of 12,000 mystics in the East Libyan desert. Toads fell on the South of France, ruining the tourist season. The Red Sea parted, grounding the largest supertanker in the world together with its cargo of crude oil, thus returning the oil to its home in the ground.

There was a sudden rush of neutrinos in Lead, South Dakota.

There was a tremendous rash of miracles all over the globe, miracles that went unnoticed in the general chaos of randomly ringing telephones, spurious bills, current fluctuations, blackouts, brownouts and pinkouts, of rusty water, dazed salmon, bullish and bearish markets wildly plunging, animals speaking, quoting Shakespeare, labor unions inexplicably demanding lower wages and longer hours.

"It is a bit of a mess down there," Buddha said. "Oh, well."

21

"I got orders to go on a mission," Junior Arkwright was telling Miss MacHunt. He was sitting on the edge of her desk, his shoes swinging against the rug, gazing down into her face. She sat in her chair and gazed back.

Barney charged through the room, followed by Hadley Grimm and Josh. Pete Boggs trailed along last, still holding his empty martini glass.

"Hello," he said, giving a little wave of his fingers to Junior and Miss MacHunt as he weaved past them.

"What was that all about?" Junior asked as the four plunged down the stairs to the cryogenic chamber in the basement.

She shrugged her gorgeous shoulders. "I don't know." The shrug fluffed up her long blond hair. "How long will you be gone on this mission?"

"Hard to say," Junior confessed. "I don't understand it at all. The orders say I'm to assassinate the president of Arizona."

"But that's a state!"

"Yes, I thought so. It wouldn't have a president, would it?"

"But what about our plans? You promised me you'd retire." Her plump lower lip protruded temptingly.

"I know, dear. I did, but . . ." He was interrupted by a roar from the basement. When it stopped he began to talk again, only to be interrupted once more by the entrance of Prudence Nisenvy and A. Spencer Sparling, who had been summoned by telephone to Boggs and Boggs, much to Spencer's relief. His expensive leather trousers had preserved their purity, crease unwrinkled and clean.

"What do you suppose is going on down there?" Junior asked, still scuffing his shoes on the carpet. Miss MacHunt gave her magnificent shrug again, her hair billowing over her shoulders. Prue and Spencer disappeared through the door.

Barney screamed. Penny's body was resting quietly on a metal table covered with frost. Tiglash Apsu, bent over her serenely draped form, was breathing hard. He was apparently attempting a revival, his tiny eyes glinting redly in their pouches of fat, his bald bullet head gleaming in the flickering fluorescents.

He half-turned, startled by the shout. Barney was in the act of running across the vinyl floor, hand up in his best Sumerian swordsman attack, when the lights abruptly flared and froze everyone in position, a freeze-frame pinning them all — Hadley withdrawn, hands up as though defending himself, Josh about to run to Barney's aid, Pete Boggs grinning foolishly, eyes unfocused.

It was a tableau. Time had stopped.

"Aha-ha-ha," Gilgamesh said, stepping around the frozen forms. He tapped lightly at Tiglash Apsu's gleaming pate and was rewarded by a dull clang.

"What the hell's happening?" Penny asked, sitting up.

"Well," Gilgamesh said, "things are a bit messed up, as you can see. This fellow here, bending over you, is a Rumanian. He's been receiving his orders from a computer, but doesn't realize it; it seems he has, in a peculiar way, fallen in love with you."

"Why?"

"Because you're dead."

"Yuk." Penny wrinkled her nose. "He must be some kind of pervert."

"Mmm. Meanwhile, over here" — Gilgamesh stepped over to Barney, hand raised in attack — "we have your former husband, or your husband formerly, Barney Gamesh. You and I also knew him as Enkidu."

"I remember all that now. But I don't understand. Why are they all petrified like that? And that boy over there, at the bottom of the stairs. That's our son, isn't it, Enkidu's and mine?"

"In a manner of speaking. All our lives are getting a bit mingled just now because of this emergency. Usually everything is kept carefully separate. And they are all frozen because we are working on a different time plane. You probably just came from a Holiday Inn?"

"Hey, you're right. We took over the kitchens, Haig Despot and I."

"I hear you," a voice said. "Haig Despot here, breaker, breaker."

"Where are you?" Penny asked, looking around.

"I'm at the Holiday Inn. I took over the manager's office and have the computer here at Deathwest. Things seem to be going to pot where you are, I must say."

"We're working on it," Gilgamesh said. "Anyway," he went on, "things have gotten so boggled up we've been sent here to be on the spot, as it were."

"But why? And who sent us? I still don't understand." She slid off the table and began to walk around the room.

"I'm not too sure who sent us," Gilgamesh said. "There are more time planes than just these two, you understand? The blue light of the Wisdom of *Dharma-Dhātu* is another, for example. And we're here because we're connected, all of us."

Penny was only paying half attention. She was standing beside Barney's frozen form. She ran her finger down the line of his jaw. "You know," she said, almost to herself, "I think he did change."

"Oh, he did," Gilgamesh said, bending to peer into Hadley Grimm's face. "He did, he changed a lot. He became quite a hero. And I missed him, tried like hell to get him back. No, I didn't like death at all. Aha-ha-ha, no indeed, didn't like it at all."

"Mmm," Penny murmured, her forefinger lingering on Barney's chin. Barney didn't blink.

"Well," Gilgamesh straightened. "We're here to try to sort all this out. Barney, it seems, has gotten into a bit of trouble. He helped me, so I'm here to help him."

"I remember. He saved your life."

"I owe him."

Barney charged across the room at Tiglash Apsu, hand in the air for his sword chop, the blade presented, a *tegatana* to the neck. Tiglash, turning at the same time, grunted in surprise.

Just as Barney was about to swing, he noted from the corner of his eye that Penny's body was gone, the table empty.

Surprise and shock followed one another, rippling from his eyebrows to his feet. He forgot his attack and scurried past Tiglash into the wall.

Tiglash, raising his hands to defend himself, pivoted with his attacker and kept on turning, spinning like an over-weight ballerina.

Prue Nisenvy and Spencer stopped, astounded, at the top of the stairs.

"Aha-ha-ha," Gilgamesh laughed. He and Penny stood in the shadows of the far corner of the room, watching. "This is kind of fun, this ability to speed things up and slow them down. Comes with being on the second level of existence, the one beyond the 'real' one."

"Are we alive?" Penny asked.

"I suppose it depends on what you mean by that," Gilgamesh answered. He hitched his scarlet cloak around himself, pulled up his pleated kilt, and grabbed his sword hilt. "Not the way we were, I guess."

"But this is my body, or was." Penny had wrapped the sheet around herself, toga-style. One hand held a knot of material at her shoulder while she gestured with the other.

"Aha-ha-ha, that's your body all right," Gilgamesh leered.

"Oh, you know what I mean," she said. "It's freezing in here."

"You were frozen; that is, your body was. You can thank Barney for that; if he hadn't had you frozen we'd have had to start all over, you know, as a baby. But now I think we'd better get to work and not stand around yakking like this. After all, it's an emergency." He gestured at Barney, in the middle of his rebound off the wall, a large surprise on his face.

It was the surprise at Penny's sudden disappearance, of course, combined with the physical shock of hitting the wall. So Barney shook his head to clear it, which was long enough for Tiglash to close his meaty fist at the end of his pirouette and swing at Barney. At that moment Barney bent double to catch his breath, and the swishing sound of Tiglash's fist sailing through the air over Barney's head was suddenly drowned in a weird whistling roar as the crematorium furnaces in the next room started up. The conveyer belts began to move.

"What the . . ." Pete Boggs said, leaning oddly forward at the waist.

"What do you suppose is going on down there?" Junior asked for the third time, and for the third time Miss Mac-Hunt shrugged the question off.

"You promised," she said, "that you'd quit."

"And I will. I will!"

"What are we doing here?" Prue asked Spencer. "Who called to tell us to come here?"

Spencer didn't respond. He was staring at the conveyer belts, picking up speed at the other end of the room.

"Breaker, breaker," Haig shouted from a loudspeaker on the wall. "You'd better do something. McWhirter's trying to pull the plug on me. If he gets into Deathwest things'll really be messed up. And he's taken over the crematorium. He's going to try to feed everyone into it. He's really snapped!''

"We're working on it," Gilgamesh shouted back, over the noise. "But I don't have any real experience with computers. We need Barney."

"I can't help from here," Haig answered. "Somebody better get in there after him."

"Do you think we can get Barney?" Penny said, looking at him bent double, hands around his stomach, eyes wide in a strange appeal, staring up at the metal table.

"We'll have to," Gilgamesh said. "So we will." His drawn sword poked tentatively at Tiglash Apsu. It was like trying to skewer a granite statue. "Wrong time frame," he muttered. "We'll never get anywhere like this. That madman in the computer is the one that's putting this pressure on us. We'll have to get in there after him."

"Just you try," McWhirter grated from the speaker.

"Wooden Nickel!" Penny shouted. Strangled electronic sounds came from the speaker.

"Here . . ." she heard. More crackling static.

"Oh, he can't help you, ha-ha-ha," the demented McWhirter cackled. The whine of furnaces increased in the next room; the belts began to fly.

"We must do something," Gilgamesh said. "This McWhirter is on our time plane *and* dismantling the world, too."

"Barney can handle McWhirter." Penny had boundless faith, and this was something new.

"Aha-ha-ha, and boy are you ever right. Here goes."

Josh ran into Tiglash Apsu, off balance from the haymaker swing, and Tiglash toppled. The noise of his crash to the floor was muddled in the general din of belts and furnaces, Barney's gasping and Prue's sharp cry: "Joshie, whatever are you doing here? And with that awful man, too."

When Pete Boggs heard Prue's voice, his dazzled head swung around. He grinned foolishly, his thin lips slack, his midbrain steeped in alcoholic lethargy. "Hah?" he said.

Josh didn't hear Prue, but instead called to Barney. The instant he said his name, however, Barney vanished with a loud popping noise.

"What the hell's going on around here?" a voice roared from behind Prue, a voice loud with authority and thick with command.

Pete's eyes swiveled to take in the stranger at the top of the stairs. Sergeant Masterbrook had his police .38 drawn and ready for trouble, a stern look on his face.

"Hah?" Pete said again.

"Drop it!" Sergeant Masterbrook said, gesturing with his pistol at Pete Boggs' martini glass.

"Hah?" Pete said.

"Who do you think you are?" Prue asked, turning around, the mustard gas seeping under the door of her mouth.

"Everybody move!" Sergeant Masterbrook commanded. "Nobody freeze."

"What am I doing . . . Where am I? I feel strange." Barney was dusting his pants and glancing at Tiglash Apsu, sprawled awkwardly across the floor, his head and back three inches in the air, congealed there.

"Barney!" Penny shouted.

Barney turned, and there she was. He stared. He bit his tongue. He chewed his lip.

"Penny . . . ?" He blinked. "Penny, your body."

"Barney, we've got to hurry. McWhirter has taken over the furnaces, the belts, this whole building. You've got to do something."

"Do something. Yes, do something. Penny, I thought I'd lost you. I was trying to get you back; something went wrong, but I was trying to get you back. Penny, I'm . . . I'm sorry."

"Oh, Barney. I know that. You showed me that in Uruk."

"You remember! It *was* you there! Oh, Penny . . ."

"Barney, I think perhaps we'd better hurry. McWhirter
. . ." Penny's voice faltered, though, a shy colt.

"Oh. I had an idea about getting in there after him, the
way we put McWhirter into the computer in the first place.
But if time is short, I might not be able to help. Where am
I?"

"This is a different time plane," Gilgamesh said, stepping
from the corner shadows, his sword still drawn and glinting
in the odd greenish light. "Don't worry, I'll be going with
you."

"Gilgamesh! What are you doing here?"

"We can talk later. McWhirter is a real danger on this
time plane too. He can act as fast as we can."

Barney looked at Tiglash Apsu, suspended inches from
the floor, still falling. Josh was gazing straight into Barney's
eyes, calling his name. Then Barney noticed Hadley Grimm,
sunken into himself, and saw A. Spencer Sparling trying to
shrug Prue Nisenvy's shriveled hand off his arm. Prue herself
had turned to confront Sergeant Masterbrook, who waved
his gun importantly.

"What a scene," Barney said. "We must be moving awful
fast for everyone to be slowed to a standstill like this. But of
course, McWhirter can work in picoseconds; I guess that
makes us even. But Penny, how can I ever . . ."

"Barney, please," she pleaded wistfully.

"OK, OK. I can handle the computer circuits, but we
need someone who can understand the particle theory."

"What are you talking about?" Penny asked. "We've got
to hurry."

"No. We can't rush this. If we intend to hunt that man
down inside the computer network we need all the help we
can get. After all, McWhirter has been living inside there for
weeks . . ."

"You call this living?" McWhirter broke in. "Ha-ha-ha."

"Living inside there for weeks," Barney repeated. "He's used to it. Let me think."

Gilgamesh said, "Meanwhile that McWhirter is demolishing the fabric of civilization and playing around with very basic energy patterns in the universe — life, death . . ."

"And good and evil," Barney said thoughtfully.

"Well, Penny is right. There is a certain urgency about this. It'll be just like when we went after the Huwawa, eh, Barney?" Gilgamesh smiled. "Together, eh? Aha-ha-ha."

"I'm having a vision," Hadley Grimm said abruptly, very loud in the clanging, whirring, roaring din of the basement.

"What'd he say?" Spencer asked.

"He's having a vision," Prue said. "This is a swell time to be having a vision. This place is nuts." She glanced downstairs at Pete rummaging in a closet of supplies.

"I found it!" Pete exclaimed, pulling out a bottle. "I found it!"

Sergeant Masterbrook waved his gun threateningly, but no one noticed.

"Jesus," Prue said.

"Pure grain, it is," Pete shouted, holding the bottle up. Then he unstoppered it and poured some in his martini glass, miraculously unbroken and undropped. Toasting Prue, he drank it.

"I'm having a vision," Hadley Grimm repeated in the same stark, loud voice. "I see a Holiday Inn, solitary in a field of corn stubble. It looks like Iowa."

"Sounds deadly," Prue said in disgust.

"That's right!" Hadley shouted. "It is the Holiday Inn where . . ."

"Gah!" Prue spat, the round levels of wrinkles in her face rippling, the early stages of whirpool, maelstrom: turbulence. She towed Spencer down the stairs.

Sergeant Masterbrook followed behind, holding his gun at his waist. Much of the authority had left him, but he still wanted more than anything to be in charge. "What's going on here?" he asked, but too softly for anyone to hear. He repeated it louder.

"You are an officer of the law, are you not?" Prue demanded. He nodded. "Well, that man" — she pointed at Tiglash Apsu's inert form sprawled on the floor — "that man was assaulting a body. A woman's body. We all saw him." Her best trial voice.

"And where is this alleged body?" Sergeant Masterbrook was glad to have discovered a possibly real crime.

"Now that is a problem. I suspect habeas corpus is involved here. I expect you'd better find that body."

"Find the body. Right. Good idea." He put his gun away and began to walk around the room, opening drawers and cabinets. Josh watched him, a bemused smile on his adolescent face.

"What the hell are you doing here? You ought to be home in bed," Prue hissed at him, forgetting it was the middle of the afternoon and he didn't live with her anymore.

He vanished with a loud pop.

"Don't I know you?" Josh asked Gilgamesh. "You look very familiar."

"I was your godfather in another life. You might remember it now that we're on this plane," Gilgamesh said.

"Aha, yes. Sumer. In Uruk. Barney, I remember it." He looked around. Pete Boggs, glass at his lips, grinning foolishly; Prue, a disapproving frown turning to astonishment nested in the congested wrinkles of her face; Hadley Grimm gripped in the ecstasy of his vision; Tiglash Apsu flat on his back on the floor, arms outstretched; and Sergeant Masterbrook questing a closet for the missing body.

"Spooky, isn't it?" Josh remarked. The living members of the group were frozen. A silence like glue, a library paste silence, and a thick green light. A feeling in the air like the feeling after the sound of a huge gong has died away, like a silent echo.

"Spooky isn't the word for it," Barney said. He was glad

Josh was with him. And Penny, and Gilgamesh. He had everyone.

"Barney," Penny urged. "We . . ."

"I have everyone," Barney said, beaming. "Everyone I love."

"Oh, Barney, I have so much to tell you. I've been to a Holiday Inn, but I guess you know that, and . . ."

"Yeah," Barney said, "I went to one too, a Deatheast, and they weren't expecting me. It was very strange . . ."

Gilgamesh was beginning to jitter. "You people sure get distracted easily. I really must insist on the importance of our mission here. We all have to get inside that computer system and hunt down McWhirter. And need I remind you, Enkidu, Barney, my friend, that it was you that put him in there."

"I know," Barney said, contrite.

"Well, perhaps you could fill Josh in on the details before we go."

"Right," Barney said. He gave Penny a tender look and took her hand. Josh smiled. "Well, Josh," Barney said, giving Penny's hand a squeeze, "I don't quite understand the hadron interactions in the memory chips and thought you could help us out. McWhirter will jump every time we get close to him, move himself to another location, probably at random. We must devise a way to follow, some trail we can sniff out. Will he leave a trace for us to track?"

"Let me think." Josh sat down on Tiglash Apsu's large stomach and thought. "I've got it!" he said.

"Got it!" Sergeant Masterbrook, shouted, opening a closet full of frozen bodies. "Here it is."

"That's silly." Pete Boggs giggled. "Those are clients."

"Now which one of these bodies was this person allegedly assaulting?" The policeman ignored Pete.

"None of them. The body he was assaulting — and we all saw it extremely clearly, didn't we? — was lying on that table there. The metal one. It has apparently disappeared the same way Joshie did."

"It's stainless steel," Pete said, trying to be helpful. He thumped the table with his glass.

"Yes, well, there is certainly no body on this table now," the sergeant said. "And what is that man drinking? And who is he?"

"It's yellow and green, just like a Holiday Inn in Iowa," Hadley informed the group. "There's a woman with yellow fingers, pointing. She resembles the woman who gives the driver's license exam."

"Yellow and green? You mean like that stuff Pete's drinking?" Prue asked. She watched Pete pour himself another drink.

"Say, this does look funny," Pete said, staring in his glass. "It should be clear."

Upstairs, Miss MacHunt said, "Oh, I'm so glad. Then we can be together, always."

"Yes," Junior said, a lopsided grin zigzagging across the lower part of his face, "always."

"Smells like some kind of embalming fluid to me," the sergeant stated, joining the small knot of people surrounding Pete

A tremendous crash jerked them all around. A steel door had slammed open above the conveyer belt, and the first of Pete Boggs' imported Hong Kong coffins crashed through the room on its way to the crematorium.

"No!" Pete shouted, lunging through the group around him to protect his precious casket, but it was already slamming out of the room through another steel door.

Pete got bumped aside by the next coffin coming through, and no one, in all the confusion, noticed Tiglash Apsu climbing dazedly to his feet.

Josh stood up. "It's like this," he said, his pale young face slightly greenish in the fast-time light. "We'll convert ourselves into patterns that will be viable inside the computer, then the cross-channeling effect of S-matrix theory would enable —"

Barney cut in. "This whole room could act as a Josephson Junction — electron tunneling. We could take a quantum leap into the computer."

"How do you suppose you got here?" Gilgamesh asked pleasantly. "You had to make a quantum jump to this time plane, another energy state. We're on a level with McWhirter, but *outside* the computer."

"Please," urged Penny, "hurry."

Barney gave her hand another squeeze. "You're very beautiful. I missed you."

"Barney, we did so well in Sumer and so badly in Sunnyvale. What went wrong with us?"

"What happened to a lot of people, I guess. We forgot something important."

"You sure did," Gilgamesh interrupted. "You forgot that there were other things in the universe besides yourselves, separately. You forgot that everything is connected — most of all, the two of you are connected. And now myself and Josh here, all of us are connected. Nothing can exist without every other thing."

"That means McWhirter," Josh said.

"That means McWhirter," Gilgamesh agreed. "We needed him. The universe needed him. Patterns."

"How do you know all this?" Barney asked.

"Oh, I've been around," Gilgamesh said with a smile. "Around and around, a thousand times alive. We all finally move up to this level, but there are others above us. Things more fundamental than the quark, patterns."

"This is a pattern," Penny said, trailing her finger down the line of Barney's mandible.

"Yes," he said.

"No!" Pete shouted. "My caskets. My imported caskets.

My computer has gone crazy. It's burning up all my caskets."

"It sure is," A. Spencer Sparling said. "Don't worry about
it, though. Death is a rip-off. You ought to go through SUM
and gain control of your life."

"Aaaargh," Pete screamed, lunging for Spencer's neck.
His hands wobbled through the air like a pair of grappling
hooks. "I've been through SUM, you son of a bitch." He
seized Spencer's throat and began shaking him. "I've been
SUMmated. I've even been MOMmed, you son of a bitch!"

"Here here, now," Sergeant Masterbrook said placa-
tingly, holding Pete's quivering arm. "Here here now."

Tiglash Apsu stood behind the group, dazed, pounding
his forehead with his meaty palm.

"Don't here here me, you son of a bitch," Pete shouted at
the policeman.

Tiglash Apsu swayed on his feet, and slowly his eyes
cleared, came into a kind of focus. He found himself staring
at the back of Prue Nisenvy's neck.

"Death is not a rip-off!" Pete shouted into Spencer's
congested face. He lifted Spencer up and down a couple of
times, emphasizing his point, and breathed into Spencer's
face a wind redolent of embalming fluid and dry martinis.
"Death is a good, clean, decent, profitable business. Death is
my business. It's SUM that's the rip-off. *You* are a rip-off.
MOM is a rip-off."

"MOM," Spencer squeezed out through his constricted
throat, "is not a rip-off."

"Is he talking about a robbery?" Sergeant Masterbook
asked Hadley Grimm.

"The sky is low and gray," Hadley said, "but the Holiday
Inn is very busy."

"Is this guy nuts?" Sergeant Masterbrook asked Prue.

She thought he was referring to Spencer. "I don't know,"
she said. "I haven't been through SUM myself."

"Breaker breaker," Haig's desperate voice shouted. "Do you copy? This is Wooden Nickel."

"We copy," Penny shouted. "What is it?"

"Do something. McWhirter is arming missiles. I'm afraid he's going to start firing. If they go off, there won't be enough room at the Holiday Inn."

"What about the President? He's the one with the codes, after all."

"The President is bowling. No one can disturb him when he's bowling."

"Oh," Penny said.

"What's a president?" Gilgamesh asked.

"Kind of like a king, but sillier sometimes," Barney told him.

"Oh."

"Uh-oh," A. Spencer Sparling, eyes bulging, tried to point.

Everyone wheeled around.

Prue's screams had been drowned out by the terrific rumbling of coffins whizzing through the steel doors into the cryogenic rooms and out again to the crematorium, one after another, all of Pete's stock — French Provincial, Louis Quatorze, Early American, Queen Anne, Empire, Baroque, Swedish Modern — rushing into the maw of flame.

Pete dropped Spencer and pointed too, too stupefied to speak. Tiglash Apsu was halfway up the stairs, Prue's struggling form slung across his broad back. Somewhere in the dimness of his brain he was thinking of kissing the hand he could not bite.

"Halt!" Sergeant Masterbook called. "Halt or I'll shoot."

"You can't shoot," Spencer said. "You'd hit the lady."

"That's no lady," Pete managed. "That's Prue Nisenvy."

"Well, whatever she is, she's being kidnapped," the sergeant snapped. Tiglash stumbled out of sight toward the reception room. "After them!" He rushed up the stairs, waving his gun. No one followed him.

"Prue Nisenvy will always be with us," Pete said owlishly, blinking his brown eyes. "Always."

"There's a canasta tournament at the Holiday Inn," Hadley Grimm said. "Everyone is dead."

"He's developed a fondness for the dull white light of the *devas*," Penny said over McWhirter's maniacal laughter from the speaker. "He was probably frightened by the glorious blue light of the Wisdom of *Dharma-Dhātu*."

"I guess the thought of death maddened him," Josh said. "You'd have to want to live pretty much to try a head transplant. Junior Arkwright told me the body wouldn't even really work, just pump blood to the brain and keep it alive. He would have been totally paralyzed."

"Probably," Gilgamesh said. "Nonetheless, he's a crazy dead man who's taking over the world and is going to destroy it. He's got a lot to learn, that man."

"All he wanted was a working body," Barney said. "He was going after Penny's. It was the one he knew most about. We put everything about her into the program. I wanted her back too. What does that make me?"

"You've learned something, though," Gilgamesh said. "You can't have her back. Not that way. And now you're going to try to undo what you did."

"What will happen to us?" Penny asked.

"We move up a level," Gilgamesh said. "The blue light of the Wisdom of *Dharma-Dhātu*. There's no going back."

"But it's going to be dangerous, isn't it? I feel it."

"Just like Enkidu, Barney," Gilgamesh laughed. "Of course it will be dangerous. That's the point. Just like the Huwawa, eh? Aha-ha-ha."

"I was afraid of that," Barney muttered. "OK, then. Let's go."

"Barney! We're going together. You're a hero."

"Penny, I know. Or is it Punumma?"

"Both. I love you, Barney."

"Hey! What about me?" Josh grinned. "I'm part of the family."

"Me too." Gilgamesh laughed again, a hearty, booming laugh that echoed in the eerie silence.

"All together, then?" Barney asked. "I love . . ."

They nodded and disappeared into the network.

"What was that all about?" Junior asked Miss MacHunt after Tiglash Apsu had hurried through the room with the struggling Prue Nisenvy across his back.

She was about to answer when Sergeant Masterbrook scurried past without a glance at them, waving his gun.

It was raining again; Tiglash Apsu lumbered away into the gray curtain, Prue beating futilely at his back with her fists and nails, to be pursued forever by Sergeant Masterbrook, the spector of Sunnyvale.

"I'm having another vision," Hadley Grimm said to the suddenly quiet basement. "It's either the Apocalypse or the dawning of a new day."

"Phooey," Pete said, pouring himself another drink. "Phooey and double phooey. This stuff is pretty good. Have a drink?" He offered one to A. Spencer Sparling.

"Thanks," Spencer said, "I think I will." There was a fizzle of flame from the next room where the final coffin returned to the ashes, a fizzle and a soft fall of ash.

"Does MOM mean an end to death?" Pete asked.

"Probably not," Spencer said, taking a drink. "Probably not."

Caroline MacHunt, seated at her desk, smiled up at her lover and shook out her full blond hair.

"Maybe we could open a shoe store," she said.

"Why not?" Junior Arkwright answered.

FINAL REPORT

"You see," said the voice. "I told you it was all con-nected."

Buddha was shaking his left foot, massaging new life into it, rubbing away the tingling. He pushed his plump fingers between the toes, and hadrons spun, pions poppled, patterns grew and formed, flowed and changed, decayed and grew again. "Aaaah," he sighed. "That's better."

"And I know it's all connected," he said over his shoul-der. "I know all that. Now don't bother me. I'm busy."

He wiggled his toes, and they flew into vast circuits of the earth's computers, the mad big one pursued relentlessly by the four heroic smaller ones, staving off yet once again the final printout, the net result.

He crossed his legs again, pulling his left foot up and over the right thigh, and settled deeply into the full lotus. He sighed and placed his pudgy hands just so, the circle and the open palm, against his knees. He looked at his knees for a moment (a moment just long enough for a universe to form, evolve, collapse, and lay a Cosmic Egg). Everything was connected: ∞.

And then he smiled.

A very sweet smile.